ABOUT THE AUTHOR

SAMIR AMIN is one of the world's foremost radical thinkers. He has been director of the United Nations African Institute for Economic Planning and Development, director of the Third World Forum in Dakar, Senegal and was a co-founder of the World Forum for Alternatives.

A LIFE LOOKING FORWARD

Memoirs of an Independent Marxist

SAMIR AMIN

*Translated by
Patrick Camiller*

ZED BOOKS
London & New York

A Life Looking Forward: Memoirs of an Independent Marxist
was published in 2006 by Zed Books Ltd, 7 Cynthia Street, London N1 9JF, UK,
and Room 400, 175 Fifth Avenue, New York, NY 10010, USA

www.zedbooks.co.uk

Copyright © Samir Amin 2006
Translation © Patrick Camiller 2006

The right of Samir Amin to be identified as the author of this work has been
asserted by him in accordance with the Copyright, Designs and Patents Act, 1988

Designed and typeset in Monotype Van Dijck
by illuminati, Grosmont, www.illuminatibooks.co.uk
Cover designed by Andrew Corbett

All rights reserved

No part of this publication may be reproduced, stored in a retrieval system or
transmitted, in any form or by any means, electronic or otherwise, without the
prior permission of the publisher.

A catalogue record for this book is available from the British Library
Library of Congress Cataloging-in-Publication Data available
Library and Archives Canada Cataloguing in Publication Data available

ISBN 1 84277 782 3 Hb
ISBN 1 84277 783 1 Pb
ISBN 978 1 84277 782 4 Hb
ISBN 978 1 84277 783 1 Pb

Contents

ONE	Childhood	1
TWO	A Student in Paris	31
THREE	Cairo, 1957–60	82
FOUR	Parisian Interlude, January–September 1960	104
FIVE	Bamako, 1960–63	109
SIX	Professor of Political Economy, 1963–70	152
SEVEN	The Political Context, 1960–98	168
EIGHT	Director of the Institute for Economic Planning and Development, 1970–80	198
NINE	The Third World Forum	221
TEN	Towards a Common Front of the World's Peoples?	240
	Notes	256
	Index	258

ONE

Childhood

Ancestors and parents

Ancestors do matter. They matter not because of some blood inheritance – I have never had any time for that sort of thing – but to the extent that the culture and ideology of which they were part have been transmitted to us across successive generations. Certainly my own family, on both my mother's and my father's side, reminded me from time to time that the education they were giving me was a 'legacy' to which they were firmly attached. This is not to say they were traditionalists; on the contrary, what they shared with their ancestors was a vanguard way of thinking and a system of values.

My father's family belonged in part to what was known as the Coptic aristocracy – a misleading term, in fact, because it involved a line of descent going back only to the second half of the nineteenth century, whose 'founders', unusually for Egypt at that time, had built their social position (and sometimes their landowning wealth) on the advantage of a good modern and scientific education. Intermarriage meant that they always kept the same names: the Wahbas (my paternal grandmother's family), the Wassefs, the Ghalis and a few others.

Some children of these families remained only 'intellectuals', little interested in riches, who led in material terms the lives of ordinary petty bourgeois. Among them were the ancestors my father respected most: the Ibrahim brothers and Mikhail Abdel Sayed. Mikhail has a place in the history books, as a journalist and publisher in the 1860s, but my father told me that Ibrahim had been a stronger person, a 'republican', in the age of Khedive Ismail when that was very rare indeed.

I remember well my paternal grandfather, Amin: his facial features, his kindness towards my sister and me. A railway engineer by training, he should (or could) have become a 'director' (that is, at that time a minister), but the British prevented it for a simple and rather amusing reason that my father explained to me in 1937, shortly after my grandfather's death. He knew French well and used it with my mother and my maternal grandparents, but he always spoke to me in Arabic. With the British, he pretended not to speak English – which was untrue – and insisted that any communication should be in Arabic, forcing them to translate all their requests in writing. In one case, when the British Army asked him to transport 'about X tons of material', he replied to them in Arabic: 'I don't know what about means, tell me exactly the weight of your machines so that the Egyptian state can charge you the exact price for conveying them.' And, of course, the British were furious. Leaving Alexandria's Cairo Station, where he was manager, he would walk chuckling to himself to the Trianon or another café on the other side of the street, where he would drink his *zibib*[1] and play trictrac[2] with the local Greeks and Armenians, shamelessly conversing with them in fluent French or English.

I never knew my paternal grandmother – a Wahba who died young in the 1920s, when my father was a student in Strasbourg. She had inherited from a relative, I'm not sure whom, a large area of land in the still undeveloped Raml area of Alexandria, which the Khedive Ismail had generously given to one (or both) of the Abdel Sayeds in return for a favour. (Mikhail was one of the pioneers of modern Arabic publishing, and I am told that Ibrahim – the 'republican' – was also a very good writer.) With a remarkable lack of business acumen, they then sold the land in order to buy a family house in Shubra, which, if it still exists, will by now certainly have become an indescribable hovel. My parents displayed the same family trait in 1942, when some Greek (or was it Levantine or Jewish?) landowners, panicking at the advance of Rommel's army, offered them for a song huge stretches of Nileside agricultural land opposite Zamalek: what is today the Cairo district of Dokki. 'We're not going to become gentlemen farmers', they replied, turning down the proposition.

My father was a Wafdist, out of a combination of (anti-British) nationalism, democratic anti-monarchism – he told me that the Egyptian monarchy, after its age of glory from Mohammed Ali down to Ismail, had been rotten ever since Tawfik's betrayal in 1882 – and an attachment to the remarkable secularist trends in Wafdism. This enthusiasm for democratic and secular values later explained his guarded attitude to Nasser: chance had it that he was visiting my sister and me in 1952 when he bought a copy of *Al Ahram* on boulevard Saint-Michel and joyfully read the news of the takeover, but after 1956 and the nationalization of the Suez Canal (which he also heartily supported) he warned me that 'we' (i.e. the communists) were on the wrong track supporting the narrow-minded officers, who at bottom were nothing more than fascists and Muslim fanatics. 'You people knew well enough the nature of the regime between 1952 and 1954,' he said, 'and you suffered so much from its brutality, so how can you fail to see its limitations today?'

One of the reasons for my father's judgement was Nasser's revival of 'Nationalist Party' discourse, in the style of Ahmad Hussein's Misr al-Fatta, which had expressed pro-Nazi sympathies during the Second World War 'out of hatred for the British'. I had been at the Lycée in Port Said at the time, where the young Egyptians (nearly all of them politicized) divided into 'pro-communist' and 'pro-Nationalist Party'. My father was happy that I belonged to the former group, and he never lost an opportunity to tell me: don't get carried away by Ahmad Hussein and his gang; they're a bunch of imbeciles who can't understand why the Nazis are much worse than the British.

My maternal grandmother Zélie Démoulin – born soon after the Paris Commune, in 1874, at the town of Château Porcien in the Ardennes – was one of the descendants of the French revolutionary Jean-Baptiste Drouet, who played a role in the arrest of Louis XVI at Varennes in 1791. (I am not sure of the precise line of descent: I think it was through the Labourets – the name of my great-grandmother, who married a Démoulin. In any event, the three names – Drouet, Labouret, Démoulin – have often been linked in marriage and appear to be quite common in the Argonne–Ardennes region.) My grandmother was quite proud of this ancestor, who was also active in the Babeuf movement in the closing years of the eighteenth century, although he later served as an Imperial *sous-préfet* under Napoleon. Still considered a 'regicide' by complicity, he was then forced to hide under the Restoration and may have moved a few dozen kilometres away from the Argonne region in the Ardennes, where he is said to have used the name Labouret or Démoulin to conceal his identity. As for my grandmother's first name, Zélie, this was quite fashionable in the late nineteenth century, but she told me she had been given it in homage to the Communard Zélie Camélinat.

My maternal grandfather – Albert Boeringer – came from a family of artisans in Alsace (Guebwiller), who spoke only broken French. After the German annexation in 1870, and a few years before his birth in 1875, his parents had nevertheless opted for France and gone to live at Suippes, in Champagne. 'We Alsatians,' my grandfather once explained to me, 'helped to make the [French] Revolution and we know the meaning and price of liberty; we didn't want to be treated as German sheep, docile and submissive to the mood of their aristocrats.' A democratic political choice, therefore.

My two grandparents became schoolteachers, as did many craftsmen's children in those days.

Grandfather was a freemason and socialist, and – as his army book makes clear – it was because of this that in 1914, despite his age, he was switched from his original posting at the rear to a more dangerous frontline position, where he was seriously wounded in the early months of the war. His courage and concern for others (protection of his fellow soldiers) were recognized in a citation and the many medals he received. He died quite young, in 1940, largely as a result of wounds that had continued to fester.

The education he gave me was remarkable for its socialism, anti-colonialism and anti-fascism.

Grandmother – whom my father called Voltaire, for her unruly white hair as well as her ideas – was living with my parents in Port Said at the fall of France in June 1940; her 'Gaullism' is evidenced by her France Libre membership card, which at first made her virtually unique among the pro-Vichy emigration in Egypt. (Only later, after 1942, did it rally en masse to the 'Gaullist' cause.) In fact, she could find no 'French authority' capable of registering her decision, and so she had to use the services of a British officer to pass on her letter of application to the Free French in London.

My maternal grandfather and grandmother were each the eldest of a family of six children, some of whom were still alive when I went to France in 1947. Pol, my grandmother's youngest brother, had emigrated to Russia and worked on the production of Crimean *shampanskoe*, then returned just before 1914; his wife was a Frenchwoman who had spent her childhood and adult years in Russia, spoke Russian as well as French, and had all the manners of a Russian woman. Happy to see that I was a communist, and therefore 'pro-Russian', she helped me learn some of the language during school holidays that I spent with her in Reims. Grandfather's youngest sister, Emilie, a midwife who ran the local maternity service, lodged my sister during her years of study in the city.

My grandfather had insisted on returning to Alsace in 1919, and my parents had actually met in Strasbourg as medical students in the 1920s. It was a happy meeting between the line of French Jacobinism and the line of Egyptian national democracy – in my view, the best traditions of the two countries. I certainly owe a lot to them.

Father and Mother also had a social vision of problems. I would not necessarily say socialist, but in the end it came to more or less the same. In the privileged class to which I belonged, people were insensitive to the wretched lot of the working classes and considered it quite 'natural'. Father and Mother, however, never stopped telling me that it was neither natural nor acceptable, and that all it meant was that society was badly constructed. I remember one occasion (if not the precise words) at the age of 5 or 6, when I got out of our car in a popular district of Port Said (as doctors my parents went there quite often) and saw a child picking up rubbish from the ground to eat. When I asked: 'Why is he doing that?', my mother was in little doubt: 'Because the society we have is bad and forces the poor to live like that.' 'Then I'll change society', I promised. 'Good,' she replied, 'that's what's needed.' When she told this story forty years later to my friend André Frank, who had asked her at what age I became a communist, she said: 'As you see, since he was 6.'

My father showed proof of this social sense, beyond anything present in Wafdism, in the way he managed public health affairs in Port Said, eliminating malaria, for example, through means I would not hesitate to describe as 'Maoist'. In Egypt Thursday is the last day in the school week, and he had the idea of a children's game that consisted of going to the ponds, gardens and other places infested with mosquitoes and sprinkling a little *siberto* (methylated spirits). Organized by charge nurses and other helpers under the leadership of Abdel Ghaffour (my father's, and later mother's, loyal nurse during their professional career in Port Said), the children received a picture at the end by way of reward. Total expenditure: next to nothing. Result: the virtual disappearance of malaria from the town, leading the health ministry to enquire about the origin of the miracle. My father received a medal, which I found long after his death at the bottom of a drawer, together with an unfinished letter to the minister that he probably thought pointless.

This social sense also explains why our family felt such a strong sympathy for the USSR after 1941. We all saw communism as the long-awaited solution to the social problem, and when the Soviet consulate set up shop on the ground floor of our house in Port Said we on the first floor translated our sympathy into a firm friendship with a number of Soviet officials.

When my mother joined my father in Egypt in 1927, she found herself at Qift, in Upper Egypt (province of Kena–Luxor), where he had the post of health inspector and general-purpose state physician. The choice of location was interesting, because our ancestors on that side came precisely from Qift. My mother did not think for a moment of not working, so she followed my father and looked after anyone who needed it – and there were plenty of those. Her detailed recollections added up to a priceless testimony that deserved to be recorded for history. Much later, a friend of mine who worked for Cairo television thought she would like to do it, but the opportunity had been lost as my ageing mother no longer felt able to focus her mind sufficiently.

My father used to do his rounds on horseback, and my mother (Odette) followed behind on a donkey that was given the name Odet because he was as stubborn as she. They crossed the Nile with local farmers and animals, on rafts placed on goatskins or earthenware *zir*. Medicine covered everything imaginable: caring for the sick and especially children (whom the mayor collected in a makeshift village clinic); measures to protect against epidemics; hygienic inspection of the water supply, markets and schools, and instruction of local officials on possible improvements; small-scale surgery, autopsies of people killed in the characteristic local vendettas (usually gunned down in a sugar field), and so on. Most of my mother's and father's friends were Egyptian or foreign (mainly French or British) archaeologists, who kept themselves busy sifting through the rich local soil. Agatha Christie was married to one of them, but my parents never met her – I think she had left before their arrival. My parents loved to spend time relaxing in Aswan, at the Old Cataract hotel; and in Cairo they also liked to go to Shepherd's, the world-famous hotel on Opera Square that burned down in 1952. It was a time when tourism was reserved for the wealthy, and people such as the king of Belgium, who used to meet in hotels of a bygone luxury. My father rapidly developed certain habits and, knowing how to speak to people, became a familiar face in all these places.

My parents' choice of residence and profession was certainly not common in Egypt at that time. The health minister, a colleague and friend of my father's, did not conceal his surprise: how could my mother have agreed to follow him to Qift, a sweltering hole in the back of beyond? 'Egyptian wives never do that, madam. They stay in Cairo with the children and let their husbands roam loose in the sticks.' 'I would find that impossible', she replied. 'Besides, I am fond of Upper Egypt; I am learning a lot there. I have the opportunity to practise my profession more than full time. I like the local people, with all their strength and qualities. I have no problem feeling completely Egyptian there. The rest – the discomfort, the heat – you soon get used to it.'

When my father later asked for a 'permanent posting' in Port Said, so that my mother could have a proper career (that is, rich clients who would allow her to treat the great majority for nothing), the minister of the time said to him: 'Think carefully, Farid, you'd be sacrificing too much. You have a fine career in front of you, but you must know you can keep getting promoted only if you agree to keep changing jobs and moving house.' My father answered that he had already given it careful thought: he would not sacrifice his wife's career, however unusual an attitude that was in Egypt or elsewhere. And, for his own part, he could do more in Port Said than by struggling up an administrative hierarchy whose limitations were already quite apparent. What happened later proves that he kept the promise he made to himself.

Childhood memories

I had a particularly difficult birth and early infancy. Born prematurely with jaundice, I could take nothing by mouth and even retched up any water I tried to swallow; they kept me alive only with huge injections of serum. That lasted for a year. If my mother had not been a doctor, combining constant vigilance with the power of maternal love, I would certainly not have survived. Indeed, my parents' colleagues advised them to let me go, as there was a high risk that I would be mentally handicapped. 'Hydrocephalous' was the word one of them used, looking at my large head atop a puny body. 'Shitephalous' was my grandfather's answering description of him, in conversation with my mother.

This happened in the Nile delta, somewhere in the country between Zagazig, Abu Kebir and Abu Hamad. I was twelve months old, sitting on my mother's knee in our Ford convertible. Obviously I don't remember the moment, but I can still picture the Ford, which my parents must have used up to 1938. My father had gone off to visit somewhere in his capacity as health inspector. A peasant woman approached the car, caught sight of me and started chatting to my mother, who explained to her why I was little more than flesh and bones. The woman then persuaded my parents to go home with her, where she gave them a herbal mixture. It can't possibly do any harm, they thought. And in fact the cure did have an effect: a few days later I was able to hold down water, then milk and a little soup. I was saved. On my father's proposal, the herbs in question came to form the basis for an Egyptian pharmaceutical preparation. And since then I seem to have kept a sturdy constitution. Still, I continued to be very careful until late adolescence, as I was told that I would need to follow a strict diet for my liver to recover completely: no cakes, no cream, no chocolate… Family friends were often amazed at my willpower and admiringly remarked on it to others. Even when I was invited somewhere with other children, I refused to eat any of the cake that was offered me.

When they were living at Qift in Upper Egypt, and then Abu Kebir in Lower Egypt (where my sister Leila was born in 1930), my parents used to spend holidays at the sea in Port Said; they took a liking to the town and eventually decided to settle there, when I was little more than a year old. My maternal grandparents, both schoolteachers, retired there soon afterwards to be close to their only daughter. Mother immediately started working in a private clinic of her own, while Father was health inspector for the Canal province. Our grandparents therefore kept a close eye on my sister and me. I loved them with all my being and still have very fond memories of them.

My grandmother had admirable qualities of both heart and mind, always calm at the most difficult moments, always intelligent in her judgement. She had proved those qualities during the 1914–18 war. Leaving Reims just before the Germans entered, she bravely and efficiently led a column of refugees between the front lines with the help of an army map and compass. She was lucky enough to die instantaneously while doing a crossword, in 1973, a few months before her hundredth birthday. She never lost any of her lucidity, and even in her nineties was always on for a spot of feasting.

'Where are you going?' she once said to me around midnight, after I had returned from a trip. 'To the Coupole.' 'Wait, I'll get dressed and come with you. You know how much I like oysters, especially with a good white wine.' A truly extraordinary person. Early on, she got me to read and love the fables of La Fontaine, whose wit and perceptiveness she shared. She did not make us do any homework: she thought that school was enough and that the rest of the time was for children to enjoy themselves, to extend the range of their knowledge in other ways. She therefore spent a long time discussing with us, giving us a taste for books. I have been an avid reader ever since.

My grandmother was very particular about her appearance. She never stopped making and repairing high-class dresses, coats and hats, sometimes at the limits of the extravagance that her great beauty made possible. I remember one hat decorated with a rather unusual owl, which made my grandfather laugh. I must take after him. He paid no attention to how people dressed, and it is said that in class he did not think twice about wiping the blackboard with the tail of his jacket. My father, on the other hand, had the severe elegance of a good Egyptian bourgeois. So did my mother.

The large rooms in our magnificent house showed to advantage the furniture, carpets and objects that my grandmother tracked down at Dialdas, the Indian antique shop on Port Said's main shopping street, rue Farouk. She took meticulous care of everything, using a feather duster to chase away the invasive dust of Egypt. 'You'll tickle them so much they'll end up laughing', my grandfather used to say. Perfect order in the home, never any breakages.

My grandfather also played an important role in my early education, although I was only just 9 when he died. He was a social, political being, who spent long hours in cafés watching and chatting with various people. His favourite was a little Baladi café at the entrance to the market, run by a Greek (as so many were in Egypt at that time). He could have long, mainly political discussions there with ordinary people, Egyptian or Greek canal workers, and never tired of arguing for his anti-fascist, anti-colonialist and socialist positions.

Grandfather came to fetch me from school at four o'clock. He bought me the same kind of spicy *bastarma* sandwich that he ate himself, and like all children who imitate 'grown-ups' I soon found it delicious. My mouth still waters when I think of it. Every day my grandfather repeated the same sentence: 'Don't tell your mother, she'll think it's bad for you and you won't get any more.' I kept the secret. It was only thirty or so years later that I finally plucked up the courage to tell my mother.

On Thursdays and Sundays my grandfather took me on a long walk to the docks; we took the ferry to Port Fouad and its gardens (where we picked mushrooms after rain), or sometimes went even further to the salt marshes or the Raswa or Gamil bridge. This long time together allowed my grandfather to educate me about a whole host of things, including boats but also political matters. From 1935 to 1937, ships bound for the conquest of Ethiopia regularly passed through the Canal, and Italian troops would assemble on deck to give their fascist salute and shout their slogans. Grandfather looked at them and responded with a V-sign, suggesting that I do the same or make some other gesture such as turning my back, lifting a leg and farting as loud as possible. 'That's how you should greet fascists.' Of course, it was great fun for a child of 5 or 6 to be allowed to do that. 'But be careful,' he said, 'you can only do that to the fascists I point out. I forbid you to do it to anyone else at all.' Okay. So, I asked what fascism was, and my grandfather took the opportunity to begin my political education.

I am not one of those who think that childhood memories are necessarily happy; that can hardly be the case for people whose early years were lived in extreme poverty. But I am lucky enough to be among the privileged ones who really can look back to a happy childhood. I have fond memories of certain places: the casino gardens and the kindergarten in the centre of town; the Place de Port Said and its huts on stilts, where in summer Father's friends from Cairo nibbled at *baklava*, *mesh*,[3] *fisikh*[4] and other delicacies, some typical of Port Said; the 'children's beach' at Port Fouad, where my sister and I spent whole summer days in a sea often dotted with harmless dolphins that were the opportunity for some extraordinary games; and the beach at Gamil near the 'beacon' and the ruined 'Fort Napoleon' (in fact, dating from the time of Mohammed Ali), where we picnicked *en famille* at weekends. Of course, all these places are much larger in my memory than they were in reality: the Lycée classrooms and yard were in fact very small, the garden forest where we played hide-and-seek consisted of a few shrubs, and so on. Two exceptionally fine buildings were the casino itself, a masterpiece from 1900 with large glass verandas, and the Eastern hotel–restaurant–garden, a monument to the glory of steel designed by a pupil of Eiffel. My parents took us there often. My sister would have ice cream and I a *granita* (an Italian word used in Egypt for a lemon, mango or guava sorbet).

When we were little, we had a maid, Fatma, who was as kind to us as a mother, with a beautiful face I remember very well. Our parents taught us to respect her – which was not usually the case in relations between bourgeois and their maids. She used to spoil my sister with ice cream, chocolates and Egyptian pastries; she made a really wonderful *kunafa*.[5] For me, the only delicacies that fitted my diet were sesame bread and those sugar candies with Syrian pistachios, whose taste I have never forgotten. But Father – who was anxious by nature and very particular about hygiene – tried to put my sister off the ice cream sold in the street by telling her that its chestnut colour came from human excrement; while I invented the story that the chocolate creams were made with pureed cockroach. Nevertheless, her weakness got the better of her as soon as she stopped hearing such things.

I saw Fatma again in Port Said in 1952. She had been married against her will to an old man, and was then a young impoverished widow who regularly visited our home. Her eldest child, by then a 15-year-old girl, took after her in the great beauty of her face and body – illiterate, but with plenty of pluck. When I asked her what she intended to do, she answered with neither fear nor shame: 'I'll get rich, I know how to; there are lots of rich men in Cairo, I'll go to them, I can use them.' I don't know if she ever succeeded.

This reminds me of a beautiful *djinké* I once saw at the presidential palace in Abidjan – that is, a kind of strong traditional hetaera, with a gold-embroidered boubou. I asked her, 'Are you from Senegal?' 'Yes.' 'Do you like Ivory Coast?' 'Yes, a lot.' 'Why's that?' 'Because I like rich old fools, and [looking around her] there are lots of them here.' 'Bravo.' It was a fine introduction to our conversation that evening, which was certainly more amusing and enjoyable than any I could have had with the dignitaries present at the reception.

At the beach, my father played the funny role of an Egyptian bey who enjoys the sea but looks at it a long time, then gradually moves from town dress (complete with tie, tarboosh and shoes) through beach costume (the same, only with straw hat instead of tarboosh, sandals instead of shoes, and no tie) to bathing costume (one-piece black swimsuit, bathrobe and baseball cap), sitting comfortably at each stage with a Turkish coffee beneath a sunshade, before finally going to test the water. The ceremony had my mother in stitches, she who loved to spend a long time in the sea, like my sister (a fish, they called her) and like myself (who conquered my fear of the water through sheer willpower). After a 'light' lunch of mezes followed by *kufta*,[6] kebab and grilled pigeon from the Gianola store, together with beer or *zibib*, he went to visit his neighbours for long discussions of business affairs, social life and, of course, politics.

There was also the Sunday ritual at the Café Royal, where Father took us around midday. He ordered mezes and beer or *zibib* for himself, and a cake or ice cream for my sister, while I had the right to a lemonade and a nibble or two at the mezes. Again he moved from table to table, or others came to ours, to chat about various things. For me it was an opportunity to listen to some good Arabic, and afterwards Father summarized (in good Arabic) the essence of what was supposed to interest me.

Father also took me to various places in a four-wheel barouche (his favourite kind of carriage), either on a tour of the *administrations* where he knew everyone, or to visit a friend who was holidaying or passing through: usually a senior official (the Canal governor, a judge or ministerial colleague), but perhaps a fellow doctor, a writer (he was very friendly with Youssef Idriss), a Wafd politician (Makram Ebeid, for example) or simply some good friends such as the Hamza family or Samiz Gabra.

At home everyone was fond of good food: especially my grandparents and father, and to a lesser extent also my mother. Any occasion was good for a slap-up meal: Egyptian, Muslim and Coptic festivals, and French ones too. We therefore had the pleasure of celebrating Christmas twice (on 25 December and 7 January), the end of Ramadan, the Kurban Bairam (the Turkish term then used for Aid el Kabir), the Quatorze Juillet, and so on. Each time my grandfather would himself prepare large plates of carefully chosen cold cuts, while my grandmother made roast quails, legs of lamb, *blanquette de veau* (which she loved especially, until the end of her life), *lapins à la moutarde*, vine leaves with lambs' feet, pigeons with *ferik*,[7] *fatta*,[8] the whole range of stuffed vegetables – everything to be found in the best Egyptian and French kitchens. And all this was washed down with fine wines, as until the war champagne and burgundy were imported from France by the caseload.

We often drove outside Port Said. Around 1938 the Ford convertible was replaced with a blue Chevrolet, into which we could all just fit for a trip along the Canal to Ismailiya and Suez (a good pretext to 'eat shark' at the Port Tewfick casino), or down to Cairo to visit my father's sisters (Hélène and Mounira) or to conclude some 'administrative' business, or else to visit some friends in Lower Egypt, at Zagazig or thereabouts. Some memories are better than others (children do not always like car trips), and others have been completely swallowed up by a Khamsin sandstorm.

In those days, Port Said was not a drab, characterless city. Built at the same time as the Suez Canal, it faced the Sultan Hussein Quay with a row of six-storey blocks and large wooden balconies in a perfect *fin de siècle* colonial style. The Belle Époque casino jutting out over the harbour entrance had the permanent spectacle of ships awaiting their turn to pass through the Canal. The Eastern Exchange would today be a listed building if British and French bombing had not destroyed it, like the Casino, in 1956. The headquarters of the Suez Canal Company survives as a fine example of the oriental colonial style, but the no less striking British admiralty, a little further along, was pulled down in one of those ill-tempered political gestures that I can understand but always find regrettable. In the same way, they toppled the bronze statue of Ferdinand de Lesseps at the entrance to the pier, which in those days had the harbour and the sea alongside it. My grandfather used to take me there to breathe in the sea air, especially on stormy days, and to observe in detail the landing of the fishermen's catch. But since then the steady retreat of the sea has cleared a lot of land for the property developers. The pier now has the beach alongside it, while the lighthouse is almost in the centre of town. A fountain on the Quay, decorated with a hideous but mercifully small statue of Queen Victoria, has also been destroyed – which is a pity, as it would have borne witness to the bad taste of the imperial British! Further inside, the middle-class city had its perfect series of dated districts (1890s, 1920s, 1930s), most of them built by Italian architects, but now all that has gone. First, there was the military aggression in 1956, when bombers took pleasure in setting fire to popular districts (the Manakh) and machine-gunned people trying to escape over Lake Menzaleh. Then came the property speculation of the new comprador bourgeoisie, which completed the city's destruction after 1973. The illusion that the 'free port' started by Sadat would become a centre of wealth led to the demolition of whole districts (including the Sultan Hussein Quay, now bearing a name I can never remember), and their replacement with vile concrete blocks reflecting what one imagines to be the taste of today's nouveaux riches. A prefabricated plastic supermarket where the Casino once stood!

The city was not only architecturally beautiful but bubbling with life, a compulsory stop en route to India or China for the great liners of P&O, the Messageries Maritimes and the Netherlands Navigation Company. Their thousands of 'passengers' daily thronged streets chock-full of fine objects from the East, and a flotilla of little bumboats, their fearless owners able to bargain in any language under the sun, set off to ply their junk to each passing ship. This had led to the development of an open, inventive culture, capable of skilfully fusing Indian curry and Port Said shellfish into a local cuisine.

Yet there was also the terrible exploitation of labour, at its worst in the case of the 'coalmen'. At that time ships still ran mainly on coal, and they used to fill up in Port Said where there were no machines or cranes to help with the job. Narrow planks were placed at a steep angle between the quay and the deck of the ship, and men constantly ran up them carrying a huge sack of coal or back down to pick up another one. They were landless peasants, scrawny but still strong enough for their few remaining years of life, whose labour-power was mobilized and offered for sale by unscrupulous dealers. Many a fortune in Port Said had been built in this way, supplemented by trafficking in the hashish that fishermen collected from accomplices on board ship, with the usual risks that poor people run in such situations. A whole mafia of pursers and Egyptian and foreign (Maltese, Italian, Greek, French) compradors was at the disposal of the big capital represented by the shipping companies. For me, the image of those poor wretches in tatters singing and working in conditions of slavery, often falling exhausted to the ground (or even into the sea), will always sum up the nature of actually existing capitalism. It convinced me at a very early age just how despicable was the social system associated with it.

At that time Port Said was the most advanced city in Egypt. Many years later, when I read Lucien Bodard's extraordinary account of the founding of Shanghai,[9] I discovered the analogy with the history of Port Said. It was truly an invented city. On the marshes of Lake Menzaleh, at the entrance to what would become the Canal, the early developers had created an artificial island simply by throwing sand into the water until land emerged from it. There had been no machinery, of course: tens and hundreds of thousands of people from all parts of Egypt, in the best pharaonic tradition, had 'moved mountains' using only their bare hands, spades and jute sacks. Either their village head (*omdah*) or provincial governor (*mudir*) had selected them because of their daredevil reputation, or they had been eager to get ahead and seen it as a way of escaping the straitjacket of family life and village tradition. Most had died in the process, but the survivors founded the avant-garde Port Said that provided a home (or a stopover) for port and canal workers, for the kind of sailor on multinational ships to be found in all the Mediterranean and Indian Ocean ports, and for hashish traffickers. The most unscrupulous, or most fortunate, among them became affluent or even very wealthy compradors, new 'notables' very different from those of rural and aristocratic Egypt. The city had therefore for a long time been electorally almost 100 per cent Wafd, with active nuclei of trade unionists and communists who commanded some attention. But all that is now history, carried away by the wars of 1956 and 1967, the post-1973 isolation of the city and mass emigration, the Palestinian intifada, the return of émigrés with a little (or a lot of) money from Saudi Arabia and other Gulf states, the illusions bound up with the 'free zone'. A population of shopkeepers has come dramatically to the fore, living off the sale of 'duty-free' goods ranging from textiles and assorted junk to modern domestic appliances. Droves of Egyptians from Cairo and elsewhere who somehow manage to get their purchases past customs, together with the corrupt officials, soldiers and policemen who wave through whole truckloads, have become the main sources of the new prosperity. The reactionary, mercenary fundamentalism of political Islam, imported from the Gulf, finds here highly favourable terrain.

War and the *lycée*

The war years, from 1940 to 1946, were those of my time as a pupil at the French state *lycée* in Port Said.

After the Germans reached Crete in 1941, Egypt itself seemed to be threatened by the movements of Rommel's army, although we knew that the main front was in the East, where the Soviet army was facing alone the full brunt of the Nazi forces. We were firmly and unhesitatingly on the side of the Soviet Union, always anxious but confident that the strength of its system would finally prevail. Now unreservedly pro-communist, I stuck up a picture of Stalin in my room.

In 1942 Rommel's offensive took him to the gates of Alexandria. Some (especially the Maltese and Jews) were panic-stricken and fled all the way to South Africa, while Egyptian petty-bourgeois and reactionary circles close to the monarchy prepared to welcome their German 'liberator'. My father considered these to be cretins (*mughafallin*) and bastards (*mugrimin*), one day supinely pro-British and the next day (when for once the British were on the right side) mindlessly 'patriotic'. He therefore supported the Wafd's decision to join the government after the arrival of British tanks: it was not always easy to explain, and many of the Free Officers of 1952 are known to have then been on the side of the king. In any event, we were very worried and for a time my parents considered moving to a village in Lower Egypt if the Germans broke through; we even went there to see a strange friend of my father's whom I knew as Sheikh Ali, a kulak who received us with the customary feast of turkey, goose and so on. My father had a number of friends who seemed pretty weird in my youthful eyes. When one of them, Gomaa, ended up in prison as a counterfeiter, my father felt sorry for him: the poor guy, victimized like that; those nice, beautifully crafted banknotes wouldn't have done Egypt any harm! Besides, Gomaa was a generous soul and had given a lot of the notes to people in need. In the end, it wasn't necessary for us to go and live with Sheikh Ali. A few weeks later came the victory at El Alamein.

Port Said was a garrison town, filled with British and especially colonial or allied soldiers: black South Africans, Indians, Greeks (the most leftwing), Poles belonging to General Anders's reactionary army, and Free French who had distinguished themselves at the Battle of Bir Hakeim in May–June 1942. (Much later I became friendly with one of these, Marcel Faure, when he came to Mali in 1961 to work for the new anti-imperialist regime of the African Democratic Rally.) The dense military presence generated the usual series of raucous incidents, mainly centred on the hostess bars littered around town that were the haunt of the *gonella* (an Italian loanword meaning 'skirt'): that is, girls wearing daring clothes that were new to Egypt.[10] These girls gave life to some merry old cabarets, like Cecil's Bar where, much later, Isabelle and I saw the extraordinary dancer Tahia Carioca.

In our home, ordinary Free French soldiers were always welcome at table. As in the 1914–18 war, my grandmother thought it normal to offer a delicious meal to men in the short time they had before going back to the front. Our Maltese neighbours in those days – the Zarbs – had converted their villa into a family hotel catering to garrison officers and civilians whom the war had washed up in Port Said, including a number of teachers at the *lycée*. We saw a lot of all these people, and I remember that the political discussions were often lively.

The air raids, almost nightly for a time between 1941 and 1942, brought the war home to us in the shape of blackouts, sirens and anti-aircraft fire that seemed to fill the whole city. Civilians usually took shelter in their own cellars, but many of these were ill-suited for the purpose and collapsed on their heads after a direct hit. My grandmother therefore persuaded the Zarbs to dig a covered trench in the garden, so that we would die on the spot if a bomb fell right on top of us – a zero probability, or so she claimed – but would be safe and sound if it fell three metres away. General Voltaire – as Father called her – proved to be right.

The Zarbs, their guests and ourselves were joined in the trench by a number of 'old ladies' – mostly Italian neighbours, such as my mother's dressmaker, who were living in humble circumstances. Christian to the extreme, but only moderately courageous, these ladies used to annoy my grandmother, who never lost her calm and spent her time there chatting to the children, telling stories, laughing, drinking (there was some good wine in the trench) and toasting the bombs that failed to explode. I remember her clinking glasses with a very nice Scottish officer, a man of advanced political ideas who was never seen without a bottle of whisky. Or she might read some Balzac or a detective novel. One day, in her characteristically mocking tone, she said to the noisy Christian ladies: 'You should shelter in the cathedral over there. It's a holy place, and certain to be the best protected by all your fervent prayers.' Much laughter from the unbelievers in the trench! And perhaps a brief lull in the sighing and moaning. 'Bravo, Voltaire!' my father said.

My father's main task then was to organize the city's hygiene so as to ward off epidemics; there were no antibiotics, and the danger was real in the army as well as the poorer districts. He was very efficient in the job, calling together all doctors and establishing a dictatorship over them. This made it just possible to avoid a terrible outbreak of pulmonary plague, which he was the first to detect after becoming distrustful of the burial permits that a colleague had given to several members of the same family. He gave orders for the forcible evacuation of a whole district (near the city market) and the control of all movement into the area surrounding it. In the end, the total number of deaths was kept to a hundred. A few days later we were terrified when Father suddenly went to bed with a high fever, but it turned out to be only a case of paratyphoid.

All this made my father so popular that, when he died in 1960, the funeral procession mobilized the whole city, and President Nasser (or his secretary) thought it wise to send his personal condolences.

Political debate became more heated in 1943–44, as the war neared its end. The post-war camps gradually took shape: on one side, those who sought to restore the pre-war imperialist and colonial order; on the other, those who wanted the defeat of fascism to pave the way for social transformation, or even the triumph of socialism. The signal for conflict came from the cruiser *Averof*, where Greek sailors, marginalized by Churchill lest they support the communist EAM resistance movement, mutinied and demanded the right to participate in the fight for their country's liberation. Groups of Egyptian workers and employees, trade unionists and progressives, immediately created a network of hiding places for the rebellious sailors, while the Egyptian police – a few months before, pro-Nazi and supposedly anti-British – shamelessly collaborated with the British authorities in hunting them down.

The French, nearly all in the employ of the Suez Canal Company, had mostly been reactionary clericalists or members of the royalist Camelots du Roi – in any case, a snobbish milieu with which we never mixed. Among the noteworthy exceptions were Dr Rivet (brother of the famous anthropologist Paul Rivet) and especially the Diuzets. The father, a Breton sailor in charge of one of the *pilotine* motor boats that used to brave storms to find ships on the high seas, naturally at once became a friend of my father's. The daughters, Alice and Yvonne, a few years older than my sister and myself, remained loyal friends of my sister and mother.

The Maltese – the Zarbs to us – were spontaneously pro-British, but neither bigoted nor colonialist in their mentality. Although their views were not the same as ours, they were very nice neighbours and their children our playmates. Mrs Zarb was originally from Hyères in Provence – she described to us, with an ecstasy I later discovered to be perfectly justifiable, the offshore island of Porquerolles – and she married young and came to live in Port Said. Her eldest son, Antoine, was married to a Greek woman, Catherine, whose father, having come from a Greek island 'with holes in his knickers' (to quote my father), had worked hard selling bread in the street, then opened a baker's shop and built it up into a successful business. But, instead of feeling proud of this thrifty, hard-working father, the children carefully concealed the origin of their wealth. My father used to laugh and compare them to those mediocre English drunkards, proud of their degenerate ancestors going back four generations, inept in every sphere of activity, and not even capable of happily squandering their monstrous legacy. Another son, Robert, found himself trapped in Grenoble in 1940, where he had been studying medicine; he joined the Resistance and, having been lucky enough to survive Mauthausen, returned to Grenoble and set up as a doctor. The youngest son, Raymond, a little older than me, became a chef in one of the most fashionable London hotels and once received me there with his characteristic generosity. He had a marked sense of humour and used to make fun of his snobbish English customers, claiming that they were unable to distinguish a Dover from a lemon sole, or even from a herring.

At the end of the war, young people in Egypt rallied to anti-imperialist and socialist positions, especially in the schools and universities. Cairo University became the centre of the huge popular movement of 1946, and revolutionary students formed the core of the Students' and Workers' Committee that helped build an organization bringing together intellectuals and workers. The conditions for this had ripened during the war years, with their massive politicization of young people. The French *lycées* were in the vanguard in this respect, by virtue of the high quality and progressive character of the education they gave. I remember that some of my own classmates had also been with me at primary school: Mohamed Sid Ahmed, for example, who became a prominent communist intellectual and journalist. The director of the Port Said post office, a friend of my father's who used to give me as a treat cancelled stamps from the first day of issue, had a son, Hassan, who was one of the leaders (I was another) of the group of 'young communists' at the Lycée. We literally fought in the recreation yard against 'reactionaries' who refused to accept that only communism and the USSR could free us from colonialism and feudalism. Hassan was killed in the street battles that took place at Port Said in 1956.

Among my young foreign friends were Adrien Corcondilas, a doctor from Athens, and Ljubomir Voivodic, whom Isabelle and I met again by chance on the Île du Levant after he had married someone born there.

Egyptian adult society, or at least that part of it which we knew, was less marked by the kind of radicalism I have been describing. My father, a social being par excellence, used to visit an incredible number of friends and their families, and he would often take me along with him. At the Hamzas, he put constant pressure on the eldest of a string of brothers to allow the girls in the family to continue their studies – which was still very rare in Egypt at the time.

One of these girls, Awatef, who was a few classes higher than me at the Lycée, owes it to my father that she was able to take her baccalaureate and study medicine in France. She remained very close to my mother after Father's death and, until she herself died recently, to me and Isabelle. Her husband Salah – who died young – was extremely generous and had the kind of social sense of humour that one sometimes finds only among big drinkers (of which he was one). Long evenings in his company never seemed to tire either my mother or grandmother.

Awatef therefore escaped the unhappy fate of her sister, Malika, who married very young one of the Soudan boys. The Soudans were nouveaux riches Port Said style, their fortune made from the 'handling' of ships. The father was very respectful of tradition and unfamiliar with even the smell of alcohol, but the same certainly could not be said of the sons, ten or twenty years older than I, who used to spend their evenings at Gianola's or a cabaret, often returning in a rather indecorous state. One day, when one of them was brought back dead drunk, the father asked my mother to come and 'look after him'. Out of fear, he muttered: 'I ate some fish that's made me ill.' 'Which fish is that?' the father asked. '*Samac bolonachi*', my mother replied laughing. (It was the name of a brandy produced by a Greek in Egypt.) And the old man ended his days firmly believing that that there was a bad fish called *bolonachi*.

So, Malika was married to one of these fellows. She used to spend her days sitting on a sofa in a tailored suit. I went to visit her – at the age of 8? – and sat next to her on a tenth of the sofa, totally absorbed in calculating that the circumference of my torso was smaller than that of one of her thighs. She was brought one large *tesht*[11] after another, covered with Egyptian pastries, dates and bananas that she ate without respite. Later I understood that this frightening bulimia had been her way of rejecting a forced marriage; the poor thing did not live to a ripe old age.

Among those who later became my friends was Wadie Ghattas, then living in the Zarbs' family hotel. My father undoubtedly helped him to get a job as one of the first Egyptian executives of the hateful Suez Canal Company, and after its nationalization in 1956 he helped the Canal to operate properly in spite of the sabotage that the French organized before their departure.

The director of the French state *lycée* was a man from Marseilles, Victor Martin, who stood out from the French colony in Port Said by his vigorous secular republicanism. His younger brother Fernand – who taught at the same *lycée* – went back to France and became the Socialist mayor of Vitrolles (long before it fell to Le Pen's fascists!). His wife was one of my teachers, whom I remember for her severity but also her perfect sense of justice. Until the second grade I was not easy to handle: mischievous, playful, and often deserving of bad marks. I also organized the 'playing up' of teachers, so that it was impossible to run classes such as 'literature' that we (or I) did not like. More precisely, we used to pay an organ-grinder to set up his instrument beneath our classroom window (left open because of the heat), and to play non-stop for an hour the same tune, which I, of course, still remember today.

The militant secularism of 'Father Martin' (as he was known) meant that most of the bigoted 'Canal Frenchmen' preferred to send their offspring to the Christian Brothers, who rightly came in for our mockery because of their stupid teaching and the poor results they achieved at the baccalaureate. Half of the children at the Lycée were therefore Egyptian – from the aristocracy and intellectual classes but also the petty bourgeoisie – and the rest were (largely Jewish) Levantine 'foreigners', from families of traders and professionals. We got along well, of course, and I had friends in every milieu – as I fortunately always have had. One unusual case, the son of a Breton canal sailor, was the future admiral Yvon Noël, who was already crazy about boats and used to go with me visiting cargo ships, liners and even warships, when his father or mine could obtain the necessary permission. But only the Egyptian pupils were politicized. Our reading was therefore precocious. Henri Curiel had opened a bookshop in Cairo – Mustafa Kamel Square – where we could find all the 'classics of Marxism' and use them to understand better the history we were taught: *The Eighteenth Brumaire, Civil War in France, The Communist Manifesto,* Stalin's *History of the Bolshevik Party,* and so on. The most reckless among us (that included me) embarked on Marx's *Capital*, although we probably did not get much out of it.

I have explained elsewhere[12] that I first embraced communism as a protest against the ignominy of social injustice, and that the national, anti-imperialist dimension of this revolt came only later. This was the opposite of the itinerary followed by most of my Egyptian comrades at the Lycée, but in the end we converged by drawing an equals sign between imperialist domination and social injustice.

Some of our teachers did not disapprove of our reading; some even encouraged it. Both history and geography, which I liked enormously, were taught in a generally progressive spirit. In particular, the classes in Egyptian history – which were certainly better than in Egyptian schools – led naturally to the conclusion that a country like ours could not accept its subaltern status as a semi-colony, and that this status had been imposed as the result of 'betrayal from within' – by feudalists, compradors and the monarchy. The classes in French history laid great emphasis on the Revolution, and it seemed clear to me that it had not brought history to a close but, on the contrary, opened it up. What was necessary was therefore to continue the revolution, to expand it to the rest of the world, including Egypt, and to deepen it by going beyond its bourgeois limits, towards a socialist democracy that the Jacobin Left and Babeuf had heralded at such an early date.

The quality of teaching at the *lycées* in Egypt had a lot to do with the position of French culture in a country occupied by the British, which had been formally independent since 1922 but was still in fact under the foreign yoke. France, though an imperialist country like Britain, had been eliminated by its rival in Egypt, and so the teaching at the French state *lycées* did not aim to train cadres for the system in place but, on the contrary, took up a cautiously critical position towards that system. The teaching of Arabic there, on the other hand, left a great deal to be desired. It is not that the school authorities sabotaged it out of imperialist prejudice: the teachers were actually selected and appointed by the Egyptian government, and they were still Azharists whose methods, based on learning by rote, were unacceptable for the kind of pupils that we were.

Edward Said's memoirs have brought home to me the gap separating the French *lycées* from the English schools. Victoria College was evidently a horrific place, whose ultra-reactionary, pro-imperialist and racist teaching was administered by a body of teachers who operated as prison warders. Said suffered from this to such an extent that he came to feel 'out of place' (the title of his autobiography) and 'at odds with himself'. The function of the British colleges was to deracinate children and turn them into servants. The *lycées* produced something very different: in the best cases, an enriching kind of dual cultural affiliation. I do not find it surprising that so many Egyptian communists passed through the *lycées*, but none at all through the English colleges.

It was the quality of the education which, from the third or second grade on, made me a good, even very good, pupil. My interests were divided, as I liked maths and physics as much as history. One teacher, Melle Thalieux, noticed this and gave me additional reading material and exercises in advance of the general course, as did my maths teacher – a corpulent, highly likeable Levantine Jew whose name I have unfortunately forgotten. I felt that they treated me as an equal, and they did not give me marks except for official purposes at the end of each term: 20 out of 20. My baccalaureate results – the top ones in Egypt for my year – filled them both with enthusiasm, and Melle Thalieux wrote my parents a letter (which I came across much later) recommending that I study theoretical physics, as 'a rigorous and demanding mind'.

I was therefore admitted to the Lycée Henri IV in Paris in 1947, first in elementary maths (for which I got one of the highest marks, if not *the* highest, at the Académie de Paris) and then in higher maths.

Of course, the Lycée and politics were not my only preoccupations. As to my sister, her temperament was very different from mine: intelligent and generous, if 'emotional', but also terribly lazy. At the time she was a 'small fat girl' (later to become thin, even skinny). She did not accompany me on my long marches with Grandfather, because after the first hundred metres she said she felt 'tired'. So, she had her own friends: the Zarb girl (Mizou), Leila Ghandar and Leila Samir; the 'three Leilas', as they were known, formed for a time an inseparable trio of beautiful young girls. As my sister showed no enthusiasm for her studies, my parents thought that a convent school might suit her better. But she did not last long there: the 'pampering' that was its secret formula was unbearable to a spirit like hers, educated in equality and justice. She therefore returned to the Lycée, where she completed the secondary cycle before leaving for France in 1947 to study pharmacy. As Leila was not interested in politics, this separated us a little and we had different friends, but we were still able to spend the summer together as teenagers on the beach, from morning to night. Later, she had the kind of healthy reactions that I expected of her, when, though still not really 'politicized', she withdrew to La Ciotat after her divorce and voted communist. 'They're the only ones who are worth anything', she used to say. Her health turned out to be delicate over the years – and she developed the asthma that probably contributed to her death at the age of 55. She had a happy childhood, beginning with Abu Kebir; she loved its splendid *gamousses*,[13] which – *mater dixit* – she used to mount and refuse to get down from.

I also like *gamousses*, but in my case this came much later, together with my liking for animals in general. One of my best childhood friends was Jocky, our grey Scottish terrier. My grandmother and grandfather could do anything with him, even remove a bone from his throat without any problems. I could not do that, but I had no difficulty playing and rolling in the sand with him. It was a great tragedy for me when he was run over by an army lorry.

One of our favourite activities was going to the cinema. There were several in Port Said – the Kursaal, Empire, Eldorado, Rialto – so we were probably able to see all the films of Laurel and Hardy, the Marx Brothers and Charlie Chaplin. *Modern Times*, *The Gold Rush* and *The Great Dictator* have remained firmly in my memory; the hilarity with which we watched Benzino Napolini[14] reminded me of what my grandfather had said about the cretinous nature of the fascists. Later there was the excellent series of crime films based on Agatha Christie, and the light American movies (especially the musical comedies, which made my mother laugh until she cried at the stupidity of those yelling women). It was the same yelling that my sister and I liked to listen to on the wind-up gramophones that we never forgot to take with us to the beach on Sundays. My father used to get annoyed and go and sit further away; his favourite music, which he listened to religiously on the wireless at home, was the still young Oum Kalsoum, or musicians from the riverside district of Rod Al-Farag in Cairo, where he went for hours (sometimes with my mother) to listen to that ancient Egyptian music which has now vanished.

Despite the war, we still lived in affluence in our middle-class home, in a port city that did not want for anything. Huge lunches and dinners followed one another as my grandmother, with the help of a succession of cooks, continued to deploy her fantastic talents as a chef; often we were joined by Egyptian notables and Allied army officers, some of whom were certainly politically interesting. In my earliest days with Grandfather, there was that great drinker of cognac and smoker of hashish Mansi – a strange man who, with his walking cane and tarboosh (not commonly worn by domestic servants in Egypt!), always came late because he had been running after the maids; he liked to draw their rounded bottoms in the air with a gesture of his hand. Mansi eventually emigrated in 1945 and, finding himself in Naples, married an Italian woman and reportedly opened a restaurant with her. A typical Port Saidian! The Ethiopian Haile, doubtless a peasant but with an elegant, haughty bearing, was proud to have fought with the Negus against the Italians before taking refuge in Egypt; he left again in 1941 to join the Ethiopian liberation army. Then there was Sharaf – the talented cook who later made a fortune in Saudi Arabia – who was a convinced member of the Muslim Brotherhood, endlessly though not ostentatiously saying prayers. He was great friends with my dog Jocky. Later, when repression hit the Brotherhood around 1948, my father and mother helped him get rid of his arsenal (an old hunting rifle and two pistols) by taking them to throw in Lake Menzaleh, so that Father could then sardonically invite the political police commander to search his house for weapons. Awad, a Nubian, I knew only sporadically: he soon left for France, and later joined a group of musicians that the Soviets helped to form in the Nasser period.

Above all, there was the previously mentioned Abdel Ghaffour, whose original experience as a male nurse working for my father, together with his narrow eyes, had led my grandmother to baptise in the nicest possible way, 'the mosquito inspector'. After Father died in 1980, my mother began again to receive a factory clientele – in particular, girls packaging tea at Brooke Bond. Ghaffour helped her with her tasks and kept her supplied with cigarettes, which she chain-smoked to cover any odours produced at the sweatshop and exhaled during medical examinations. Three packets a day: and yet she lived to be 94, showing no signs of anything wrong with her heart or lungs. As to Ghaffour, he loyally stayed on to look after our home, from 1980 – when it was virtually abandoned after Mother broke her leg and left for Paris – until it was finally sold in 1992. Alas, the purchaser then destroyed this magnificent villa, to make a bigger profit on the investment by building a hideous apartment block.

Mother and Father were both good doctors. At Strasbourg University in the 1920s Mother had been one of the top medical students, and the reminiscences she could have written about her work in Upper Egypt in the 1930s and in the factories of the 1960s would have been a major document for historians of the country. Father had already shown signs in his student years of an unfailing diagnostic intuition, but he chose to become a doctor working for the state, in the firm belief that Egypt's main problem was not treating the sick but reducing the chances of illness. Then, soon after the war, he retired from state service to specialize in social medicine, using all his energy to force the bosses – and the state that took over from them – to respect the health of factory workers.

The two families – the Amins and the Boeringers – were not noted for their religious zeal. My sister and I were baptised (Catholic) only at the age of 8 or 9, when my parents realized that it was better for us, as Egyptians, to be classified in one of the 'community' pigeonholes in which everyone anyway had to be confined. Ever since, I have had profound contempt for that kind of 'identity' discourse. My two grandparents were freemasons and Enlightenment-style freethinkers. To the best of my knowledge, my grandmother never set foot in a church; she liked to quote the old radical slogan: *ni Dieu, ni maître!* But she had a copper figure of Christ on her bedside table – an object that a young Breton soldier had given her before expiring in the 1914–18 war – and she thought highly of Jesus Christ as the first communist. My father was no more interested in religion, but he thought that at the great Coptic feasts he should display all the external signs of belonging to his community. Once or twice a year he therefore went to the Coptic church in Port Said, where the archpriest immediately invited him to sit in a comfortable seat in the first row. He took me along once in every two or three times. I felt enormously bored, although I must say that the ceremonial splendour and the beauty of the songs left quite an impression on me. The archpriest routinely gave Father some bread soaked in wine (the Orthodox communion), without enquiring whether he had fasted (he certainly hadn't), and Father took this while mumbling a few Coptic words that were incomprehensible to me, and I suspect to him. I myself went through a mystical phase around the age of 11 or 12, but it did not last long. As to my sister, I would say that she was more a superstitious person than a believer.

My grandfather and father were very fond of each other. But, when my father died, the two idiots who ran the Port Said cemetery – the Catholic and Orthodox priests – did not think it permissible to bury the two men side by side. My mother therefore negotiated a burial plot straddling the two areas held sacred in the respective faiths. The ashes of my grandmother, sister and mother are in three urns occupying the same compartment of the Columbarium at Père Lachaise cemetery in Paris.

TWO

A Student in Paris

I was a student in Paris from 1947 to 1957 – that is, between the ages of 16 and 26. In *Re-reading the Postwar Period: An Intellectual Itinerary*, I tried to give an account of these decisive years for my intellectual and political formation: how I understood the period and how I think of it today, with the benefit of hindsight. At the same time, I attempted to retrace the stages of my theoretical evolution concerning capitalism and socialism. I shall not go over again what I had to say there about my Parisian education and my later professional and political life, but shall focus on the more personal side of my memories.

The Fourth Republic

The years from 1947 to 1957 were the period of the Fourth Republic, which I experienced as what I would today call a permanent crisis. The project of a people's republic, based on the three forces of the Resistance (PCF, SFIO and MRP[15]), had been defeated with the rejection of the draft constitution of 1946 and the adoption of the one that would last from 1947 until the demise of the Fourth Republic in 1958. Whereas the MRP had quickly taken the initiative in breaking the anti-fascist front, the SFIO had wavered until January 1948, when it broke off relations with the PCF and rallied to the US-led camp in the Cold War. The Marshall Plan, which was proposed in April 1948 and immediately accepted by the French government, therefore marked the end of the immediate post-war period. The signing of the Atlantic Pact in July 1949 was the natural sequel.

The Fourth Republic was not strengthened as a result; indeed, we may wonder how it was able to survive for another ten years. One-third of French people – those who voted communist – remained attached to the project of a people's democracy, while another third – those close to the Gaullist RPF – were hostile to pre-war parliamentarism and its post-war revival. The governments of the Fourth Republic, which had neither the strength nor the courage to break with the legacy of the Third, were therefore bound to be weak, resting as they did on the remaining third of the electorate that fluctuated between the 'Centre Left' (SFIO plus the Radicals) and the 'Centre Right' (MRP). As to the colonial world, despite the communist participation in government, the Gaullist regime had already in 1945 launched into the Sétif massacre in Algeria, the bombing of Damascus and the beginning of the dirty war in Indochina. The Fourth Republic then became mired in endless repression and warfare: from the savage crushing of the insurrection in Madagascar (1947) through the first Vietnam war (until Dien Bien Phu in May 1954) to the Algerian war (which began with the uprising on 1 November 1954), and, after some minimal concessions to the movements in Morocco and Tunisia, the headlong rush into the Suez adventure in 1956. Only then did it finally embark on timid self-criticism and grant a degree of autonomy to the colonies of tropical Africa (February 1957).

This same weakness gradually led France to fall in with the American plan for Europe, thereby giving up the weight that it might have carried in European and world affairs. The turn began in June 1948, with the tripartite agreement on Germany, and continued with the US pressure for German rearmament in 1950, which came as a surprise only to those who were blind to the logic of their choices. In October 1950 France tried to counter these moves with a proposal for the integration of West Germany into a European Defence Community (EDC) – a project that limped along until its final abandonment in August 1954, two months before the Federal Republic joined NATO as a full member. The dual communist and Gaullist opposition to this US policy for Europe saw off the ECD idea, but it did not manage to come up with a convincing alternative, simply because there was not enough in common between the social forces and ideologies mobilized behind the opposition.

It is good form nowadays to argue that the Fourth Republic inaugurated the construction of economic Europe, through the adoption of the Schumann Plan for a European Coal and Steel Community (in December 1951) and the Treaty of Rome (in March 1957). But that is to forget that, at the time, neither the Europeans nor the Americans saw this kind of economic integration as an alternative to US-dominated Atlanticism, but rather as its natural complement driven by the exigencies of the Cold War.

The gradual weakening of the communist opposition, including the erosion of its electoral base, combined with the timidity of the Centre governments to produce a fatal slide to the right, heralded by the comeback of Antoine Pinay, now at the head of his Centre National des Indépendants, and the discredited pre-war *notables*. As concession followed concession, France's secular tradition came to be eroded by the principle of subsidizing independent schools. A compromise uniting this classical right with Gaullism was therefore bound to put an end to the Fourth Republic, and the Algerian crisis of May–June 1958 served as a launching pad for the end of the Fifth Republic. With the Communists isolated, the Socialists and Radicals were defeated in advance.

The rather colourless picture that I have drawn here does not take into account the economic recovery begun under the Fourth Republic and continued under the Fifth. Nor do I wish to suggest that the Fifth Republic was a step forward: on the contrary, its presidentialist constitution was a serious setback for the principle of democracy. To be sure, the right-wing bloc that took shape in 1958 around General de Gaulle, in the hope that he would continue the Algerian war and maintain colonial rule in tropical Africa, was fortunately 'betrayed' by its leader. But the 'European' option that the Fifth Republic substituted for the imperial options of the Third and Fourth republics was conceived in a way that would lead to today's neoliberal impasse and eventually restore the American hegemony that de Gaulle wished to limit.

In any event, our image of the Fourth Republic was certainly colourless during my student days in Paris. When I say 'our', I mean the revolutionary young communists and numerous former members of the Resistance. Believing that the strategic vision of a people's democracy had not been decisively defeated, we argued that the slide to the right could be reversed through a combination of struggles on the social front, the anti-colonial front and the anti-Atlanticist front of the Cold War. And yet, on all three of these fronts, the struggles gradually lost momentum.

The great strikes of November–December 1947 ended with a split in the trade-union movement and the creation of Force Ouvrière. From that time on, no social movement was able to regain the dimensions of 1947, especially as the material situation of the popular classes underwent a certain improvement. In 1949 bread rationing ended, and by then the major reforms of 1945–46 – the nationalizations, the establishment of a social security system – were beginning to bear fruit.

The mobilization against the war in Vietnam never lost momentum. By making it impossible for the government to send conscripts there, it helped the Vietnamese people to achieve victory more rapidly than they might otherwise have done. The Vietnamese know and say this themselves. However, the attitude of the French working classes, and of the Communist leadership, to the Algerian war was very different: a wait-and-see attitude, to say the least, as displayed in the PCF's support for Guy Mollet's government in 1956, in the vain hope of reconstituting a 'united Left' amid the gathering crisis of the Fourth Republic. Not only did this offer no prospect other than the use of conscripts to fight the war to the end; things became even worse with the Suez adventure (October–December 1956) and the unconditional rallying to the Zionist project. Those who resisted this pro-colonialist degeneration – some young 'leftists' and a few older people like Jean-Paul Sartre – pointed forward to the 1968 renewal of the Left, when a powerful social movement, resulting from deep changes in French society, would produce militants and ideological themes of a different kind. But this is to jump ahead of the period we are considering.

The mobilization against US hegemonism and its Cold War evolved in the same way. It reached its height during the Korean war (1950–53), but the violent clashes with the police at the great demonstration of 28 May 1952 against General Ridgeway, ending in the arrest of Communist leader Jacques Duclos, were not followed up with any similar actions. It should be said that Soviet policy at the time contributed to this weakening. For the moments of relative calm in the Cold War – which Soviet diplomats, to their undoubted credit, managed to achieve – were unfortunately accompanied with an opportunist discourse that could only obscure the true nature and project of US imperialism. At another level, Stalinism was wreaking havoc: the workers' revolts in East Berlin (especially in 1953) and Poznan (1956), and above all the Hungarian uprising of summer 1956, were condemned in a wooden language devoid of any attempt at critical self-appraisal; even the Twentieth Congress and Khrushchev's famous 'secret speech' threw little light on things; and the Chinese comrades' still muffled criticisms, which began in 1957, were rejected out of hand. In these conditions, it is understandable that the anti-US/anti-Cold War front should have softened into a pacifist movement, in the weakest sense of the term, incapable of grasping the nature of the main enemy or of its equivocal opponent. We know that the crushing of the Hungarian insurrection put an end to powerful mobilizations of the Western Left against the first Cold War.

Once history has taken its course, it always seems to have been inevitable. Those who fitted into it appear as realistic – history 'proved them right' – while the others appear as utopian. I belonged, and still belong, to the latter group. I believe, even more strongly than in my youth, that history can take more than one course, that several alternatives are always possible (though not all alternatives: some are real utopias in the trivial sense of the word). To fight for the course that is best in humanist and socialist terms – that is, for a 'creative utopia' – should be the alternative chosen by those who want to change the world, not merely to adapt to it. History is not determined in advance – as the failure of nearly all long-term predictions happily proves. Those who, out of fear, timidity or worse, let themselves be carried along by what seems to be the prevailing current bear a grave historical responsibility, for their choice strengthens the chances of success for the very current they claim to be fighting against. Such was the choice, in fact, of the people in charge in Moscow and of the French Communist leadership. In France, the project of a people's democracy was not ridiculous. The permanent revolution that had characterized the country since 1789 made it possible to envisage something going beyond bourgeois democracy, as part of what I today call the long transition to socialism. If this option had been victorious, it would not have turned France into some kind of Poland subject to the diktats of Moscow. On the contrary, it would have helped to change the European balance of forces and perhaps helped the countries of 'actually existing socialism' (which actually had little that was socialist) to find a left solution to their impasse, instead of turning to the right as they did forty years later. Revolutionary France might once again have placed itself at the head of the movement, instead of lagging behind, as it does today, in a neoliberal, Atlanticist Europe without a future. 'Realists' will say that that was impossible, since the inherent weaknesses of French capitalism in relation to the Anglo-American or the German model allowed no other option than to try to 'close the gap'. The argument carries some force, as it rationalizes what actually happened, but it is by no means beyond debate. The great revolutions that shaped the long-term development of the world – the French, Russian and Chinese revolutions, in modern times – were not produced by the greatest advances of capitalism. Against such a linear view of history – which is refuted in the long term – I put forward the idea of progress through uneven development.

The Lycée Henri IV (1947–49)

My sister and I left for Europe in August 1947, together with my mother and grandmother. Father, who knew everyone and liked to do things his way, had negotiated our trip with the captain of an oil tanker.

We landed at night in Genoa, after dallying long enough outside the port for little boats to come and take the huge load of cigarettes, bananas and other contraband – and for the captain to count the wads of notes in full view of everyone. From there we took the train to Paris, via Bardonnechia and Modane. It was a long journey in those days, with a change of trains at the frontier and a mass of paperwork.

For me it was the discovery of a completely new human and geographical world, after a childhood and adolescence in which I had never been outside Egypt, or even the little triangle formed by Port Said, Suez and Cairo. (Only much later did I get to know Upper Egypt, the western oases, the Red Sea and Sinai, and appreciate the unique beauty of the region from which some of my ancestors had come.) The Canal and Lake Menzaleh were beautiful in their way and still move me. I will never shed my memories of the (still broken) Gamil bridge, or of the long trips running to keep up with Jocky, behind the migrating birds that inhabit the countless bushy islands in the lake marshes. Many years later, I was fortunate enough to see there with Isabelle the 'green ray' whose pursuit, in a novel by Jules Verne, had once made me so feverish.

Yet the beauty of the trip on open seas, the coasts of Crete, the straits of Messina illuminated by fireworks, the sight of Stromboli erupting: these were things I had never imagined. Then came the Alps, which I discovered with wonder, together with the peaches of Italy. From the train window, I felt amazed to be travelling across a land empty of people. I was used to the roads of Lower Egypt, where you literally see one village after another and the fields always have people working in them.

I lived at the Lycée Henri IV as a boarder, both in the 1947–48 school year (when I passed elementary maths more than respectably) and in 1948–49 (when I passed higher maths without difficulty and graduated to special maths in the next year). Life at the Lycée was by no means as dull and monotonous as people often say. First of all, I was an active member of the Communist Party, whose offices were fairly close at rue Linné, which we reached by walking down rue de la Montagne Geneviève; they were then very poor neighbourhoods, and rue Mouffetard, in particular, was quite unlike what it is today. The Lycée's chief supervisor, Toulice, readily gave us permission to go out by day or night, actually valuing the fact that this made it easier for us to be politically active. At the Party branch for the Fifth Arrondissement, young people and old, workers, housewives and intellectuals all rubbed shoulders with one another, seriously discussing everything with an open mind. It was here that I met René Maublanc (he gave us a taste for serious philosophy), Marcel Prenant and many other leading academics, who, like the working-class members, did not hesitate to give their opinion and to have it discussed, thereby creating the best possible framework for a training of real value. Nor did people of the stature of Paul Langevin or Frédéric Joliot-Curie think twice before coming to listen to workers and young people express their point of view. Of course, we got together to sell *L'Humanité* – at the Mouffetard market on Sundays, as well as on special occasions such as the great strikes of November–December 1947, when classes were suspended at the Lycée and we had a few weeks to work 'full time' for the Party before returning to our families. Materially, life was still difficult, but even the bread rationing, the abominable food and the unheated dormitories scarcely seemed to matter.

At that time, secondary education was still elitist, with the democratization of intake only just beginning. The great majority of boarders and non-boarders, being good bourgeois children little interested in politics, tended to be on the right and offered us nothing likely to make them our close friends. I therefore remember only the exceptions on the left: Jacques Cormon, the son of a French settler from Oubangui-Chari in Central Africa; Paul (later renamed Saul) Friedlander, the Czech Jewish refugee, who, despite our attempts to persuade him not to go to Israel, emigrated there and became an ideologue of Zionism; Lazare Rosensztroch, a loyal friend in later decades, whom Isabelle met again in the Tenants Federation; Guy Béard, the future Lebanese mathematician and major singer; Vazguen Ovanissian, later member of the Tudeh Party of Iran,[16] murdered in prison by the Shah's police; and the Syrian Constantin Kodsy.

Our communist minority at the Lycée had no intention of allowing ourselves to be pushed around. We therefore solemnly warned the organizer of the bullying in higher maths that, if one of his henchmen tried anything again, we would go and literally 'smash his face' so that he ended up in hospital. This put the wind up the great leader, and so his cohorts made do with bullying the stupid, reactionary majority who were prepared to put up with this odious tradition.

I do not have the literary talent to do justice to the Paris of those days. Paris has always been and remains a beautiful city, where I have always felt at home, as I do in Cairo or Dakar. After the war, it was still marked by the slums and poverty it had inherited from the nineteenth century. The apartment blocks and historical monuments, which had not yet been given the Malraux facelift, were uniformly grey or black with dirt. There were still so few cars that you could safely cross any boulevard or avenue without having to use a pedestrian crossing. Yet it was a fascinating city, and I soon got to know all its districts and hidden corners. A lot has been written about the *zazou* jazz scene of those years, but it did not make such an impression on me. In Paris everyone has his or her own world.

How did we enjoy ourselves? The Lycée was not a prison but a kind of third-rate hotel, with an even more dreadful restaurant. But, so long as we attended classes, we could go out whenever we wanted. The supervisors, who had nothing in common with their military-style counterparts at other *lycées*, were by and large students no more than five years older than ourselves, who performed their tasks to earn a little money and to benefit from the quiet of the study rooms and dormitories. They did not cause us any trouble. When we thought we had finished our study assignment (quite quickly, in my case), we simply went 'over the wall' (actually, straight out of the gate) without feeling obliged to stay there yawning, chatting or messing around. In the evening, the supervisor on duty discharged his own responsibilities, and those of the Lycée, by making a list of the absent names and handing it to the concierge, who, for his part, left the front door unbolted and asked us not to wake him during the night; we were only too happy to leave a slip of paper on the allotted table ('Samir Amin, returned, X o'clock'), and in the morning he simply ticked the name of everyone who had returned and that was the end of the matter. Nevertheless, not many students took advantage of this system. The great majority, who had been brought up to respect conventional discipline, did not think it was possible and were perhaps even afraid of the city, of their own freedom. The minority to which I belonged, most of them of political activists and by no means bad students, may not have had 'all the rights', but they certainly had the right to act freely. Toulice did not hide his view that 'hassling' pupils was not the right use of discipline, since liberty was the best school they had, and that we should not be blamed for anything so long as our teachers were happy with us. So far as I am aware, nothing seriously untoward ever happened – although it is true that, in those days, drugs were virtually unknown, at least among young people.

I remember the times when our little group of three – Jacques Cormon (often joined by his sister), Guy Béard and I – 'descended' on some local night clubs. *La Rose Rouge*, where we listened to jazz or Juliette Gréco, was one of them. (As chance would have it, I later discovered that Isabelle had been at the Lycée in Bergerac with Juliette during the Occupation and got to know her well; she remembers her mother and sister, the return from Dachau, and her attempts to find Juliette at the Lycée, only to discover that she had left for Paris.) Guy Béard, already a fine singer himself, used to drag us to the cafés in the fifth arrondissement, where he would play his guitar with real talent. He continued to study maths and became an engineer, but then gave it up for the singing career that made him famous. When we met again many (twenty, thirty?) years later, we fell into each other's arms; we had not forgotten each other.

A tramp with a maths background set himself up opposite the Lycée and, for a bottle of the most ordinary red wine, would solve any problem for us in a few minutes, so that all we had to do was copy it out again neatly. This gave us all the more time for other activities. But Toulice used to repeat: 'Don't use him too much, it's not good for either your education or his health.'

I was still an adolescent, of course, though quite mature intellectually and politically. It was therefore a pleasure to spend time in Reims at Aunt Mélotte's, where my sister was staying; we ate well (incomparably better than at the Lycée!) and were able to rest and read. The Christmas and Easter breaks were spent with my sister in London (then still a sad city) or in Austria, where I discovered the pleasures of skiing. During the long holidays, my mother and grandmother came to be with us for two or three months, and we would go to Brittany, the Vosges, Alsace, the Massif Central and, above all, the Alps. When she had been a student, Mother had caught pleurisy (then a very serious illness) and spent a long time convalescing at Megève. She liked it very much there, and we used it as a base in July and August for coach trips through all the great mountain passes of France, Switzerland and Italy.

In Paris, I did not go out often except for political activity. Perhaps on Sunday to the cinema or one of the little Greek restaurants in the Quartier Latin (La Grèce, L'Acropole, etc.), or the Vietnamese Luu Dinh (behind the Contrescarpe), where I am today probably one of the customers who has been going there the longest.

I began to have doubts about my future 'career'. I certainly liked maths and physics, and had no difficulty with the coursework, but I was sure I had a political temperament and said to myself that these subjects would leave me little time for anything else. So, why not switch to political science and economics? Without telling anyone, I therefore enrolled in October 1949 at the Faculty of Law (a law degree then being necessary to study economics) and in the preparatory year for political science, which I could take without a competitive exam because of my good baccalaureate results. My teachers reacted strongly when they found out, writing to my parents to explain that I had the makings of a physicist and would waste myself in the pointless tittle-tattle of the so-called social sciences. But I stuck to my guns, and my parents gave their blessing in the end.

Trips east: 1948–49

In summer 1948, the World Federation of Democratic Youth (WFDY) organized a youth camp in Yugoslavia for the building of the Zagreb–Belgrade highway. The incipient break between Moscow and Tito led to the cancellation of the project, and those already registered (including Lazare Rosensztroch and myself) were reallocated to railway construction in Czechoslovakia. I therefore made the journey through the French and American occupation zones in Germany to the Czech frontier at Cheb, where we were collected and taken by train and lorry to Višovice (Zlin province) in Moravia. The countryside was beautiful, the camp pleasant, and some of the Czech and French people I met there are still my friends.

Of course we had a lot of political discussion, especially about Titoism, and I must say that, although in general we automatically adopted the Cominform position, the 'Titoist betrayal' did not seem as evident as they would have had us believe. For most of us, it was more a question of 'mistakes' in defining the political line, and we were shocked by the fanciful suggestions (later hardened into formal accusations) that the betrayal went back to the time of the anti-Nazi resistance. I still had a keen memory of that magnificent chapter in the history of the Yugoslav people, news of which had percolated through to us in Egypt.

We were too young to remember the Moscow show trials of the 1930s, and this made it easier for us to swallow the Stalinist version of events popularized in the official *History of the CPSU(B)*. In any event, Trotskyism seemed a dead end, especially for those of us from the third world who thought that it made no sense to wait for revolution in the advanced capitalist countries. The wave of new trials was only just getting under way in the people's democracies, and anyway we would be convinced fairly easily by what was said about them. The terrible parody of logic that drew an equals sign between 'mistake' and 'betrayal' was beginning to penetrate people's minds. Dogmatic Marxism–Leninism taught that there was only one correct line, which the Party (or, to be more precise, its leadership) had to discover. The idea of pluralism was gradually becoming strange or even alien to us. No doubt we were right not to place all ideologies on the same footing, and so we accepted the classical Marxist (not only 'Marxist–Leninist') critique of bourgeois ideology and its truncated conception of democracy. But the rejection of pluralism was extended to debates within the 'camp of socialism', with the disastrous result that socialism itself came to be thought of not as a relatively unpredictable objective dependent on the complex course of working-class struggles and gradually converging streams of perhaps diverse origin, but rather as a model that could be known in advance in all its details. And that model, of course, was the USSR.

The rejection of pluralism, reflecting a mechanistic and deterministic reduction of Marxism that I accepted like everyone else at the time, masked the opportunism of the Soviet ruling class and allowed it to endow all its manoeuvres with theoretical legitimacy. It would take me a few more years to understand the true nature of the Soviet system (which I now describe as 'capitalism without capitalists').

It should be said, however, that our own experience of true Stalinism lasted for only a short period – let us say from 1948 to 1956. The turning point for us was not the Twentieth Congress but, on the one hand, the Maoist critique that began to take shape with the Great Leap Forward in 1957, and, on the other hand, the development of particular angles of vision among many communists in Asia and Africa. I have already written about this in *Re-reading the Postwar Period* and shall not return to it here.

It was in Višovice that I met Jacques Vergès, in rather amusing circumstances. We used to receive our meals in tin dishes and had to wash them each time before being served again. Jacques and I, independently of each other, discovered the least unpleasant way of doing this: namely, to hang the dish by some string to the branch of a tree and then throw it into the river. It was as we were effortlessly collecting them from the water that we introduced ourselves and immediately took a liking to each other. Jacques, like his twin brother Paul, had joined the Free France movement and taken part in the Liberation, thereby earning a well-deserved halo of glory. Intelligent, courageous and combative, he had all the qualities that command recognition. I, and Isabelle, continued to be close friends with him so long as he remained what he had been (especially during the Algerian war, when he took up the defence of the FLN). His later evolution created a distance between us, when he opted for cynicism and his well-known defence of unacceptable causes.

Jacques's father, Raymond Vergès, a Communist deputy in the overseas territory of Réunion, lived in modest accommodation on rue du Cherche-Midi, which he shared with Paul and Laurence (Paul's wife), a PCF full-timer. We often visited the whole family and their friends, now also friends of ours, especially the working-class Renauts and their teacher daughter Martha, who was married to a physicist, Kieffer, from Luxemburg. I have warm memories of the times spent there, in the evening and on Sunday at midday, when we had long political discussions of every kind. We also travelled to Dottignies in Belgium, the home of Jacques's girl friend Colette, and were regular visitors to their place at rue des Artistes in Paris. When the couple separated, after their return from a period in Prague, they lost all influence over their son, Jacquou, who drifted in the way that teenagers often do in such cases. In 1965 I found him strumming a guitar beneath one of the Paris bridges, and took him with me to Dakar, where Isabelle managed to put him back on the rails.

When the three or four weeks at the Višovice camp were over, I did not feel like returning straight away to Paris. So Lazare and I decided to spend some time in Prague – a city whose beauty struck me again when I revisited it a short time ago. We 'hid' ourselves in university hostels with the help of some friends we had met in Višovice, proving that the system was not as efficient as it was often said to be.

In Prague I continued discussing Titoism with Stania Dubkova, the friend who hid me away in the university hostel on Opletova Street. The Yugoslav Communist Party, she argued, had won the people's support through its heroic leadership of the anti-fascist resistance; it had therefore developed positions of its own, which it found natural to express, and it was for this reason that the Cominform wrongly characterized them as 'nationalist'. The other, mostly puny, CPs of Eastern Europe had been artificially swollen by the massive recruitment of opportunists who had contributed virtually nothing to the anti-fascist struggle, and who therefore understandably felt obliged to keep their mouths shut and do Moscow's bidding. For my part, I tried to convince her that Tito's 'strategy' was wrong, my only (shaky) argument being that respectable independent Parties such as the PCF or

PCI shared the Cominform's point of view. It was a dialogue of the deaf, but it would never have occurred to me to 'denounce' Stania – proof that, after all, Stalinist control had its limits. I never saw Stania again, and I don't know what became of her.

When we were finally discovered, we had to find another way of continuing our holiday for free. Lazare was already feeling tired and went back to Paris, but I and Jacques Vergès decided to go and work in the Sudetenland, where labour had been short since the deserved expulsion of the Germans. We saw there the full horror of Nazism, which had been supported by all those good Germans who are nowadays held up as 'victims' in their own right. My work, hardly the most productive, consisted of tossing hay and sorting potatoes. But the little I managed to earn made it possible to think of a fourth stage in my journey. I took the train to the High Tatra mountains and crossed them on foot to Zakopane, in Poland, where I came across a famous pre-war resort that sheltered a strange assortment of *ancien régime* aristocrats trying to spend what remained of their fortune before it was seized, and revolutionary (not yet really bureaucratized) communist cadres taking a short holiday. The two groups, which did not get on too badly, consumed a prodigious amount of vodka between them. From there, I went on to Krakow and stayed with a Polish friend I had met in Višovice – Akwilina Gawlik, a young communist who had survived Auschwitz and become a good critical activist. In Krakow I was contacted by the organizers of the Peace Conference due to be held in Wroclaw, in which I later took part without having any real credentials. I have a very vague memory of the big speeches, the faces of Picasso, Joliot-Curie and the Soviet leading lights.

Back in Paris at the end of September, I found my mother worried because I had only told her where I was, not when I would be returning. A cousin of mine, Mansour Fahmy, who worked at the Egyptian embassy and enjoyed all the benefits of the diplomatic corps, had once kindly invited my mother, grandmother and sister to join him on a car trip outside Paris (a rare occasion in those days). When he had asked my mother how I was, Grandmother had seen her worried look and hurried to reply in her place:

'He's off camping in the Vosges, so we're not expecting to hear anything from him.' How we laughed afterwards! Mansour had known my whereabouts all along but, good friend that he was, had never breathed a word about it.

The next summer, in 1949, I took part in the Youth Festival in Budapest, with a delegation of colonial students put together by Jacques Vergès. I was the only Egyptian, but there were a number of Syrian, Iraqi and Iranian communists, as well as a large group of Vietnamese and a sprinkling of North Africans, Madagascans and other Africans. Some travelled through Austria and were subjected to many tiresome checks and provocations at the hands of the American occupation forces. For my part, I found a place on the Polish ship *Batory* from Southampton to Gdynia, then on by train to the Festival, and my return via Vienna went fairly smoothly thanks to Soviet help in getting me between the occupation zones.

We certainly had a good time in Budapest and saw a number of fine shows – but not much else. The political atmosphere had hardened a lot since the previous year in Višovice: no more frank discussions, only speeches and applause. In Summer 1951 Isabelle took part in the Festival in Berlin and came back with similar impressions. On the *Batory* to Gdynia, she had shared with a French comrade her doubts about the wisdom of certain Party slogans, but others overheard this and responded with what she described as a 'Pavlovian reflex'.

After 1949 I rather lost interest in visiting Eastern Europe, even if I continued to hold perfectly Stalinist positions. The next time I went there was in 1961, from Mali, when I was given the opportunity to visit the whole of Yugoslavia together with Isabelle. We found it a beautiful and friendly country, and I would go there often in the 1980s to the great gathering of all manner of socialists and communists, held at the marvellous Hotel Croatia in Cavtat. It was then that I began to sense the gradual deterioration that would lead the country to its dramatic ruin. As for the Soviet bloc proper, I only went there twice again: once in 1965 to Moscow and Leningrad, and once in 1990 to Central Asia. But of that, more in a later chapter.

Establishment of the new world system: 1945–57

As we can now see, the first decade after the war established the system that would come into its own in the 1960s before lurching into crisis in the 1970s and 1980s. In *Re-reading the Postwar Period* I have already discussed how we experienced that formative moment at the time, and how it appears to me today with the benefit of hindsight. This frame of reference is important, because my own options were governed by it, but all I can do here is repeat the bare outline, adding a little more detail in connection with regions directly affected by the movements in which I was personally involved.

The success of US strategy in Europe and Japan was rapid and total, thanks to the unconditional support it received from the whole bourgeoisie and all social-democratic parties in these countries. It was a hegemonic strategy which, from the outset, emphasized the constitution of an anti-Soviet military bloc; the key dates are those associated with the introduction of the Marshall Plan (1947), NATO (1949) and the Treaty of San Francisco (1951).

Faced with this deployment, the USSR remained in an isolated and defensive position until the middle of the 1950s, forced to enter into a new arms race to challenge the US monopoly in the military field. At Yalta, Moscow had obtained the right to form a buffer zone in Eastern Europe, but no more, and the establishment of pro-Soviet regimes there came up against various difficulties that it never really overcame. Only after the death of Stalin (1953) and the Twentieth Congress of the CPSU (1956) did the USSR launch a new strategy to break out of its isolation and forge an alliance with the third world. The Bandung Conference of 1955 was the first herald of this. In any case, although the Soviet Union started catching up with the West at the military level (the first sputnik went into orbit in 1957), the Hungarian uprising in 1956 demonstrated how weak the system remained.

The true obstacle to US hegemonist strategy came from the national liberation movements in Asia and Africa, which, from 1945 on, were determined to achieve the independence of non-European nations from the colonial yoke. Up to this day, imperialism has never found the terms of a social and political compromise that could allow a system of rule to stabilize in its favour in the countries of the capitalist periphery. I interpret this failure as proof that such a compromise is objectively impossible, that the polarization resulting from capitalist expansion creates an objective situation in the periphery that is potentially revolutionary and always explosive and unstable.

In the fifteen years after the end of the war, the structure of the world political system underwent radical transformation. For the first time in history, the system of sovereign states was extended to the whole planet, as a result of struggles mobilizing all the peoples of Asia and Africa. Imperialism never made a single concession in this direction without their having to fight for it. The formation of the international system that marks our age did not follow from something that capitalism wished, required or even planned, but on the contrary from struggles that contradicted the logic of world capitalist expansion, so that the latter was forced to adjust – successfully, it is true, at least in the short term – to the process of transformation. Now, the hegemon of the post-war system – the United States – was in a better position than the waning colonial powers to carry out this adjustment, and sometimes even appeared to favour the way things were going. But, although this appearance to some extent corresponded to reality, as far as concessions to the weakest national liberation movements and de facto acceptance of the neocolonial compromise were concerned, the United States placed itself at the head of the imperialist coalition in order to combat radical movements, whether they were led by Communist parties (China, Vietnam, Cuba, etc.) or intransigent nationalists supported by a popular movement (Nasserism, Arab and African socialism).

In this perspective, the great flow tide of national liberation (1945–75) that preceded the ebb tide may be said to have scored considerable achievements for the whole of Asia and Africa, and, through a kind of solidarity effect, Latin America. The most striking advances were in China, where national liberation merged with the struggle for socialism. Reading Mao

Zedong's *New Democracy* in 1952, soon after its publication, I took the basic position that ours was no longer the epoch of bourgeois revolutions (which were now impossible because the local bourgeoisies had thrown in their lot with the project of imperialist expansion) but the epoch of socialist revolution. On the periphery of the capitalist system, socialist revolution was developing by stages in an uninterrupted strategy: the democratic, anti-imperialist revolution of national liberation, led by the proletariat and its (Communist) Party, in close alliance with the peasantry, would neutralize the national bourgeoisie and isolate the enemy feudal–comprador bloc, creating the conditions for a rapid transition to the stage of socialist construction.

In Vietnam and Korea this strategy ran up against imperialist military aggression. Both the first Vietnam war (1945–54) and the second (up to 1975), as well as the Korean war (1950–53), were proof of the collective resolve of the imperialists to oppose this movement.

These earlier experiences were therefore the yardstick for the success of the national liberation movement, since it seemed evident that any liberation which did not go that far would not have completed its route. We thought that the objective conditions for this already existed in Asia and Africa, beginning with Egypt.

Like all young Egyptians at that time, I was excited by the radicalism of the popular anti-imperialist and social movement, which reached its peak on 21 February 1946. The communist movement – which, despite its youth, had gained the respect of everyone in Egypt whose patriotic and social feelings had been roused – was the only force that dared to oppose a monarchy detested by politicized layers among the working classes and the radicalized petty bourgeoisie. It therefore seemed to have the capability to lead a Chinese-style or Vietnamese-style united front. Repression continued: in fact, modern Egypt had known no genuinely democratic period, so great was the fear of communism among the exploiting classes and the imperialist masters. But this did not prevent the red flag from flying over the Nile valley, as we put it, and indeed, in those days, a genuine bourgeois democracy would undoubtedly have allowed the communists to win large sections of the masses and perhaps even the elections. Neither the bourgeoisie nor the Western powers could accept such a risk.

The creation of Israel and the first Palestine war (1948) gave some respite to local reactionary forces, but the very defeat of 1948 ensured the downfall of the monarchy, the central political pillar of imperialist and reactionary domination. From 1950, the electoral victory of the Wafd (which had been compelled to denounce the unequal treaty of 1936), together with the beginning of guerrilla operations in the occupied Canal Zone, signalled that an anti-feudal, anti-comprador revolution was a real possibility. The Cairo fire of February 1952, the dismissal of the Wafd government and a period of acute governmental instability finally led to the *coup d'état* by the Free Officers (July 1952), which simultaneously aroused hopes of social advance and cut the ground from under the feet of the progressive forces bearing the country's future.

Nevertheless, having fuelled hopes of Western support and made every concession to obtain it, Nasserism came to understand that nothing could be expected from the United States, whose main objective, since the Tripartite Declaration of 1950 (USA, Britain and France), had been to control the whole region through regimes subservient to it, relying in particular on its two military extensions (Israel and Turkey) and forcing the Arabs to accept military pacts that took over where the British and French protectorates had left off. When Nasser rejected Washington's proposal of a Baghdad pact in 1954, he became the target of an offensive drive to topple him. It was at this same moment, in 1955, that the Bandung front took shape and the USSR broke out of its isolation by offering support to third world national liberation movements. The supply of Czech weapons to Egypt prompted the final decision to overthrow Nasser (October 1956), which France and Britain had been proposing in response to his support for the Algerian FLN and the nationalization of the Suez Canal in July. This last colonial adventure was jointly mounted by London conservatives and Paris socialists, who had forgotten that they could take action only if it suited American plans, and only under American instructions. But the defeat of the expedition opened a whole new chapter for national liberation in Egypt, very different from the conditions of the previous decade. The bourgeoisie, in Egypt as elsewhere, seemed to regain control and leadership of the liberation movement – contrary to the theory that had held sway since 1945.

The Mashreq, the eastern half of the Arab world, was preparing to challenge the fragile equilibrium that had been built in the interwar period. We had not failed to notice the founding of the Baath Party, which would preside over the region's destinies from the late 1950s; we doubted the sincerity of its anti-imperialist positions and found disturbing its somewhat fascistic style. Since the events of 1945 in Algeria and 1952 in Tunisia, we had known that the days of colonial rule in the Maghreb were numbered. But who would lead the liberation? Would the Moroccan monarchy and the Tunisian bourgeoisie, to which France had handed over power in 1956 following the outbreak of war in Algeria (on 1 November 1954), be capable of imposing their neocolonial order? Would the powerful people's movement, represented by the Algerian FLN, overcome the anti-communism of its leaders, all too easily fuelled by the slavish adherence of local CPs to the ambiguous attitude of the French Communist Party?

In Iran the strength of the Tudeh Party filled us with optimism: the chauvinism that the Shah was able to exploit over the Soviet withdrawal from Azerbaijan and Kurdistan (in 1945) proved to be short-lived, and from 1951 to 1953 the events surrounding Mossadegh's nationalization of oil pointed ahead to the great battles of the future. However, Mossadegh's eventual defeat cleared the way for a quarter of a century of the Shah's bloody dictatorship. In 1954, Iran joined Turkey alongside the United States in the battle to subordinate the region to American pactomania.

Since 1945, the liberation struggles in Asia and Africa had been occupying the centre of the global arena. In our view, since the USSR and China – isolated and on the defensive – were able to give us only moral support, we would have to rely on our own forces. The liberation wars and guerrilla campaigns in Southeast Asia seemed to us to have the same potential as the victorious battles in China and Vietnam. So, when reactionary or moderate nationalist forces gained the upper hand in the early 1950s, we thought that we were witnessing a temporary reverse, not the beginning of a new era in which the conflict between imperialism and third world countries would present a very different configuration.

This is why we also considered the partition and the consolidation of Congress rule in India to be major imperialist victories that had brutally halted the development of a Chinese-style war of liberation. The diplomatic rapprochement between Nehru's India and China, and the signing of the treaty on Tibet in 1954, seemed good in themselves but in no way modified our judgement of the Congress Party. The next year, beginning with Bandung, things began to look rather different.

Until the late 1950s, I shared the Soviet-inspired 'Marxist–Leninist' view of the nature of socialism and its construction in the USSR. I did not yet realize that my incipient analysis of capitalist polarization made it necessary to rethink the challenge of actual capitalist expansion in terms other than the contrast between bourgeois revolution and socialist revolution in the periphery, which were the terms of Marxism–Leninism and even classical Marxism. Some of us were certainly not duped by the rosy propagandistic vision of the Soviet system and its growing perfection: our travels in the 'socialist' countries had revealed to us the lack of democracy, and we had read enough to be aware of the violence of the repression. Yet two other realities, which are not always taken sufficiently into account, seemed to us more important than the 'imperfections' of the Soviet system.

The first of these was the hatred and hostility that the Western powers displayed towards the Soviet Union – one need only think of McCarthyism or, thirty years later, the 'evil empire' rhetoric of Reagan and Bush – which made us think that its system posed a real danger to capitalism. Moreover, we correctly saw that the Soviet regime was on the defensive, and I never believed for a moment that any Western politician who was not a complete idiot could take seriously the idea that Stalin intended to invade Western Europe. Our position of solidarity with the Soviet Union did not require total belief in its system. But we were used to thinking that, since 1492, the Western powers had never intervened anywhere in the world to defend a defensible cause, and that without exception their interventions had always been harmful to our peoples. We therefore understood, almost spontaneously, that capitalist imperialism could never accept the refusal of any country to bow to its dictates, and that it was just such a refusal which the West held against the USSR.

The second reality was our critical judgement of bourgeois democracy, much more critical than that of many Western progressives. We could see every day how democracy was systematically denied to our peoples, and how Western diplomacy invoked it only when that tactically served its interests. Nothing has changed in this respect. Nevertheless, our argument was not valid at a psychological level, for socialism – or even any popular advance towards socialism – must by definition be more democratic than any bourgeois democracy. We bent the stick too far in the other direction. When it was a question of our own countries, we passed a severe judgement on the democratic deficit of the populist nationalist regimes. We were right to do this, but we should have seen that the argument also applied to the USSR.

With regard to the 'general crisis of capitalism', to use the Soviet concept of the time, our view was very optimistic. We thought that objective conditions throughout the third world were essentially the same as in China, and that the radical development of national liberation in the direction of socialist revolution was the order of the day. The emergence of a new national-bourgeois thrust, beginning with Bandung, subsequently proved that our analysis had been too simplistic. It should be borne in mind, however, that we did not think that socialist revolution was on the agenda elsewhere than in the periphery of the system.

From 22 rue Saint Sulpice to 7 rue des Carmes

In October 1949 I enrolled both at the law faculty and for the preparatory year in political sciences. From the beginning, it was my intention to complete a doctorate in economics, but the years of law that I had to do first were of only very moderate interest to me. I therefore decided to put my main effort into political science, which would give me the opportunity to study the things I liked most. After the preparatory year, in fact, I opted for international relations.

In those days French universities were very different from what I encountered later, as a teacher, after 1968: they were quaintly old-fashioned in their formalism, standards of dress, abuse of lectures and failure to keep courses up to date. They were also elitist in the nineteenth-century sense, as France was only just beginning to experience the massive spread of secondary education that would eventually swell the higher-education sector, in a context of profound social change.

Law students did not attend lectures – or, at least, I cannot remember setting foot in a lecture hall throughout my undergraduate years. Instead, I showed up in April or May to buy some duplicated lecture notes and speed-read them in a café, but the results were not so brilliant as I had to repeat my first year and graduated only in June 1953.

Meanwhile I had finished at the Institute of Political Science (*Sciences Po*) and obtained my diploma in June 1952. Some of the lectures there were interesting, especially Jean Baby's on Marxism, and the course work itself was compulsory as well as intelligently designed. The lecturer Michel Debeauvais, a communist member of the Resistance and death camp survivor, became a personal friend of mine.

Following its nationalization in 1945, the formerly reactionary and elitist Institute of Political Science was undergoing quite a boom; its function – at least in the case of the administration and finance departments – was to prepare students for the entrance exam to the newly created École Nationale d'Administration (ENA). The ENA supplies ministers and principal private secretaries, prefects and chief executive officers – people both on the right and on the left (that is, supporters of the Socialist Party, as communists were marginalized and developed their own tradition of cadre formation). Modesty inhibits any mention of these august names, which include those of statesmen who reached the very top of the ladder in the Republic. But, whether as friends or acquaintances or political opponents, I and others of my generation mixed with an incredible number of those who today 'administer' France, and engaged with them in sometimes serious, often stormy debates.

The PCF's influence at the Institute was so great that it organized two separate cells; they used to meet at the Party offices in an indescribable hovel on rue Dupin that has now been replaced with a modern block. It was not unusual to come across a rat as you climbed the ramshackle staircase, passing overcrowded rooms and flats and often blocked toilets that gave off every imaginable smell. Isabelle got to know hundreds of such places in her later work at the Tenants Federation. The legacy of the 'liberal', unfettered capitalism that had been the norm until the war, they gradually faded from the landscape in Western Europe thanks to the social policies which fear of communism forced the bourgeoisie to accept in its own self-interest, but they have never completely disappeared from the big American cities, are making a comeback in post-Thatcher Britain, and will perhaps become a part of life on the continent if the neoliberal turn is continued. Such is the 'normal' law of the market – that is, of the one-sided domination of capital.

The Party cell meetings, which were held weekly, or more frequently if special activity made it necessary, saw serious and lively discussions. Contrary to the image presented of them nowadays, communists were by no means a herd of yes-men – even if they did end up internalizing the logic of dogmatism. A perfect illustration of this process was the expulsion of Selsevic, an Egyptian-born Yugoslav, who sided with the Cominform against Tito yet was accused of being a 'Titoist infiltrator' simply because it was necessary to find and expose one. When the secretary of the Paris Federation came to a cell meeting to demand his expulsion, he could put forward only the stupidest of arguments: Selsevic smoked Balto cigarettes instead of the workers' Gauloises; he had expressed a wish to have a motor-cycle; he was living with a Bulgarian woman (I never understood what was shameful about that!). And yet, his best friend Farag Moussa, who had known him as a teenager in Cairo, voted along with everyone else for his expulsion. Subsequently expelled from France too (this time for his communist affiliations!), he sought refuge in East Germany, in the naïve belief that the truth would one day be established. But he was arrested in East Berlin and sent to Czechoslovakia, rearrested, thrown into prison and released only after many years.

We used to spend a lot of time in the *Sciences Po* entrance hall, discussing everything under the sun, organizing petitions, trying to get students to come on demonstrations. The friends that Isabelle and I made in those days have mostly remained our friends, even if circumstances have put a geographic distance between us. I am thinking of Farag Moussa, André Vanoli (later director of the French Central Statistical Office – INSEE), Barthélémy (a top civil servant at the Public Finance Department), Éliane Mossé, Andrée Lacarrère and the lawyer Viviane Le Marc (who later went into alcoholic decline and was killed by her alcoholic lover in a Nanterre slum).

It was also at *Sciences Po* that Isabelle and I first met in 1950. We were at once strongly drawn to each other, and a few days later we were beginning a life together. Isabelle likes to point out that she was less Stalinist than I – or not Stalinist at all, with a more anarchistic temperament that happily complements the other mere half of myself that I would describe in that way. (This semi-anarchistic side I perhaps owe to my grandmother, and the other side to Egyptians and Alsatians who have very little in common with the Gascony of Isabelle's father or the Champagne of my grandmother.)

Already during my school years I used to spend quite a lot of time at 22 rue Saint Sulpice, where Jacques Vergès was living. After his return from Višovice he had founded an association of anti-imperialist students, baptised the Ho Chi Minh Association, and he and I formed the communist nucleus of it that tried to act within broader organizations of colonial students to move them beyond spontaneous nationalism – the most active being the Vietnamese (whose leaders then included Vo The Quang and Do Dai Phuoc), the students from Réunion, the West Indians (Justin, Fardin et al.), the Madagascans, the Africans who later founded the famous FEANF (Abdou Moumouni and Malik Sangaret are two of my oldest friends from the region), the Egyptians and Syrians, and the North Africans (who used to meet at 115 boulevard Saint-Michel).

So, in June 1949 I went to live in a tiny room at rue Saint Sulpice, in a building which before the war had been a brothel much used by senators and Catholic prelates (a concealed door in a religious souvenir shop on the ground floor made it possible to climb the stairs without being seen), and which after 1955 became the four-star Hôtel du Sénat. At that time, however, it had been 'nationalized' and placed at the disposal of students from Réunion. Jacques Vergès had staged a *'coup d'état'*, driving out the rich reactionaries and, in the name of internationalism, freeing rooms for other colonials from Vietnam and Africa, including myself. The Conseil Général de la Réunion and Parisian support bodies had cut off their student allowances, but we did not have to pay rent – only a contribution to the minimal costs of electricity, water and (very basic) heating. It was far from being a comfortable hotel, then, but it could be used as a place for meetings, and as the offices of the *Étudiants anticolonialistes* magazine that functioned between 1949 and 1953. Dull it certainly wasn't. The police raided it on the slightest pretext, often as the result of some provocation. It was easy enough for them to get people expelled from France, without having to give any justification; that is what happened to Farag Moussa, who had to continue his studies in Geneva. The concierge of the 'hotel' was Mère Simone, an unusually obese woman, probably recommended by the CP, who was nice enough but not very efficient and rather dubious in matters of cleanliness; she used to sit motionless behind the grimy counter watching our comings and goings. Her shady husband, Père Lulu, spent his time drinking with the owner of the corner café (it is now a fashionable boutique), which was also frequented by the local police. When Isabelle came to join me, we had the right to a larger room, with a view over the roofs of Paris. For us it seemed palatial – which was not difficult in those days.

At *Étudiants anticolonialistes*, where I was one of the editors, I also had the task of supervising the manual typesetting and correcting the proofs. I liked setting the lead letters and reading them back to front, and I came both to learn a lot about print workers and to enjoy their company. It was a very agreeable milieu, cultured and anarchistic.

Isabelle and I used to eat in the university canteens, which were not exactly great, or – when our finances permitted it – at a Greek, Chinese or Vietnamese restaurant in the Quartier Latin. It was at one of these, on rue du Sommerard, that Comrade Long (what has become of him?) served us triple portions and charged us for a single – making up for it with his rich customers, he said. We also ate cheap and delicious Chinese soups in a (now vanished) cul-de-sac behind the Gare de Lyon, filled with Chinese restaurants that each had an opium den in the back room. It was then that I first got into my lifelong habit of working in cafés, which were better heated than No. 22, and whose noisy anonymity I found much more propitious than the deadly reading rooms I hated so much in the university. The Relais de l'Odéon thus became a kind of annex of No. 22.

Farag too lived at No. 22. He had picked up a stray kitten from somewhere, which he baptised Bouny and used to feed on sardines and chocolate (his own favourite brand, probably). When he was expelled from France, we inherited the cat – a nice creature, like all animals – and set it up at Isabelle's parents' house with a garden in the suburbs. It continued all its life to go crazy at the sound of a chocolate bar being opened – childhood memories for it too.

Our life at No. 22 kept us so busy that we felt little need to go outside Paris. Sometimes we took a cheap break that proved to be more tiring than restful, for example, three or four days' camping at Bonneuil-sur-Marne (the suburbs of Paris!) or, just once, a little further to Caen. At No. 22 we organized merry 'dances', some of which got a little too merry under the influence of drink, or were livened up with a slightly phoney lottery that served to bolster the finances of our community or the magazine. The Quatorze Juillet used to be livelier and more popular than in later years, when car ownership spread and Parisians got into the depressing habit of escaping the city whenever possible. Once, I remember, a nouveau riche at the wheel of an American convertible, accompanied by a vulgar blonde, tried to make his way down the little pedestrian-thronged rue Grégoire de Tours, and Farag on the pavement, cool as a cucumber, slapped the guy so hard in the face that his cigar fell from his mouth. The irate victim got out of his car and made a rush at Farag, but then stopped in his tracks when he realized just how solidly built he was. Farag kept his composure beneath a shower of insults, while the crowd, which had not really witnessed the original incident, asked what was happening. 'Nothing,' Farag answered calmly. 'He must be raving mad. Look how he shows off his wealth.' Farag simply wanted to show us that you can always come out on top if you keep your self-control.

Among my friends at No. 22 was Abdou Moumouni, the physicist who subsequently installed a famous solar energy laboratory at Niamey, in his native Niger. Abdou had been the victim of political repression (at the Lycée Saint Louis, I think), and we had welcomed him to No. 22. Although he was a sun specialist, his head had always been in the clouds (or 'on the moon', as we say in French). One cold wintry evening, when Isabelle saw him sitting on the pavement opposite No. 22 and watching the snow fall, she asked him what he was doing. 'I'm looking at the moon', he replied. I could tell many such stories from the time he lived in Bamako, in Mali.

We spent a lot of time on political activity, which for me fell into three areas of equal importance. First, naturally enough, there was French political life; I could not imagine living in a country without taking that seriously, and for me there is no problem in being a convinced internationalist. Apart from the PCF, we were also active in UNEF, the French students' union, where we already came up against Le Pen and his fascists. Street demonstrations often turned violent, and the police intervened repeatedly to protect the fascists, as was only natural. Isabelle remembers that once Le Pen, surrounded and in a tight corner (but not even roughed up), was saved by a police charge under the direction of the local commissioner. Le Pen escaped unharmed in the commissioner's car – no doubt they went off to have a drink together – while the cops took away the communist activists and gave them a beating. Yet, as usual, it was the squad of fascists who had initiated the violence.

Political activity in France had some remarkable, if also questionable, intellectual dimensions: profound discussions took place every week on politics, history, literary and artistic criticism. But equally, or more, important for me was the struggle within 'colonial' organizations, and No. 22 offered the ideal setting to conduct this in an anti-imperialist, internationalist spirit that could unite young people from Asia, Africa and the West Indies.

First of all, we responded to each major event in the liberation struggle of the people to which we belonged: the trial and sentencing of Madagascan deputies, the Casablanca riots of December 1952, the deposition of Sultan Ben Youssef of Morocco in August 1953, the vicissitudes of the Vietnam war and later the Algerian war (Guy Mollet's humiliating visit to Algiers in January 1956, the boarding of the Moroccan plane carrying Ben Bella in September 1956), the troubles in Tunisia and the return of Bourguiba in June 1955, the concessions of 1957 that paved the way for the autonomy of France's African colonies, and so on.

Isabelle and I did not conceal our joy at the news from Dien Bien Phu in May 1954; the disgusting war in Indochina was finally ending in victory for the side that deserved to win. As internationalists through and through, we hated French imperialism as much as any other, just as it would have been normal for a German to rejoice at the defeat of Hitler. I felt the same when the Americans were driven from Saigon in May 1975, and laughed at the television pictures of US generals, stolen art objects under their arms, jostling one another to board the last helicopters. Recently, on a visit to Vietnam, we had the opportunity to discuss Dien Bien Phu and to read what Bigeard wrote following his return to the scene of the battle.[17] Isabelle then had an interesting exchange of letters with Bigeard, who seems to have been more a victim of the system than one would have thought.

I followed especially closely the events in Egypt and the Middle East: the Palestine war of 1948, the CIA's *coup d'état* against Mossadegh in Iran (1953), Egypt's renunciation of the treaty of 1936 and the beginning of guerrilla operations in the Canal Zone (1951), the Cairo fire of January 1952, Nasser's *coup d'état* of July 1952 and its aftermath in 1954, the arrests of communists between 1952 and 1954, and the nationalization of the Canal (July 1956) and the Suez war (October–December 1956), to which I shall return shortly. More generally, the great Bandung conference (1955) and the beginning of the Sino-Soviet split (1957) were major turning points in the history of the contemporary world.

We believed that our responsibilities – and perhaps our capacities – required us to give more systematic thought to strategies of national liberation and socialist construction. This involved a dual task: to theorize the fundamental problems associated with capitalist expansion (the subject of my doctoral thesis[18] and my lifetime preoccupation), and to engage in more directly political reflection on the relationship between national liberation and socialist construction, and therefore the future of our countries in the Third World.

The Anticolonialist Students Liaison Committee, of which Jacques Vergès was general secretary, played an important role in the years from 1948 to 1954 and, in the longer term, helped to radicalize young men (few women in those days!) who later became active politicians in their own countries. This called for a combination of great strategic firmness and tactical skill. We had to remain close enough to the 'nationalist masses' for them to accept us, while also trying to move them beyond a spontaneously anti-imperialist nationalism towards 'socialist class consciousness'. We had to engage in permanent dialogue with the existing leaders of national liberation movements, sometimes 'exposing' those who compromised themselves with the French or American imperialists, but sometimes assisting them to take an important step forward. Jacques Vergès placed his great talents at the service of a cause that deserved the commitment of all our capacities and willpower.

The leading bodies of the PCF, to which we remained loyal in principle, did not always understand the finer points of our strategy and tactics, and sometimes characterized us – according to circumstances – as 'petty-bourgeois nationalist deviants' or left or right 'opportunists'. They did this in the dogmatic, wooden language that became all too familiar over the years.

With hindsight, the essence of the problem seems quite straightforward. The political line set out in Zhdanov's report to the Cominform on the international situation (September 1947), which divided the world into a camp of socialism (and peace) and a camp of capitalism (and war), seems to me not to have been wrong in itself, as a response to the Cold War unleashed by the United States, but to have involved a simplification at several levels. In choosing war and peace as the central focus of mass action, it gave priority to defence of the encircled Soviet Union and Eastern Europe and thereby inspired a dangerous reduction of the camp of socialism (and subordination of revolutionary strategies) to the interests of the self-styled socialist states. This is the reproach that Maoism would later lay at the door of the Soviet leadership. Furthermore, Zhdanov's simple dualism obscured a fundamental contradiction within the 'camp of capitalism', opposing the colonized peoples of Asia and Africa to the imperialist heartlands and their American protector – the very contradiction, in fact, on which we based our activity in the Committee of Anticolonialist Students. Zhdanov fell into the trap laid by the Americans, for they too described the world as divided into two camps: a demonized communism and the 'free world', as if the dominated peoples were free within it.

It was even possible to interpret the Zhdanov doctrine in a way that indirectly flattered French imperialist chauvinism, so that the task of the peoples colonized by France was no longer to fight for their own liberation but to struggle alongside the PCF to bring France (and therefore its dependencies) into the camp of socialism. Interestingly enough, many of our worst enemies in the Party – ultra-dogmatists such as Annie Besse – later became apologists for the most banal anti-communism. But meanwhile they hauled us before 'commissions of inquiry', chaired by sad mediocrities like the Seine Party secretary Raymond Guyot. Things turned so ugly that it was necessary to go right to the top, to Party leader Maurice Thorez himself, who, it must be said, ultimately ruled in our favour. Thorez had the makings of a great French politician, and I think he realized that many of the young people in question would play a role in their own country, and that it would not be a bad thing if they were friendly to the PCF and France (or, anyway, a certain France).

It is not surprising that those with the most dogmatic rhetoric, actually the most servile rather than the most convinced, should have so easily passed to the other side of the barricades. It is almost a general law of human behaviour. I remember one of the men in charge of the CPSU's ideological censorship, Oleg Bogomolov, a past master in the art of wrenching quotations out of context, who never failed in his duty to castigate 'deviationists' (including myself, whose 'petty-bourgeois' theory was supposed to have overemphasized the global polarization within capitalism). Well, in September 1991, scarcely two years after his party had lost its ruling position in the USSR, this officiating priest at the Academy of Sciences suddenly declared himself a straightforward 'anti-communist'. I was present when he said this, at a conference organized in Budapest, and I could not stop myself bursting into laughter. 'Gospodin Bogomolov,'[19] I said, 'if this is indeed the man I am thinking of and not someone with the same name, seems to have been converted to anti-communism just a couple of weeks ago. But rest assured, I have known him for thirty years and I have always considered him an anti-communist.'

The points I have just been making on the nature of the epoch, which are central to my book *Re-reading the Postwar Period*, led me to engage in constant discussion with the future leaders of independent Africa and a series of brilliant Asian and African intellectuals, as well as to contribute to the debates in Egyptian communism, most notably in the polemic between Hadeto and the CP and in the pages of the journal *Moyen Orient* (from 1949 to 1953). The friends I made in the process – above all, Ismail Abdallah[20] and Bouli, Raymond Aghion, Yves Bénot[21] and Maxime Rodinson[22] – have remained among my closest.

Raymond Aghion then had quite substantial funds from a family inheritance, which he gradually used up, with great political generosity, for the support of progressive causes. But that was by no means his only quality: he has always been sharp and precise in everything he has done. In those days he used to receive us in his luxurious maisonette in Neuilly, where we discussed the contents and other matters relating to *Moyen Orient*, which owed a great deal to Aghion's input. Yves Bénot, who offered his services free as he has always done, displayed the same qualities of generosity and modesty, as well as political courage (he had been a member of the Resistance, of course) and intelligence. Maxime Rodinson was and remained the most delightful person you can imagine, with a scrupulous honesty that one would like to find in more intellectuals, whether committed to the left or not.

Ismail, whose qualities of heart and mind are well known, was another of my few comrades who thought that the contradiction between imperialism and its dominated peoples constituted a strategic field irreducible to Zhdanovian dualism. It is certainly he who proposed that *Moyen Orient* should support the 'neutralist movement' which became the axis of struggles in what I have called the 'Bandung period' (1955–75). Together with Fouad Moursi, he then developed this idea in the direction of founding an Egyptian communist party separate from Hadeto. We could not have failed to meet again there. Bouli, whom Isabelle and I first met during this period, has not only demonstrated her literary talent but – when Ismail was later in prison – given proof of exemplary courage and tenacity. I should add that the very writing of these *Memoirs* owes a lot to her. It was after reading her own memoirs – a magnificent portrait of Egyptian society – that it occurred to me that I too might have something of interest to say.

No doubt history did not stop when my student life came to an end. I anyway have a concept of education as a never-ending process. Readers who are interested in my further thoughts about the Bandung period may again consult *Re-reading the Postwar Period*; they led me, at least by 1960, to become highly critical of the Soviet system, and therefore to have difficult relations with the mainstream communist currents during the next three decades.

Returning to a more personal note, I should say that once I had my law degree and political science diploma I thought mostly about my thesis in economics. I therefore registered in September 1953 for the higher diploma in political economy and obtained it in June 1954. At the same time, to make my maths 'pay', I registered in September 1953 at the Institute of Statistics, obtained its vocational training certificate in June 1954, its higher certificate in 1955 and its mathematical statistician's diploma in June 1956. The main course there was on the calculation of probabilities and the special mathematics associated with it. But, at that time, computers were still only at the research stage, and we were limited to what now seems the antediluvian recording of data on punch cards. Meanwhile I also made a lot of progress with my thesis, under the supervision of François Perroux and Maurice Byé. It was nearly finished when my political activity in connection with the Suez war obliged me to delay submission until June 1957.

My work method involved reading all the basic classics, as well as opening out to other subjects such as politics and acquiring historical knowledge in every dimension. An understanding of society can never come from economics alone. What this also meant, however, was that I wasted little time on mainstream economic literature, the compulsory reading of which nowadays has an effect that I would almost describe as mind-numbing.

I read a great deal – nor was I alone in this. It would never have been acceptable to 'learn' economics from the Samuelson-style manuals that are the rule nowadays. Good students used to read all the classic sources, which for me naturally meant Marx, but also Smith, Ricardo, Böhm-Bawerk, Walras, Keynes, and so on. This serious study programme forced us to deepen our Marxist understanding of bourgeois theories, to develop an immanent critique of economistic thinking, to uncover its true ideological nature and its attempts to legitimize capitalism by basing it on ahistorical mechanisms of 'universal harmony'.

The result in my case was an interesting thesis. It may not have excelled in the eyes of a mainstream academic, but I dare to say without false modesty that it was ten to twenty years ahead of what became the main current of thinking on the left, with its emphasis on capitalist polarization (later theorized in terms of 'dependence', 'world economy' or whatever). François Perroux and Maurice Byé rewarded me not only by giving it the faculty prize but by writing a letter in which they attributed the 'rarely seen' qualities of 'this exceptional thesis' to my 'wide-ranging culture'. I am not insensitive to such praise.

After returning from a trip to Egypt in October 1953, Isabelle and I left 22 rue Saint Sulpice, which was due eventually to be handed back to its owners. Besides, the running of the Réunion student community was now in the hands of a really horrible guy, Chane Kune, whose ugly grimacing face, fat body and coarse manners were strongly reminiscent of Chinese mafia compradors. He has since become a political wheeler-dealer of the right in Réunion.

In the same year, the PCF asked foreigners active in their own country's organizations (mostly underground, as in my case) not to renew their Party membership.

Isabelle and I moved for a time to her parents' house at Pavillons-sous-Bois, then had the good fortune to find a monthly let at the Hôtel de Rome, 7 rue des Carmes – a real rarity in Paris at that time.

Isabelle, having graduated from the Institute of Political Science, was working at the finance ministry, in converted royal stables from the eighteenth century, which, though splendid enough, were by then in a sorry state. Discriminated against as a communist, she was assigned to examine the files of former Resistance fighters and to determine whether any improvement in the state of their wounds made it possible to reduce their benefits. There was to be no misplaced generosity on the part of the French state. During this same period, Isabelle was fined – together with Jacqueline Meppiel, now a film-maker in Cuba – for handing out leaflets against a French colonialist intervention in Tunisia. (Yes, it was still possible for a judge to fish out one pretext or another from the thick mass of legislation.) After further punishment for taking part in a strike, she was sent out of the way to a cellar on rue de Vaugirard, where she worked alongside little old men in cotton oversleeves, sorting returned envelopes in a Balzacian setting that was hard to imagine if you had not seen it with your own eyes.

Subsequently, I think in 1954, Lazare Rosenztroch recruited Isabelle to work at the Tenants Federation, then a mass organization, which defended people against threats of eviction. The housing crisis was still acute, and – as a campaign launched by Abbé Pierre in 1954 dramatically recalled – there was a real risk of dying from the cold in a makeshift hovel. The work perfectly suited Isabelle's brave temperament, her ability to bring out the neighbours in protest and to stand up to the cops. But we also needed to think that we would soon be returning to Egypt, and teaching work would qualify her for a possible job there.

Isabelle and I have fond memories of the short holidays we could sometimes afford to take: for example, a spring week at Saint Jean Cap Ferrat, on the advice of Ismail and Bouli; or perhaps as much as a month at the village of Les Diablerets in Switzerland, in a chalet we rented with Farag and an Egyptian friend of his. Isabelle naturally had no intention of acting as a maid to us three men, and so we decided to draw lots for the housework on a rota basis. But, on the day before it was the turn of Farag's friend, he began to 'feel ill' and left. The three of us stayed on together, until Farag showed up with a pretty Italian waitress from the local café and made it a foursome; we went for long walks every other day, leaving in the morning and returning at sunset. Then there were the holidays we spent travelling all over Corsica, the very beautiful homeland of Isabelle's mother. In our little beach hotel at Algajola we were fed exclusively with rock lobsters, the owner finding it less tiring to go and draw the nets from the previous day than to go shopping in the village. Later, with the help of Reda (a real ace at fixing things), I bought an old banger to drive down Italy's Adriatic coast. We spent one holiday at Cattolica, again with Farag, then returned via the Dolomites and the Swiss canton of Graubünden, stopping for the night in the back of beyond at a little inn recalling L'Auberge Rouge. The landlord, abandoned by his wife and now living with a mentally retarded maid, had not had a customer for ages; the rooms were decorated with all manner of ancient farm implements and the floor creaked at night beneath his insomniac feet. The bedroom door did not shut properly, and there was a torrent beneath the window to carry away chopped-up body parts, so Isabelle shifted a table to prop up against the door. The next morning, the banger was still so weary from the steep slope it had had to climb that it almost failed to start. Finally, in spring 1957, with my thesis already finished, we travelled to Seville and Granada, through a Spain newly reopened to the outside world. On the way back, however, things could have turned nasty when, in a long queue for reservations, we protested at all the trading of favours and preferential treatment. The ubiquitous Guardia Civil took us to their office and accused us of 'insulting the regime', and we got away only by paying everything we had in fines. While Isabelle continued on to Paris, I alighted penniless at Carcassonne and went to pick up the copy of my thesis that had been made at Aix.

The colonial political milieu in France

My activities as a student naturally brought me into contact with broad sections of people involved in African politics. First there were the young people – mostly the first generation of students who in 1950 founded the FEANF (Fédération des Étudiants d'Afrique Noire en France). Little has been written about this milieu, but it deserves to be studied in greater depth. When I leaf through Charles Diané's collection of documents,[23] I realize that I spent hours in discussion with most of the Federation's activists: from Senegal, Babacar Niang, Cheikh Anta Diop, Mamadou Dia (the doctor and namesake of the prime minister), Baidi Ly, Ogo Kane Diallo, Maktar M'Bow (the future director-general of UNESCO), Assane Seck and Amady Dieng; from Congo, Joseph van den Reysen and Henri Lopez; from Cameroun, Osende Afana, Tchaptchet and Woungly Massaga; from Togo-Dahomey, Franklin, Tevoedjre and Behanzin; from Upper Volta, Kaboré – although a number of others, studying in the provinces, only came occasionally to Paris, and many names are missing from the list. This first generation inevitably provided many of the government and opposition leaders in the post-1960 independent African states. I developed ties of personal friendship with a few of them: especially Malik Sangaré from Ivory Coast, the youngest participant in the Bamako founding congress of the RDA – African Democratic Rally in 1946 (he is now a surgeon in Abidjan), and the Niger physicist Abdou Moumouni. Having finished my studies in 1957, I did not get to know the second generation, who began to come in larger numbers in 1955–56, just before the law granting semi-autonomy to the colonies of sub-Saharan Africa. As the training of African cadres grew by leaps and bounds, the nature of political activity began to change: the prospect of being part of the system replaced the aim of fighting it. Gradually a new class took shape, whose main concern was to cash in on its diplomas.

No less interesting were my discussions, usually as part of a delegation, with the 'politicians' of the new Africa: party leaders (whether belonging to the RDA or not), trade unionists, French parliamentary deputies or members of the Conseil de l'Union Française, many of whom either lived in Paris for long periods or visited it quite frequently. A few of the names that spring to mind are: Gabriel d'Arboussier, Léopold Senghor, Félix Houphouët-Boigny, Daniel Ouezzin Coulibaly, Hamani Diori, Sourou-Migan Apithy, Mamadou Konate, Félix Tchicaya, Sékou Touré, Bakari Djibo, Doudou Guèye and Gisèle Rabesahala. I never met Ruben Um Nyobé (did he ever come to Paris?), although younger leaders of the Cameroon People's Union – Tchaptchet, Massaga, Osende Afana (executed by Ahidjo's henchmen) and later Moumie (murdered by the French secret service) – plunged me into the debate within this more than averagely radical party, soon after the national uprising was launched in 1955. My testimony of these discussions will be sincere, but I am not sure that my interpretation of them is the same today as it was then. Moreover, although my memory is generally good, I only remember well a certain number of encounters; many others have faded and blurred over the years.

The occasion of our meeting was usually a protest against repressive measures affecting student activists, when we went as a delegation to solicit the support of members of parliament and political leaders. It is true that we did not contact the 'rotten elements' promoted by the colonial administration through fake elections, but all the others – RDA radicals or moderates, or non-RDA leaders such as Senghor – condemned the repression. They did not, however, carry sufficient weight with their own governments, whose main concern was to protect the administrative apparatuses in place. I remember Senghor once fulminating: 'Yes, they keep telling me it's a matter of communists. So what's wrong with that? When you're young you're a communist. It's normal.'

We also met these leaders to discuss burning issues of the day, perhaps the subject of debate in the National Assembly or the Conseil de l'Union

Française, such as the bloody repression in Ivory Coast (1950) or the doubts about whether forced labour had actually been abolished, or the trial of the Madagascan deputies Raseta and Ravoahangy. We expressed the point of view of the 'Anticolonialist Students', supporting the leaders' statements that we thought positive and progressive, and criticizing those we considered inadequate. Yves Bénot has given a subtle and precise account of these debates, and of the various positions taken.[24]

Most important of all, perhaps, was the opportunity that these meetings provided to discuss basic strategic issues. What did we want? What should be the aims of the anticolonialist struggle: independence, assimilation or a 'genuine French union' involving a more or less federal multinational state? Today it may seem that the only progressive option was independence, but things looked more complex at the time, especially in the period between 1946 and 1950.

For the most radical – the Cameroon People's Union (UPC), especially after the 1955 uprising and the bloody repression that continued long after 1960 – independence was the evident objective, to be associated with socialist revolution. This was the Vietnamese model, which the movements in the Portuguese colonies also tried to implement. But the UPC was the only one of this kind in the French colonies of sub-Saharan Africa.

For the Madagascans too, who had remained attached to national identity throughout the colonial period, independence was the strategic objective. Although the idea of a loose French Union was accepted (rather in the manner of Ho Chi Minh in 1945–46), it was no more than a possible concession that in no way undercut the demand for total national autonomy.

For the other countries of western and central Africa, however, things were rather less clear-cut. Here the struggle on the ground was for assimilation, in the sense of an end to special laws for the colonies and the extension of French legislation to all overseas territories. This was, to be sure, tactically irreproachable. An amusing and little-known example is the demand of African schoolteachers that 'special' cheap textbooks for the colonies should be replaced with the ones used in France – a demand that eventually led to the famous manual in which black children were reminded of their 'ancestors, the Gauls'. But we may well ask what would have been the outcome if the struggles for assimilation had won through.

The Communist parties of the French West Indies and Réunion fought on this ground and did eventually carry the day. The outcome is such a degree of economic and social dependence that it is hard to imagine that the French West Indies or Réunion could one day, for better or worse, become independent. Paradoxically, although they have become inseparable from France, they owe this to the successful efforts of communists. The right, on the other hand, which always opposed assimilation at the level of people's rights, supporting first slavery and then a colonial status, would not have prevented the movement from championing the demand for independence, as it did in the British West Indies and Mauritius.

Would the same degree of assimilation have been possible (assuming that people wanted and fought for it) in Africa? To answer this, we need to go beyond the framework of 'the national question'. For total economic and social integration does not necessarily entail the abolition of cultural specificity or national diversity. Some argue that the West Indies and Réunion constitute different nations from the French nation; others argue the opposite. But everyone agrees that Africans were not and could not become French. Thus, if I say that a 'West Indian' type of assimilation was not possible for Africa, it is not for national-cultural but for economic reasons – at least in the framework of a system that remained fundamentally capitalist. Would it have been possible in a different system? We should not forget that the PCF's strategic objective, at least in 1946, was to build a 'genuine' people's French Union, highly centralized and homogeneous in its social-economic organization but diverse in respect of the nations composing it – in other words, a multinational socialist state along the lines of the USSR. I do not know if that would have been feasible, but in any case it was not what history wanted to happen. It would certainly have involved economic sacrifices for the French people to help the ex-colonies catch up. After all, that is what Russians did in the case of Central Asia and Transcaucasia (which is why the analogy between the USSR and the colonial empires is meaningless), although history has shown the fragility of a set-up that Russians themselves apparently did not wish to maintain.

In our discussions with African leaders, we were led to pose these questions, albeit in an ambiguous and sometimes confused manner. But, as I remember it, most leaders (except those from Madagascar and Cameroon, following the Vietnamese, Cambodians, Laotians and North Africans) had given no thought to them. Most of those who were fighting for a 'same laws' type of assimilation had no strategic vision; they were tacticians and nothing more. My memory of Houphouët (who did support our activity financially) is that such matters just made him yawn, and the same was true of many others, including Sékou Touré. But there were some who reflected on the issues. D'Arboussier and Senghor, for example, though politically opposed to each other, shared the strategic objective of a multinational state in which the former colonies would be associated with France, the former believing that this would happen through socialist revolution in France, the latter that it could be achieved through gradual evolution. Curiously, therefore, Senghor was at least in this respect closer to the Communist Party than one might think.

In any event, since the French right had never wanted anything other than colonies, the idea of a French Union was not on the cards. The PCF came to realize this and gradually discarded its project of a multinational people's republic, while the SFIO, in its timorous way, effectively rallied to traditional colonialist positions. It is therefore easy to understand why young Africans took the initiative of declaring independence as the strategic goal. The Parti Africain de l'Indépendance (PAI) was a late product of this development, founded at a time (1957) when a new outline law had already sketched out independence as a possible option. No doubt a number of external events speeded up the process: the Mau Mau revolt in English-speaking Kenya (although it had few echoes among students in Paris), the outbreak of war in Algeria in November 1954 (surprising because the country had always been thought of as 'French'), but above all the UPC insurrection in Cameroon, in sub-Saharan 'French' Africa. This is not to belittle the historical importance of the PAI, and indeed I discussed many of these questions with one of its founders, my friend Abdou Moumouni. Since the outline law did not formally envisage independence, most African politicians nevertheless condemned the PAI initiative – an error of judgement on their part, of course, because independence came anyway, faster than expected, not only for the single country (Guinea) that voted no in the 1958 referendum on the official French plan but even for those that voted yes. As a result, these politicians often seemed to be 'yesterday's men' in the eyes of the younger generation.

The ensuing debate therefore inevitably led to a re-reading of the past that conflicted with the position I have just outlined. Senghor's *négritude*, summed up in the formula 'Reason is Greek, intuition is black', became the screen hiding his abdication of responsibility in the conflict with the colonial power. It also involved a misinterpretation, since the ideology of *négritude*, constructed in the 1930s by West Indians at least as much as by black Africans, had been scarcely more than a response to the challenge of racism and had no bearing on what was at stake politically in the 1950s.

The core group of anticolonialist students therefore had some success in its activity among Africans. We also tried to establish relations with movements from various African countries, and to this end I travelled to London in 1952 to meet the WASU (West African Students Union) and representatives of east and southern African movements. The Gold Coast (today's Ghana) was known to be Africa's most advanced colony, having experienced an economic take-off fifty years ahead of the fleeting Ivory Coast 'miracle', and we already believed that Nkrumah's vision of a regional, pan-African movement was the only one that corresponded to the objective requirements of the situation. But we were swimming against the current, since France's outline law was pushing a new generation of students to derive immediate benefits by falling into line with a kind of institutionalized Balkanization into 'territories/future states'. We paid special attention to Sudan, a country straddling Arab and black Africa, which obtained independence as early as 1956 when it became clear that the British were in no position to delay it indefinitely. Of course, we were also convinced that the Mau Mau armed struggle in Kenya was ushering in a new stage in the national liberation movement. It was in London, during long discussions of these issues (including the relevance of Mao Zedong's *New Democracy* for African liberation and the construction of socialism), that I first met the man who would lead the revolution in Zanzibar a few years later: Abdulrahman Mohamed Babu. We immediately became real friends and never lost touch with each other, meeting up again in the journal *Revolution* and then in Dar es Salaam.

Our activity in the North African milieu was more difficult, as we came up against a number of strongly anti-communist nationalist parties that had overwhelming support among students in Paris: the Moroccan Istiqal, the Tunisian Destour and even Messali Hadj's MNA in Algeria (despite the fact that it had initially recruited among émigré workers in France). Our isolation here was sometimes reinforced by unfortunate aberrations on the part of the PCF, such as its absurd theory of an 'Algerian nation being formed through the joint contribution of Arabs, Berbers and Pieds Noirs'. The Moroccan Hadi Messouaq played a valuable role in our discussions of this problem, but it remained difficult to plan any action to end our isolation, if only because the nationalist leaders (apart from those under house arrest) spent little time in France. We were unaware of the conflicts beneath the surface of these parties that were paving the way for the founding of the Socialist Union of Popular Forces in Morocco, the Ben Youssefist and Ben Salahist organizations in Tunisia, and the proclamation of the FLN and the launching of the liberation war in Algeria. We were little more than external observers of these developments. So, it was only later that many communists rallied to these more radical currents, without being able to gain positions of real influence within them.

The 'Indochinese' milieux were completely autonomous. In particular, the Vietnamese divided into two clear camps of their own: those who supported the liberation war in Vietnam (and often went back there to fight), and corrupt elements in the pay of Bao Dai (with whom we obviously had no contact). The position of the Cambodians and Laotians was a little different, neither of their countries being then more than marginally involved in the war of liberation. The Cambodians' historic distrust of their big

Vietnamese brother was apparent to anyone who knew how to look for the signs. I personally knew Khieu Samphan, who was an economics student like myself. But I only came across Saloth Sar (the future Pol Pot) on two occasions; he soon ended his studies and returned to Cambodia. Unscrupulous journalists have since embroidered on the issue of my 'relations' with Khieu Samphan, and I have even been described as his 'mentor'. That is a stupid calumny. He was exactly the same age as myself, and there is no way I could ever have been his intellectual guide.

As I said before, the West Indians were focused on their battle for assimilation, but they had some brilliant poets and intellectuals whose prestige was thoroughly deserved. René Depestre from Haiti, Aimé Césaire and Léon-Gontran Damas from the West Indies, were among those to whom we listened a lot, and with whom we discussed freely. Meetings with them were always refreshing.

There were a considerable number of Syrians and Iraqis in Paris, many of them tightly organized by their respective Communist parties. They were the dominant force among student activists from the Middle East, while the Baathists – or Baathists-to-be – did not yet seem to give cause for concern. My first contacts with the Arab Communist parties in the region, as with the Iranian Tudeh, go back to that time. I shall return to them in connection with the history of Arab and Egyptian communism.

Links with Egypt

In 1952, when my father, mother and grandmother came to visit us in France, we all took a few short breaks in Bormes-les-Mimosas, in the Var. The hotel keeper must have thought that Isabelle resembled me more than my sister did, because he was surprised to see us sharing the same bedroom. Noticing his confusion, my grandmother said in her deadpan way: 'Didn't you know that the pharaohs married their sister?' No more questions were asked. My parents left in August.

In September Isabelle and I set sail for a holiday in Port Said. Then we made another trip there in July to October 1953. The idea had been for me to collect Isabelle in Alexandria, but the ship to the Holy Land on which she was travelling broke down and actually put into Port Said. People used to travel a lot by ship in those days: I myself took a plane for the first time only in 1960, when I went to Mali. Usually I travelled on one of the liners passing through Port Said: the Castle Line service to the east coast of Africa, Mombassa and Durban, or P&O's to India and Australia. Or else we would use one of the Greek or Italian lines that stopped at various ports in the Mediterranean, perhaps Beirut, Tripoli, Piraeus/Athens, Cyprus or Naples. I have many fine memories of those journeys.

In the early 1950s Athens was a deeply depressing place. Savage repression was directed against communists and anyone who had sided with them during World War II and the civil war of 1945–48 (when monarcho-fascists reconquered the country with British and American support). Ordinary people looked straight through us, with our air of tourists off a ship, and spat on the ground muttering what was probably a string of insults. Supporters of the dictatorship, on the other hand, including rare former collaborators with the Nazis, looked fat and conceited as they displayed their aggressive exuberance in powerful American cars or on café terraces. We found ourselves travelling with Sistovaris, the Cairo furrier, and were welcomed by his family when we got off at Piraeus. He explained to us, in a low voice, that we should be careful because 'tourists' were not well regarded. Ah, what a fine democracy the West sponsored to resist the horror of communism! Of course we went to see the Acropolis, as marvellous as ever in its elegance and proportions. Later, I was struck by the resemblance between its façade, seen from below, and that of certain structures in Upper Egypt – a point that Eurocentric prejudice has prevented all but a few historians from seeing. But, as to Greece, I went back again only after the victory of democracy in 1981, at the invitation of George Papandreou, the Greek translator of my *Accumulation* book (when he was a refugee in Canada) and then prime minister and head of Pasok, the Socialist Party.

A brief offshore trip through Lebanon made me very fond of the country, and not only because of the Place des Canons in Beirut (alas, that whole historic centre, devastated by civil war, is now being rebuilt to the taste of the property speculators), the mountain landscapes, the treasures of Baalbek, or the cool stream at Zahlé beside which we had a delicious meze lunch. I also liked its open, cheerful and refined people, immediately sensing that these qualities, as well as Lebanon's disproportionately important place in the intellectual production of the Arab world, were the result of democratic practices all too rare in the region. I later returned to Lebanon during and after the years of civil war, when I became still fonder of it and was able to appreciate its real qualities more seriously.

In Port Said the situation was tense in the extreme. The British armed forces, on permanent alert since the start of guerrilla operations in 1951, were due to leave the Canal Zone only in 1956, under the terms of a final agreement signed in 1954. During the summer of 1953 Nasser visited Port Said incognito, received only by a handful of loyal supporters, as a popular welcome or official ceremony was not possible under the circumstances. Incredible though it may seem, for Egypt at that time, he drove around on an army lorry stripped to the waist and crowned with a laurel wreath, with an escort of four or five men shouting something or other. As chance would have it, we saw him pass from the veranda of our house on avenue de la Plage. Isabelle asked me: 'Who's that dark, handsome, semi-naked man with the large nose?' 'It's Nasser', I replied, scarcely able to believe my eyes.' 'Who's he?' 'The real leader of the Free Officers. Naguib, the president, is only a front man.' 'Where has he come from?' 'He's been knocking around the communists, the Muslim Brotherhood and [Ahmed Hussein's] Nationalist Party.'

During the summers of 1953 and 1954 in Port Said, I went almost every evening to the Nadi Wafdi, the club where politicians and activists from the Wafd party or the trade unions used to gather, and one of the few places where you could still talk. Even then, however, you had to be careful of eavesdroppers: people would first loudly declare their 'unconditional support for the blessed July revolution' (its official name), then recite a list of reservations that cancelled out everything they had said before. The club was closed down later in 1954.

The Blessed Revolution was supposed to be negotiating the final removal of the British. But we were afraid that a new treaty might simply invite their American backers to come and join them there, and indeed the treaty signed in 1954 was denounced by the Communist Party because it seemed to confirm those fears. If things turned out differently, it was only because Nasser, after meeting Chou Enlai, Nehru and Sukarno in 1955, gained a better grasp of the global strategies of imperialism and eventually decided on the nationalization of the Canal. It was also said that the Blessed Revolution would secure the British departure from Sudan – so long as it did not arrange for the British to hand over power to their 'Mahdi lackeys'. This is what happened when the country became independent in 1956, but of course the Sudanese people then had, and still have, the possibility to try to change things themselves. A note of Egyptian chauvinism began to stress the unity of Egypt and Sudan, and we communists responded by calling for the 'unity in struggle of fraternal nations against a common enemy'. But I cannot say that this was widely appreciated. At the Wafdi club, the general view was to support a multiparty electoral democracy, and people were afraid that the 'provisional' dictatorship of the Free Officers would last for ever. The Muslim Brotherhood and the Nationalists around Ahmad Hussein and Fathi Radwan also had a presence at the club. They took special care to proclaim their support for the regime, at the same time underlining the officers' declarations of 'faith' and sympathy for the ideological themes of the Brotherhood. The Nationalists recalled that in 1942 the future Free Officers had been among those who opposed the British coup d'état that reinstalled the Wafd. What they forgot to mention, however, was that the Free Officers had all sided with the King – and been manipulated by the Nazis.

All this was most instructive and disturbing. It was during this period that I had my longest political discussions with my father, who saw the Officers as primitive and anti-democratic nationalists. Wadie, who knew one officer well and was informed about their stormy meetings, talked a lot with us and confirmed my father's judgement. But my father had no view about whether they could be 'educated' (how and by whom?), or whether the Muslim Brotherhood and the supporters of Ahmed Hussain would inevitably gain the upper hand. At least he was pleased that the Officers had rid us of the monarchy and dared to carry out a land reform.

In Port Said, as elsewhere, the Free Officers tried to create the nucleus of a political party and set up their own 'liberation committee'. But, as no respectable politician or activist would agree to take part, it consisted of complete nobodies or, worse, corrupt politicians from the old monarchist right, Muslim Brothers and supporters of Ahmad Hussein. This did not augur well for the future.

During our short holidays in Egypt I made contact again with my comrades in the CP. Once I visited Ismail and Bouli in their flat at the end of Zamalek island, in Cairo, and on another occasion I saw them in Alexandria where Ismail was a teacher. It was there that I first met the great painter Inji Efflatoun and her young husband Hamdy, and we kept in touch with each other until her death in 1989. She became close friends with Isabelle, Fawzy Mansour and his wife, and we went together for long trips to the Egyptian countryside and oasis, which she loved so much and painted with great originality.

Meanwhile, in Paris, I did what was asked of me: liaison work with the PCF and PCI, 'tutoring' of Egyptian communists. There were sharp disputes at that time between the various Egyptian communist organizations, especially the Communist Party of Egypt (Raya al-Shaab) and Hadeto.[25] Concealed beneath the clash of personalities and the dogmatic jargon was a deep divergence over the perspective that the Soviets were soon to call the 'non-capitalist road'. I do not want to treat this episode superficially and hope that I shall one day be able to give a full account of it. Recently I have been working with a Cairo-based committee of 'veterans' from all the self-styled communist organizations of that time. We are honestly trying to collect all possible documentation: illegal newspapers and pamphlets, tape-recordings that supplement the growing number of published memoirs, and so on. Rather than wishing to revive past quarrels, we hope that the passing of time will have encouraged calmer analysis of the theories and strategies (explicit or implicit) put forward by all those concerned.

The second half of 1956 was entirely taken up with the Suez crisis. Isabelle and I arrived in June for a holiday in Port Said, and it was there, at the heart of the Canal Zone, that we listened to Nasser's broadcast in July announcing the nationalization of the Canal. Feelings of personal joy mingled with the immediate outpouring of popular jubilation. But I had to return soon to France, to defend my thesis, and in September we took what proved to be the last liner to pass through the Canal before the Franco-British-Israeli aggression in October. Back in Paris, I and many other Egyptian students, such as my close friends Reda and Nadra Bastouly, worked flat out supplying information to the French press and assorted organizations, and trying to 'put pressure' on the wavering embassy, where some thought the regime would collapse and wanted to ingratiate themselves with a restored monarchy.

I need hardly say that I was also very worried at a personal level. My parents were in Port Said, with a ringside view of the naval bombardment and the landing of parachute troops. Street fighting close to their house meant that some of our beautiful furniture was riddled with bullets; the holes still bring back memories when my eye falls on them in Cairo.

All this delayed the completion of my thesis by nearly twelve months. When I returned to Egypt in August 1957, I found a quite different country from the one I had known in my childhood, or even the previous year. The defeat of the coalition of aggressors had permitted a real leap forward and the nationalization of foreign capital, and settlers from abroad had left in droves. Egyptian communism was also facing a novel situation in many respects.

In June 1957 Isabelle and I decided to get married, if only so that she could obtain a visa for Egypt at a time when diplomatic relations with France were still suspended. The French police slowed things down – a Frenchwoman still had to receive permission from the prefect's office to marry a foreigner! – and the wedding itself was not exactly straightforward. I had bought an old black Ford to take with us to Egypt, but it stubbornly refused to start for our journey from Pavillons-sous-Bois to the registry office in the fifth arrondissement. A neighbour of my parents-in-law therefore took us in his minivan, arriving just as the officiator at the town hall was losing patience. Afterwards, accompanied by our two witnesses, Reda and Nadra, we had a nice trip in the south-west before I boarded ship in Marseilles. Isabelle joined me in Egypt a few months later.

The chapter of our life as students was over.

THREE

Cairo, 1957–60

In October 1957, a month after my return to Egypt, I went to Cairo for an interview with the government department for which I hoped to work. It went well and I was asked to report for duty on 1 January 1958. In the intervening period, in Port Said, I was hit by a strange illness that showed the same symptoms as gout: red swollen toes and pain that made it impossible to walk. The doctors – my parents and their colleagues – could not understand why it should have happened to someone so young. Was it due to gastronomic excesses during our trip in south-west France? It is true that there had been some. In the Dordogne, Isabelle had taken us to visit relatives and friends, including an old classmate who now owned a restaurant in Lalinde, where we had a real feast. It would be hard to find greater food-lovers than Reda and Nadra, who kept pushing us to indulge in the *foie gras* and the *confits* of duck and goose. But could that have been enough to give me gout? Fortunately it passed in a month, but six years later the same story was repeated in Bamako without a gastronomic prelude. A Yugoslav doctor Abramovic, a neighbour and friend of Koulouba's, then cleared up the mystery. 'Have you been in Ethiopia?' he asked. 'Yes.' 'Well, there's a rare disease that you must have caught from drinking water from the Nile down there; it's called *shiga*.' The treatment was effective, and my symptoms disappeared within eight days.

The Mwasasa Iqtisadia

The year 1957 witnessed the great shake-up in Egypt, when the British, French and Belgian capital that had dominated the modern industrial sectors of the economy was sequestrated. What was to be done with it? Two opposing plans took shape among the Free Officers: either to transfer ownership, with or without payment of its real value, to big private Egyptian capital (much of which, especially in the case of the MISR group, had been an associate more than a competitor of foreign capital); or to nationalize the property and create a public sector large enough to launch accelerated development of the economy. In the end, Nasser opted for the second path, although here and there, on the margins, Egyptian capital was allowed a stake in the new state sector.

This raised the question of how the enterprises were to be managed and their development planned. Ismail Abdallah was assigned to gather the necessary information: the country's leaders knew him as a Marxist economist, especially as they had jailed him as a communist in 1954 and released him only in 1956; he was respected both for his intelligence and for his national sensibility. In his view, the danger was that management functions would be assigned to a political clientele (mainly consisting of officers) who, while formally depending on various ministries, would not be held answerable for very much, with the result that fragmented control would be compounded by managerial incompetence. Ismail therefore proposed what seemed to me the best solution: an autonomous state holding institution, along the lines of Italy's IRI, which would select the directors of individual companies and set the broad guidelines for their management and growth. A body of this kind, the Mwasasa Iqtisadia (or Economic Institution), was created in 1957. Its chairman was inevitably an officer close to Nasser, but fortunately the appointee – air force officer Hassan Ibrahim – was the least objectionable choice. More cut out for honours than for sustained work, he was happy to dabble in his own private sidelines without interfering in the affairs of the institution. Its real managing director, in fact, was Sedki Soliman, an engineer by training, whose lack of corruption and capacity for hard work and meticulous organization were later demonstrated as minister in charge of the Aswan High Dam project. But Sedki Soliman also had his limitations: he was a real technocrat, with only a pragmatic grasp of economics and no political vision other than a national-populist patriotism.

Ismail, who had had the idea of the institution, was appointed director in charge of its economic decisions. As a communist, he could not have been given a higher position, but it was certainly not bad. With his strong personality and talent for argument, he was really able to influence the major decisions during his year in office, 1958. He tried to find a good team for this purpose and had obviously been thinking of me from the beginning. This was how I came to be interviewed and appointed by Sedki Soliman.

The Mwasasa was not a giant bureaucracy, and we had to avoid this typically Egyptian defect. It was therefore installed on the top floor of the Bank of Alexandria – formerly Barclays Bank, now nationalized – on Kasr el Nil Street in the city centre. I could have walked there from my home at Bab El Louk, but I always took my big old Ford.

Our little five-man team in the office next to Ismail's included Sobhi el Atrebi – who went on to become an undersecretary of state – and Yousry Ali Moustapha, who had obtained his doctorate in economics at the same time as I. (Much later, under Sadat in the 1980s, I saw him again in his prestigious office on Adli Street, where he was economics minister in the Atef Sedki government.) We had two tasks: to prepare a 'weekly bulletin' (*Nashra*) which, through analysis of enterprise problems and the presentation and discussion of decisions, would serve an educational purpose for the often inexperienced Egyptian managerial staff; and to offer in-depth studies of economic problems in the sectors relevant to our enterprises. I became especially concerned with the latter, while Sobhi took charge of most of the work on the bulletin.

My research work on the major sectors of the modern Egyptian economy – cotton and textiles, food industries, construction materials, chemicals, mining, steel and engineering – therefore involved tracing their history, analysing their problems and assessing their future prospects. I left behind a mass of studies that will be of use to students interested in the country's past and the Nasserite experience. I also looked into the High Dam project – which, after all, permitted Egypt to face without much difficulty the drought that hit the African continent in later years – and can say here that the excellent Egyptian technicians who worked on it were already aware of many of the problems that emerged later, when the dam was already up and running and new land had been wrested from the sands (though not adequately drained, because of lack of resources). Many of today's ecologists, failing to appreciate that in Egypt water is a factor without which life is simply impossible, have light-mindedly taken on the wretchedly negative positions of the Americans, who were understandably upset that the World Bank's refusal to fund the project without unacceptable political conditions had not had the desired effect (since the Soviets stepped in and eventually helped to build the dam at much less than the Bank's estimated cost).

My functions at the Mwasasa led me to take a close interest in the management of the new public sector, and to follow the discussions and decisions of its various enterprise boards. I could see how the 'new class' was taking shape, how the private interests of many of these gentlemen dictated too many of the decisions, and how the workers' representatives (one of Nasser's initiatives, excellent in principle) were being marginalized, duped or bought off.

All through 1958 Ismail performed his work at the institution with great skill. A lot was needed. For the pharaonic state bureaucracy was riddled with all manner of contradictions and conflicts, some of them worthily expressing divergent political visions, others more crudely reflecting a clash of personal or clan interests. Basically, there were four decision-making centres that disagreed more than they agreed about the direction in which the country should develop: the Mwasasa, the planning ministry, the finance ministry (on which the Central Bank depended) and the industrial bank.

At the Mwasasa, it was not possible simply to manage the public sector on a day-to-day basis; its development had to be planned. But was that not a task for the new planning ministry? Well, anyway it did not assume the task. Its technical experts – often high-quality people like Nazih Deif, my main contact there – had been geared up (or had geared themselves up) for the designing of 'growth models'. Of course, I am not hostile to models in principle; they are necessary to test the coherence of policies in different sectors or areas of the economy. However, the model should come not before but after the social and political objectives have been defined, whereas technocrats often delude themselves that they can escape responsibility for this by devising a supra-political, supra-social model. Charles Prou, who worked under Claude Gruson at the French planning think-tank and came on an assignment to Cairo, shared my opinion. Together, we tried to persuade Deif – but to no avail. In short, the Plan did not interfere with us, but it served no purpose as a reference.

Mwasasa's role in developing the public sector had to be funded, and this brought us up against the competing visions of the finance ministry and the Industrial Bank. The former, an institution as old as Egypt itself, had certain habits that it was virtually impossible to change. The Treasury had always funded irrigation and the railways, and when the economic crisis of the 1930s threatened large landowners with bankruptcy it extended this support to real-estate credit (taking over from the banks to which the landowners were indebted) and to various funds created ad hoc to limit the damage due to inflation. Each of these functions was discharged by a separate department, and the lack of communication among them resulted in considerable waste and absurdity. Moreover, the Treasury had never thought of funding industry itself, nor had industry ever demanded it, being content to base its profitability on monopoly advantages from tariff protection and access to public markets.

The National Bank, now nationalized and serving as a central bank, was in the highest degree conservative: it was meant to ensure the stability of the currency (which it did well enough), but nothing beyond that.

My absorbing study of this jumbled system of public finances later stood me in good stead when I had to delve into the equally confused Treasury accounts in Mali, Ghana (during the Rawlings period), Congo (under Noumazaleye) and Madagascar (under Ratsiraka). I discovered in Egypt that there were huge amounts of unused national wealth in the hands of the recently nationalized *wakfs* (religious trusts). But our proposals to mobilize this for industrialization were turned down, for the simple reason that the armed forces had their fingers in the pie – not only to buy weapons but also to build housing for the officer corps.

There remained only the Industrial Bank, the regime's own creation, which was theoretically controlled by the new ministry of industry (now independent of the finance ministry). Our loyal friend, the fellow-communist Hassan Abdel Razek, was the Bank's chief economist. We often discussed with him this or that project, and usually (though not always) came to the same conclusions, but we were not able to follow up our proposals with appropriate action. At the ministry of industry, which had the final decision-making powers, all the shots were being called by more or less corrupt and incompetent (or, for one reason or another, impossibly stubborn) *shilals*[26] of officers and others. It was they who 'planned' reality, in a complete disorder antithetical to the very concept of planning.

I am going into some detail here because books about the period mostly limit themselves to abstract and general descriptions of Nasserite planning, as if it had rationally applied what was written in the relevant public statements and texts, as if its 'failure' had to do with its very principle.

The year 1958 was hard, and 1959 harder still. The post-Suez honeymoon proved to be short-lived, as the regime refused to accept communist criticisms of the bureaucratic, anti-democratic vision of Egyptian–Syrian unity. On 1 January 1959, the police arrested communists by the thousand. I escaped this first round-up, but Ismail did not. We therefore no longer had a director, and the position remained vacant for the rest of the year. I no longer had 'my heart in the job', but I decided not to remain idle. I therefore continued my research with the same intensity as before, to improve my own knowledge of the reality of the Egyptian economy. The book *L'Égypte nassérienne*, which I published in 1963 under the pen name Hassan Riad (in fact, my underground name), owes a great deal to the information I collected during that period.

At the same time, I was taking my first steps in the teaching world, having been invited to give a course on 'financial flows' at the Arab

League's institute for higher education. A book based on these lectures, published by the institute later that year, put forward Egypt's first table of financial transactions, using a new technique that Charles Prou had taught me during his visit. We were well ahead of many others at that time, and the World Bank itself was ignorant of this dimension of macroeconomic analysis. But in Egypt, the instrument served no purpose in the kind of 'planning' I have described above.

My course was new and difficult, and there was no background reading in Arabic, very little in English, and only a little more in French (in the documents of the SEEF[27]) to which my doctoral students could refer. Besides, most of them had difficulty with English and did not know French. I therefore dictated and handed out a copy of the lecture, which I later used to compose the book. For the exam I set two questions: a 'normal' one, which told me who had more or less understood the subject matter; and a stock question from the course, which allowed those who had done some work to avoid a debacle. One of my students, who had been at Al Azhar, chose the course question and handed in a word-for-word copy, inserting dots here and there and sometimes accompanying them with the information 'here 8 words (or 2 lines) have been omitted'. What mark to give him? One, so as not to make it nought. He then came and accused me of being unjust, claiming that he really deserved 16.73 out of 20 or some such precise figure. When I asked him how he had reached it, he answered: 'It's easy: I used 83.65 per cent of the right words, in the right order.' It was impossible to make him understand that this proved he had no desire to master the subject. I would not be surprised if he is not today among those championing the 'specificity' and 'authenticity' so fashionable in political Islam. Indeed, Al Azhar is now taken seriously in a way that would have made my father's generation laugh. 'Doctors' in all manner of things produce incredibly stupid works, which are then 'discussed' at conferences where other university teachers listen in silence before making some respectful comment. That is the 'specificity' we are taking about. It would have made the hair of a twelfth-century rationalist stand on end.

Daily life

I won't try to describe Cairo any more than I have Paris. I also like this warm, imposing city, the only one in the world where you can find whole areas (not only buildings) from each century since antiquity. Rome has no equivalent of the little streets of old Cairo, where the walls of every house date back two thousand years. Egyptians never destroy anything: they wait for it to fall down by itself. That happens with modern buildings, but only rarely with those from ancient times. And, being generally poor, people keep everything in case it might come in handy one day: old bicycles on the roof, and so on.

In the late 1950s the population of Cairo was around two million. Today the city and its suburbs have fifteen million. In those days there were still beautiful and clean areas, sumptuous palaces, and avenues lined with buildings in the flamboyant style. The city centre, built by the Khedives in the nineteenth century, conformed to the 'Parisian taste' of the Egyptian aristocracy – sober grey blocks, all in the same style and of the same height – not the flashy taste of the false Mediterranean and its eclectic villas. They were the days before thirty-storey modern towers were thrown up at random by property speculators, in surroundings of small dilapidated houses. But, despite the urban decline for which the new middle classes are responsible, the ironical but warm character of its people gives it an enduring charm. I know its nooks and crannies well – or at least those which existed at the end of the 1950s. Between the city proper and its suburbs, the roads ran south (to Meadi) and west (to the Pyramids) through green fields of quietly grazing buffaloes, and north-east (to Heliopolis) through the desert. Now there is nothing there but built-up areas and squatter settlements, while the total surface of the city is itself two or three times larger. The old petty-bourgeois parts of town, ancient (El Hussein) or early-twentieth-century (Abbassieh, Shubra), and the working-class districts have all turned into slums. Vast areas (in Embaba) are now occupied by 'modern' shantytowns.

Isabelle and I, being city people rather than suburbanites, found a central apartment in the Anwar Wagdy building (named after its investment owner, a well-known film actor), on Mazlum Street, facing the Circassian mosque. It was a fine structure – though, as always in Egypt, not well maintained, and by now it had badly deteriorated. We had three rooms there – rather on the small size for Egypt. Luckily, the neighbours across the hallway were friends of ours: the psychoanalyst Moustapha Safouan (who was actually working in Alexandria), his wife Nimet and their children. He later moved to France, first living in Strasbourg and working in Paris, then settling for good in Paris but working in Strasbourg. We spent many very pleasant evenings in each other's homes.

My monthly salary of 35 Egyptian pounds was not considered low, but nor was it exactly a large sum. It is true that the outgoings were similarly small: 4 pounds for rent, and just one and a half piastres for a filling meal of '*foul* beans with bastarma,[28] olive oil and onions', at the clean working-class restaurant a few yards from the apartment building.

Isabelle was teaching at the Franco-Egyptian lycée in Meadi, which, like other French schools, had been nationalized in 1956; she therefore had only a local contract, with an Egyptian salary. She would leave early in the morning and come back in the afternoon, catching an overcrowded bus that was suffocating in the summer and freezing in the winter. Fortunately, she became good friends with a fellow teacher at Meadi, Zeinab Ezzet, and used to have lunch at her place. Other friends at the lycée – Melle Politi, André Ghali, the headmistress – created a nice atmosphere, but the workload and especially the travelling made it a very hard job. Isabelle is a courageous woman.

Despite the worries that always go with underground political activity, we had a happy life and often spent time together with people who have remained friends (at least in my memory, when circumstances have separated us): Amina Rachid, Mohamed and Zeinab Ezzet, Mohamed Shawarby and his wife Jacqueline Maqar, Ismail, Bouli and Inji, our neighbours the Safouans. Reda and Nadra Bastouly were still in France at the time. My sister, who had married a German working at the Goethe Institute, also lived in Cairo, in a new apartment block in Zamalek, but she moved in circles that were rather different from ours.

We took a few trips in our black Ford, but not as many as we would have liked. Once we went down the Red Sea coast and had a look at the oil wells, where a crazy engineer insisted that we go so close to the burning gas that we almost left our skin behind. Isabelle did not hesitate to jump out of his car, and this finally made him halt the circus. We also went to Alexandria once or twice – in winter, we finally saw the rain that is so rare in Cairo – but our most common destination was Port Said, when we would often stretch out the trip a little by taking the Delta road, via Belbeis and Tell el Kebir. While staying with my parents, we would look up old friends such as Awateh and her husband Salah, as well as new ones such as the Soviet consul, Shikov, who lived on the ground floor of our house. He was a very likeable man and – whatever one thinks of Soviet society – probably a sincere communist. I don't know what became of him, or whether he is still in the land of the living, but it would surprise me if he has not remained true to his beliefs. Shikov, like many Russians, found that his drink slipped down very easily; he used to come to us with caviar and several bottles of vodka, and engage in varied and amusing conversation interspersed with ever more frequent 'bottoms up'. My grandmother, who found this very funny, emptied her little glasses into a flower pot near her armchair on the veranda; no doubt the flowers suffered as a result. But sometimes our discussions were more serious. I told him what I thought of the situation in Egypt: not state secrets (I don't think I knew any, for that matter), but my own analyses. He listened attentively but said very little himself.

During the wave of arrests in 1959, the Party group to which I belonged was led by Fawzy Mansour, a model of courage and rectitude, and my friendship with him dates from those difficult times that allowed us to measure the true quality of individuals. Inji had gone into hiding in Shubra, and we used to hold our meetings there. But then someone I didn't like the look of – I seem to have a flair for spotting things – turned her in to the police; he struck me as having the face of a coward, and that probably was the reason for his betrayal. Fawzy had introduced a system of 'two successive meetings': for the first, I (or he) arranged to appear at a clearly specified time and place, but if one of us thought he was being followed (or was even unsure – there are techniques for knowing that) he did not show up and went to the 'reserve' meeting place instead. In November, there was no sign of Fawzy at two successive meetings. The conclusion: he had very probably been arrested. And he had. Shortly before, it had been decided that in such a case I would try to leave Egypt. I therefore decided to do this, with the Party's agreement.

Fortunately Charles Prou, who was in Egypt on an assignment and had half-openly discussed with me the risks of our activity, sent me an invitation from the SEEF director, Claude Gruson, for a special training course in France. I needed an exit visa, and as luck would have it Taha Rabie, the police official in charge of such matters who also had to arrange my arrest, had a daughter whom my mother had once saved from death. Taha thought that he had to pay her back. He therefore locked away the arrest warrant in his office and told me: I'll be out all day and will come back this evening to deal with my mail. I understood at once. Half an hour later the Ford was on its way, two hours later I was in Port Said, and an hour after that my father had dug up a ship's captain willing to take me on board. It was early January 1960. Faster than if I had got a plane. Isabelle would stay in Cairo until her contract expired, then join me in July at the end of the school year. She lived for some of this period at Zeinab's, in Meadi. In Port Said I could see from my father's worried look that he must have suffered a lot during this terrible year. I would never see him again: he died suddenly in October 1960 of a heart attack.

Egyptian communism

When I left for Paris in 1947, I did not yet know all the Egyptian communist organizations and their respective histories. I became familiar with these when I met some members of Hadeto who had been expelled from Egypt and gone to live in France in 1947 or 1948: Youssef Hazan, his sister Mimi, André Bereci and doubtless a few others. Soon I also heard another side of the story from Ismail, Moustapha Safouan and Raymond Aghion (whom I first met in connection with the publication of *Moyen Orient*) and gradually inclined towards their criticisms of Hadeto. Thus, when the idea came up of creating the CPE (known by the name of its paper – *Rayat el Shaab* or *People's Standard*), I joined the new party and, as I said before, held some positions in it between 1952 and 1957, in Paris. I received CPE reports on the political situation, which I translated into French and sent to the PCF and PCI, usually via Raymond Aghion. Fouad Moursi, on his way through Paris (I don't remember exactly when), gave me a pile of CPE and Hadeto documents and instructed me to draw up a report comparing the two from a point of view of our own, in the CPE. I did this, in a highly polemical tone that was to Fouad's liking, and so the report was in a way attributed to him by the CPE leadership. I have placed all these documents – the original CPE and Hadeto papers and pamphlets and the CPE reports – at the disposal of our veterans' committee in Cairo and sent copies to the Institute of Social History in Amsterdam.

Subsequently I knew many of these old Egyptian communists, and many of those still alive are today members of the Tagamu (the Party of the Egyptian Left), whose chairman is Khaled Mohi el Dine and general secretary is Rifaat el Said. The story of Egyptian communism has been the object of works by Rifaat el Said (himself a former member of Hadeto), memoirs of various old militants (Sherif Hettata, Didar-Fawzy and others), interviews and tape-recorded reminiscences. But, in my view, a real history still remains to be written: not only because the authors' background inevitably (and quite understandably) makes most of the existing testimonies biased and partisan, sometimes outrageously so, but also because they do not take the trouble to review the history with the benefit of critical, and therefore self-critical, hindsight, or to analyse calmly and methodically the explicit or implicit positions taken by each side on Egyptian society or the Soviet experience. I am struck, for example, by the fact that they think of the USSR as a distant paradise and show little interest in its problems – and that they virtually ignore Maoism and China. Egyptian and, more generally, Arab communists had little or no knowledge of the Chinese Communist Party's famous 'Letter in Twenty-Five Points' to the CPSU (1963); nor of the discussions surrounding the (very Chinese) formula 'states seek independence, nations liberation and peoples revolution' that called for a new articulation of the questions of power, culture and class struggle; nor of the ideas and debates that paved the way for the Cultural Revolution ('The bourgeoisie is not outside the Party but inside it'). If they were known at all, it was only through the deformations – not to say fabrications or falsifications – of Soviet propaganda.

My intention here is neither to dash off an essay on Egyptian communist history – this will, I hope, be the theme of a later serious study, preferably under collective editorship – nor to continue the polemics of the past. But I would like to make it clear that on the whole I consider it to be a glorious history, and the great majority of its members to have been the best children of Egypt, the most sensitive to its dramas and the most courageous in actively facing up to them. These qualities do not mean that particular individuals or even the whole movement were never wrong, or at least that our opinions today should not take account of how history has developed. Here I shall limit my remarks to three major aspects of that history: the Palestine question, Arab unity and relations with the Nasserite project.

Palestine was always an important concern for us. Soviet support for partition in December 1947, echoed by all the Communist parties of the time, gave rise not only to heated discussions but subsequently also to self-criticisms which, though doubtless sincere, do not always seem to have been sufficiently justified or cogently argued. The Third International and the Egyptian and Arab communist movements have always rightly condemned Zionism, seeing it as the expression of a nationalist and racist project to create a settler colony that denies the right to existence of the Palestinian 'natives'. The Egyptian communist movement today can feel proud that, ever since the 1940s, it supported the anti-Zionist current among the progressive Jews of Egypt. It has no reason to be self-critical on this score, despite the skilful attempts of Zionist propaganda to confuse anti-Zionism with anti-Semitism.

With regard to the partition of Palestine, it is useful to recall a fact that many have tried to overlook in polemical argument: that is, the Soviet Union and Arab, Palestinian and Egyptian democratic forces initially supported the independence of a unified secular Palestinian state open to all the country's inhabitants, including – a not insignificant concession, this – recent Jewish immigrants. Zionism, on the other hand, always rejected such a solution. With the support of a mandatory power which, while disarming the Palestinian liberation movement, allowed Zionism to arm itself and form a 'state within the state', a situation was created on the ground that worked in favour of the expansionist project. It is open to debate whether, in these conditions, a partition plan was the best or the worst way of 'limiting the damage'. We should remember that, although the UN resolution backing this plan was supported by all the Western and socialist countries, it was rejected by all the African and Asian countries which then belonged to the United Nations. On the Soviet side, certain tactical reasons may have weighed in the balance: the USSR was still terribly isolated and desperately seeking to break the US nuclear monopoly. The support that Egyptian communists gave to this tactic may have been questionable, but it seems to me that the later one-sided 'self-criticism' was too clear-cut and underestimated the complexity of the situation in 1947–48.

On the question of Arab unity, the Egyptian communist movement always adopted generally intelligent positions. It never accepted the idea of a 'multiplicity of Arab nations' or recognized a series of individual 'states' as the definitive horizon for the liberation project. But nor did it blur regional specificities bound up with a history much older than the imperialist division of the Arab world, or lend credence to the idealist theses of pan-Arab nationalism. Whereas the Egyptian bourgeois-nationalist movement (principally the Wafd) or the Unionists in Sudan denied the specificity of Sudan, the Egyptian and Sudanese communist movement defined its strategy in terms of a common struggle of two fraternal peoples against external and internal enemies. When Egypt and Syria formed the United Arab Republic in 1958, and when new advances towards Arab unity seemed possible following the overthrow of the monarchy in Iraq, the Egyptian communist movement did not hesitate to criticize the undemocratic methods of the Nasser regime and his contempt for the particular realities of the countries in question. History has proven us right, since those methods were largely responsible for the failure of the project. And, when I look back, the differences among communist organizations on this issue seem to have been relatively slight: while some (Hadeto) modulated their criticisms of Nasser, others (the CPE-Raya) more clearly supported the positions of Abdel Karim Qassim, the Iraqi leader of the time. Both positions had their weaknesses, but they were part of a generally correct political line.

The existence of several different organizations, for most of the period from the revival of Egyptian communism (1942–45) to the self-dissolution of the two parties in 1965, seemed to us unacceptable. The violent polemics between them certainly had a personal dimension, to the detriment of a sober examination of the real differences of analysis and strategy. Nevertheless, I wonder today whether the quest for unity (or its substitute: the de facto 'victory' of one organization) was not the result of certain conceptions of 'the Party' as the sole repository of the 'correct line'. A better attitude to democracy within the movement, either in a single 'Party' or several 'parties', would have encouraged a more lucid conduct of debates, without ruling out a common front in many areas of political activity.

The fact remains, however, that the multiplicity of organizations expressed differences concerning the general strategy for revolution in Egypt. Some thought that national liberation should take precedence, or – to use a formulation that may seem extreme but is not intended in a polemical sense – they believed that Egypt essentially needed a bourgeois-democratic national revolution. Others emphasized what they saw as the need to move more rapidly to the stage of socialist construction. I do not think it possible to associate these two visions directly with particular parties: they tended to cut across organizations, even if the shared dogmatic ideology of the times did not allow their contours to appear clearly. All sides based themselves on the 'quotation method', the positions of the Soviet Communist Party, a reading of Mao's *New Democracy*, and so on. The ambiguities of the debate, linked to 'personality problems', meant that the short-lived unification (1958) remained fragile, although we were all very happy that it had been achieved.

The *coup d'état* by the Free Officers in July 1952, then the crystallization of Nasserism and its further evolution from 1955 to 1961, transformed the choice of strategic perspective into an immediate and unavoidable problem. Should we support, criticize or oppose the new regime? Once again, the plethora of critical reassessments in Egyptian progressive literature, whether intended to justify or to denounce, do not usually go to the heart of the matter. For example, when former members of Hadeto argue that, having been active in the secret organization of the Free Officers, they were better placed to appreciate the progressive character of Nasserism from the beginning, this does not seem to me to situate the problem on the correct terrain.

For my part, I have argued since 1960 that the Nasserite project never became anything other than it was at the beginning: an inherently national-bourgeois project. Its populist style does not contradict this judgement. For it was the only possible form in which a national-bourgeois project could be deployed, given the weakness and comprador character of the 'liberal' bourgeoisie and the fear that the popular classes (whose support was necessary) might carry things too far. Consequently, the anti-democratic, 'statist' way of running the country did not at all indicate a 'transition to socialism'. Unfortunately, the strategic alliance that Moscow forged after Bandung with the national liberation cause in the third world, as well as the top-down nature of the Soviet system itself, did a great deal to confuse statism and socialism in people's minds.

I think that history has confirmed the correctness of this assessment. Nasserism gave way to Sadatism, as Brezhnevism did to Yeltsinism, and in neither case is it possible to describe the sudden change as a 'counter-revolution'. I myself saw it as an acceleration of tendencies within the two systems, as the new (bourgeois) class constituted in and through statism sought to 'normalize' its status. But I also said and wrote that there was nothing inevitable about what happened. An evolution to the left was also possible, although it would have depended on the maturity of socialist forces within the two societies (and others). In retrospect, I therefore have no problem describing the national-bourgeois project as utopian.

Contrary to the most widely held view, I believe that Hadeto's support for Nasserism – however critical and however much the regime's anti-communism sometimes called it into question – was a fundamentally incorrect position, based on the idea that a 'national-bourgeois stage' was necessary and positive and would eventually open out into socialism. My own view is that actually existing capitalism is a polarizing global system which inevitably gives any bourgeois project a comprador character, and that the national-bourgeois rejection of that system therefore involves a utopian illusion. I would now argue this more clearly, but in those days I already had more than a glimpse of its truth.

This is why my re-reading of the positions of the CPE-Raya, with which I fully sympathized as early as 1950–51, is different from the sharply critical view that it was fundamentally mistaken about the Nasserite project. Such criticisms, which correspond to the CPE's self-criticisms after 1956 and are today repeated ad nauseam, strike me as very one-sided and tied to a strategy whose failure has been demonstrated by history. Leaving aside secondary issues of language (a 'fascist' regime) or possible imperialist involvement, the key question is whether it was right or wrong to see Nasserism as a bourgeois project doomed to failure.

To be frank, I do not think that Egyptian communism really took on board the analysis of Mao's *New Democracy*. Hadeto never did at any time in its history, while the CPE starting thinking in that direction before 1956 but then suddenly pulled away. Take, for example, two successive reports of the CPE: one in 1955 that is extremely critical of the bourgeois Nasserite project and does not consider it a possible stage in the New Democracy (which entails a break with the bourgeois national illusion); and one in 1957 that not only endorses the 'progressive' character of bourgeois nationalism (which it might be valid to support tactically so as to deepen the contradictions with imperialism) but also analyses it as a stage (or 'non-capitalist path', to use a later term) on the road to socialism. Today this vision contained in *New Democracy*, like the limits of the Maoism that it inspired, must be criticized in the light of China's own evolution. But this does not mean that it should be replaced with something worse: that bourgeois national illusion whose stupidity is all too apparent from the catastrophic results in Russia and the third world.

So, in the 1950s, the 'left position' substituted the project of a socialist revolution uninterrupted by stages for the project of a bourgeois national revolution. Today I would say that both these positions underestimated the polarization inherent in capitalist expansion, and that Marxism has gradually become fossilized because of its failure to integrate this dimension. Both 'bourgeois revolution' (the perspective of social democrats and radical nationalists in the third world) and 'socialist revolution' (the perspective of Leninism–Maoism) avoid the real question: what kind of revolution is on the agenda when polarization makes both bourgeois revolution and socialist revolution impossible? Although it is only recently that I have expressed my analysis in these terms, its roots go back to the 1950s.

As a reader of my *L'Égypte nassérienne* may judge, my original verdict on Nasserism was harsh. Today it is more critical still: the Nasser regime did not merely suffer from a democratic deficit, nor did its populist style involve a primitive or inadequate opening to democracy; rather, it held the very idea of democracy in contempt, and behind this contempt lay the class interests of the bourgeoisie. This is also the reason why the regime was thoroughly to blame for what followed: Sadat's *infitah* policy and the rise of political Islam.

Mohamad Sid Ahmed's idea that 'Nasser nationalized politics' is worth taking seriously. It is more than a clever formula. For Nasser prohibited the clash of ideas and destroyed the two forces that had dominated the stage since the 1920s: the bourgeois-liberal modernist pole, moderately democratic and only tending towards secularism (such limits had to do with the weakness of the Egyptian bourgeoisie); and the communist pole, which associated modernization with national and social liberation. He destroyed them both systematically, not only through police repression more brutal than the country had witnessed before in modern times, but also through the closure of all venues where ideas could be openly debated. In this way, he created a huge cultural void and opened the door wide for the return of an Islamist traditionalism that had been in constant retreat for a century and a half, since the time of Mohammed Ali. He even encouraged its revival, through policies which, though geared to short-term tactics, were no less dangerous in the long term.

The traditional thinking of pre-capitalist Egypt had been on its way out for a century; Al Azhar, its central institution, paled in significance beside the modern universities. It could have been allowed to continue its slow death, but Nasser tried instead to 'modernize' Al Azhar, doubtless believing – like all dictators – that he could indefinitely control and even use it. But, through a familiar mechanism, opportunist arguments for a 'socialist' interpretation of Islam could be turned around without any difficulty. The right progressive attitude would have been to leave religion its particular sphere and to take the debate elsewhere, outside that sphere – an attitude which, in my view, would also have borne fruit within the religious domain itself, by creating the conditions for the various possible interpretations of religion (progressive and reactionary) to confront one another freely on their own ground. So, what did the 'modernization' of Al Azhar consist in? Isabelle reminds me that, when I got her to visit the institution in the 1950s, she was astonished to find that the twelfth century still existed: students literally stretched out on straw, reciting in a drone the texts handed out by their teachers. Modernization replaced this state of affairs with buildings, dormitories, refectories, lecture rooms, syllabuses, examinations and diplomas – all imitations of a modern educational system. But the mentality was not modernized. So, reform made it possible to give traditionalists a platform and a legitimacy that they had not previously had, with results all too apparent today. In addition to the tens of thousands of students who can learn only by rote, we now have thousands of 'doctors' produced in accordance with the same intellectual model. An old friend of mine once heard with his own ears, at the Al Azhar branch of the 'modern' university of Assiut, an unspecified 'doctor' explain in a lecture on *jinns* that a man could have sexual relations in his sleep with one of these mythological creatures (a female *jinna*, that is), and that he had found the material proof of this one morning on his bed sheet. When someone mockingly asked him whether a woman could have similar relations with a male *jinn*, he explained that this was impossible because it was shameful (*eib*) and contrary to religious law (the sharia), and besides no one knew of any women who had been made pregnant by a *jinn*. It seems that this lecturer is a 'moderate' Islamist, who has officially condemned terrorism. But his teaching must create religious extremists by the dozen. We are told by serious American magazines and French postmodernists that, truth being relative, belief in such things as *jinns* is just as valid as quantum theory. This is all very convenient, and there is certainly no denying that it suits the interests of the rich and powerful. *Jinns* for some, nuclear physics for others: to each according to their specificity.

Much the same may be said about the Nasserite reform that made civil rather than religious courts responsible for applying the law on civil status (which was and remains governed by the sharia): this poisoned the whole judicial system, as the obscurantists then started to argue that the sharia should be applied in all other areas, which had hitherto been governed by secular legislation. A progressive response would have been to draft secular modern legislation on civil status too, leaving it up to citizens to decide between this body of law (implemented by state courts) and religious laws administered in the traditional way. There can be little doubt that people would have increasingly opted for the modern formula. Instead, 'modernization' of the religious courts through their absorption into the civil judicial system has tended to destroy what was modern and secular in the Egyptian state. Far from reducing the confusion between the state and religion, Nasserism actually deepened it. Thanks to its 'reforms', the Egyptian justice system has returned to the obscurantism of the Ottoman era.

At the level of culture, then, Nasserism turned out to be profoundly reactionary. It is true that the effects seemed to be contained until Nasser's death, but the rot had already set in. All Sadat had to do was choose the weapon of Islam to force through his *infitah* (the comprador policy of capitulation to imperialism and Zionism), and in a trice the obscurantist forces already present in the two basic institutions of social life – education and justice – took them firmly under control. I do not know how long it will take, in the best scenario, for Egypt to extricate itself from this quagmire. To justify these huge steps back in the name of 'specificity', presenting them as 'a form of cultural resistance to Western imperialism', would be hilarious if it were not so tragic. Obscurantism can only serve the strategies of imperialism; it has never been and never will be a means of confronting the challenge of imperialism.

Arab communism generally rallied to the perspective of a bourgeois national stage and the Soviet theory of a 'non-capitalist path'. The unity of communists in Syria and Iraq, whose parties reproduced to the point of caricature such features of the Soviet model as the personality cult (around Khaled Bagdash, for example), doubtless seemed superior to Egypt's organizational fragmentation and could sometimes lead to arrogant attitudes. It is possible that communists in Iraq had stronger popular roots than their comrades in Egypt or even Syria. But nowhere did they manage to form a serious alternative to the rise of Baathism, whose ideological formula was close to Nasserism and the populist bourgeois-nationalist radicalism that was then blossoming in many third world countries. The fusion between civilian Baathists and nationalist officers, the *coups d'état* that brought the latter to power, could only serve to strengthen this family resemblance. And, as in Egypt, the communists of Syria and Iraq came to form the (perhaps 'critical') left wing of the movement, not an alternative to it.

The crumbling of bourgeois national utopianism subsequently eroded the credibility of the Arab communist movement as a historical option. Few of its members had thought the Soviet system could fall apart in the way that it did. Few had taken seriously Mao's warnings that, in the USSR but also China, the 'capitalist road' would inevitably whet the bourgeois appetites of the new class. The communist movement as a whole was therefore not prepared to face the global challenges that followed the Soviet collapse and the end of the Bandung stage of national liberation. Nor, if we judge by the recent Egyptian debate on socialist perspectives and relations with the Tagamu, does it seem to have made much progress since then. The movement is still imbued with nostalgia for the past, nostalgia for the

Soviet model, nostalgia for the age of Nasserism. But that is not the basis on which to advance beyond the limits of historical Marxism, in this region or anywhere else in the world. Of course, neither will anything good come from further capitulation to comprador forces and the related displacement of struggle to the mythological terrain of 'cultural specificity'.

FOUR

Parisian Interlude, January–September 1960

At the Service des Études Économiques et Financières (SEEF), attached to the French finance ministry, the leading light was Claude Gruson, whose genuinely revolutionary thinking had developed a coherent system of market regulation capable of serving a new social-democratic management of the historic compromise between capital and labour. He had devised the macroeconomic tools for this, and the SEEF was developing the necessary techniques. It all went far beyond an elementary Keynesian management of public finances. In comparison with the only other two conceptions of indicative planning in the developed capitalist countries – those associated with Ragnar Frisch in Norway and Jan Tinbergen in the Netherlands – the SEEF conception could assess much better the import of political and social options and formulate them in terms of precise economic policies in every field (prices and incomes, credit, money supply, foreign trade, incentives for technological modernization, finance markets). It was not simply a question of technocratic statism, as today's out-and-out denigrators of planning and regulation seek to claim. It was an effective scientific expression of a social vision for the management and development of the economy, much more elaborate than the simple German idea of a social market economy.

I could have wished for no better school during my stay in Paris. Gruson, like all those working with him, had a truly liberal spirit – and the department did not impose special tasks on anyone. This method encouraged creative initiative. We discussed and devised a project collectively, and freely put together a team to implement our own programme. Contrary to a widespread prejudice among 'organizers', the lack of anything other than a formal hierarchical discipline did not encourage people to be lazy, but rather to work more intensely on things that they found intellectually interesting. Charles Prou, Denizet, Bénard, Nataf, Durand and others were to be my teachers and colleagues for these six intensive months of my personal training.

I chose to form a two-man team with the mathematician Nataf. We had thought of a way of explaining the relative prices of products in different sectors of the economy (and therefore of influencing them through effective policies) by the ratio between self-financing and external financing in each sector. Our starting point was simple: we were living in a capitalist system where the ownership of capital counted for its beneficiaries. But the ownership structure – its actual spread among the main oligopolies and their relations with the finance markets – gave rise to different self-financing ratios in different sectors as the targets for corporate strategy, and hence to the key data of competition, supply and relative prices. Our idea was therefore the polar opposite of the unrealistic discourse of neoliberalism, in which 'the market' spontaneously determines 'real prices'. For Nataf and myself, the concept of 'real prices' had no meaning, and some time before neoliberal discourse took hold we were proposing instead a realistic analysis of the market in one of its decisive dimensions.

This idea then had to be given the form of a model that would allow its potential to be tapped. The national accounts and Tables of Financial Transactions, as well as structural surveys of different sectors and related statistics, governed the structure of the model to be devised. My role was to come up with a formulation, which would then have to be given mathematical form with a coherent system of equations expressing the major active interdependences – neither so many that the system was unviable, nor so few that it was indeterminate. These tasks were shared between the two of us, and discussed point by point. Finally, we had to put the system to use, at a time when a computer was still a large rudimentary machine. Only Nataf, the real mathematician, was capable of doing that.

I must say we had a whale of a time, and the results were no less interesting for that. The model revealed some important things: it explained why and how the structure of French relative prices differed from that of the apparent world market; it assisted the proposal of modernization policies if the aim was to bring France closer to the system of global capitalism; and it allowed for sectoral social policies to be made more effective through controlled 'delinking' of the French and global systems. The 'variable prices model' has become one of the panoply of tools in non-conventional macroeconomics. Of course, World Bank experts could never have devised such a model, trapped as they are by their idiotic preconception of the market as self-regulating by nature. Still today the Bank sees relative prices simply as crude data about which no questions are to be asked.

I can safely say that I acquired the essence of my professional training in two places: the Mwasasa in Cairo and the SEEF in Paris. After that, I felt capable of standing on my own two feet – or, rather, of continuing my own (permanent) education and confronting new problems, such as those I would find in Mali and elsewhere in the third world.

During those six months I lived with my parents-in-law at Pavillons-sous-Bois, travelling each morning by bus and metro to the SEEF building near the Louvre, which then housed the finance ministry. I used to arrive about ten o'clock and left between four and eight, depending on my mood and the pressure of work. Everything was perfect, except that I suffered from not being able to have a siesta. I later heard that, when Élie Lobel went to work there, he suffered from the same deprivation and installed a camp bed in his office. (I confess that I regret not having thought of it myself.) It seems that his very French colleagues thought it a curious habit.

In Paris I thought it my duty to make contact with the PCF and fill it in on the situation in Egypt. I saw Aghion again – although I no longer remember whether he had returned for good from his Italian exile, and whether he had already opened his 'café-shop', as I called it (that is, his art gallery on boulevard Saint-Germain, near the café where we used to meet as students). I also met the people at the journal *Démocratie nouvelle*. The editor, Paul Noirot, was open to the analyses I suggested to him, but in general I felt that the PCF found them embarrassing. After all, Moscow was happy with Nasser, so there was no point in making the French public too aware of how he treated Egyptian communists. Among the many friends I looked up was Jacques Vergès, then up to his ears in work with the team of lawyers courageously defending Algerians and risking assassination at the hands of OAS thugs.

In 1960 the Sino-Soviet dispute was in full swing. I read everything concerning it, especially the Chinese literature that was then starting to become widely available. I was immediately sympathetic to the Maoist critique of the Soviet system, which included a far-sighted warning that capitalism might one day be restored in the USSR. But the PCF had already made its choice: it supported the Moscow line without reservations. I was forced to take a certain distance from the Party.

In July Isabelle flew back from Egypt. She travelled with André Ghali, now too forced into emigration, and with the baby that his wife (Melle Politi's sister) had left him before dying in childbirth. It was a painful and truly sad journey.

Gruson suggested that I stay and work at the SEEF, but I realized that this would ultimately use up my energies and intellectual capacities for the running of capitalism. Why not try to place them at the service of liberation and progress somewhere in the third world? To remain in Paris would also, more or less, have meant sharing the lot of 'political refugees', and I knew from past contact that nothing was more destructive. I saw such people live in the illusion that they were still in their country of origin, trying to continue acting by proxy. It was contrary to my temperament.

Jean Bénard proposed instead that I go and work in Bamako. He knew what I was doing at the SEEF, and during lunch breaks there I had spoken with him at length about my 'planning' experience in Cairo and my political analyses. He and Charles Bettelheim were advisers to the new government of the Republic of Sudan (the former French Sudan), which had joined with

Senegal to form the short-lived Federal Republic of Mali, but they both thought they would be unable to fulfil their tasks properly without a good and politically reliable economist acting as their full-time intermediary in Bamako. At that time no Malian met those criteria – which scarcely surprised me, as I had not come across any Malian students during my years in Paris. Nearly all the students from French west and equatorial Africa had come from Senegal, Togo-Dahomey or Congo, virtually none from the other territories or the Sahel. On the other hand, I had met people who would become political leaders in the future Mali – men like the ageing Konaté (replaced on his death by Modibo, whom I did not know), but also Madeira Keita on the more radical wing of the African Democratic Rally. When my name was suggested to him, Madeira immediately gave his approval and on 20 September 1960 Isabelle and I boarded a plane to Bamako. I remember the date so well simply because it was also the day on which the Congress of the Sudanese Union, meeting after the break-up of the Mali federation, proclaimed Marxism–Leninism as the 'state religion'. It was not the worst of choices, and the proclamation of Christianity, Islam or neoliberalism as the state religion has proved much worse. In any event, it struck me as a welcome coincidence.

FIVE

Bamako, 1960–63

Our flight to Bamako stopped in Dakar in the early morning, at a hanger-airport that had nothing of today's modern and imposing structure. When Isabelle went to the toilet, she said it was like in Egypt: full of huge cockroaches. Our arrival in Bamako underlined the resemblances: a spiralling descent to the old airport beside the river; the Niger uncoiled like the strip of the Nile; the poor savannah stretching desert-like into the distance; the river banks green with crops; at the airport, a male population dressed in boubous,[29] reminiscent of the Egyptian *galabiyeh*.

Greater Sudan, the Arab name for a territory stretching from the Atlantic to the Red Sea, has quite a homogeneous appearance, as I was later able to convince myself in Khartoum. The French were therefore not wrong to call their colony French Sudan, which then became the Sudanese Republic (to distinguish it from the formerly Anglo-Egyptian Republic of Sudan) and shortly afterwards the Republic of Mali.

In Bamako we were put up for a month at the Grand Hotel, an old colonial building still in fine shape, with spacious rooms and verandas looking on to a bougainvillea-coloured garden stocked with mango trees, rubber plants and various fruit and nut trees. The evenings were kept lively by a colourful person at the piano bar, a man of unparalleled obesity by the name of Louis de Gonzague. A real descendant of the Bourbons, he was like a physical caricature of them – the spitting image of Louis XVI. We saw him again once in Paris, at the Coupole.

The Malian government eventually moved us into a modest villa on Koulouba hill, looking over a city lost in coloured gardens that then occupied only the left bank of the Niger. It had a population of roughly 200,000, whereas today this has risen to over a million and spread along the right bank. A narrow road wound up the Koulouba hillside, which accommodated the colonial administrative quarter, the former governor's (now the president's) palace, and three or four large ministries, including the economics and planning ministry to which I had to report. The villa itself was divided into two; our wing had a large reception room and a large bedroom, a no less spacious bathroom with rather rustic fittings (the shower consisted of a watering can that you filled by easing it down with a pulley), and a beautiful veranda. We soon improved the look of the colonial furniture, in the so-called *Louis Caisse* style, by dotting around various objects and brightly coloured Sudanese blankets. The kitchen was outside, as it often is in this part of Africa. It was certainly a pleasant spot, surrounded by gardens and trees and inhabited by sometimes over-persistent monkeys. Famished by the end of the dry season, they used to come and lay siege to us until we fed them. In fact, Isabelle has a bad memory of these creatures, since on one occasion, when she was out walking down the hill, a starving monkey attacked her and some mango-sellers and bit her on the calf. (She still has the scar today, although it was expertly sewed and is only just visible.) The preventive treatment against rabies was naturally rather unpleasant. Years later, at Nossy Bé, Isabelle told her story and that of a man bitten by a snake on the same day, who was afraid he would die and leave behind a pregnant wife. The woman with whom Isabelle was speaking then said to her: 'The pregnant woman is me, the child is this young girl, my husband is not dead, and he has told me of your own adventure.' It's a small world! There were other nasty creatures in the neighbourhood, such as a python (which visited the garden from time to time) or the more dangerous *foufouni* snakes. Once, five huge mygale spiders, measuring ten or twenty centimetres across, paid a collective visit to the veranda and gave Isabelle a terrible fright. But I should not exaggerate our little trials. Despite everything, the place was peaceful, beautiful and safe.

I was given the use of a car, but my first was a terrible Dauphine, an unstable vehicle completely unsuited to African roads. Fortunately they soon replaced it with a solid Citroën Deux Chevaux that I could drive on any terrain.

The Malian plan

My knowledge of the Sudanese Union was quite rudimentary, although its left wing (Madeira) welcomed me sincerely as a brother. I therefore considered it my first responsibility, and the first condition for anything positive on my part, to educate myself through long discussions with Madeira, Djim Sylla (principal private secretary in the planning department, who became a real friend), Idrissa Diarra (the Party's organization secretary) and, of course, many others. The conclusions I drew were probably quite banal, but they may throw some light on what followed.

The Sudanese Union (SU) had already established itself as the de facto single party in colonial times, when it succeeded in uniting all the anti-imperialist forces and isolating would-be collaborators. On 20 September 1960 it proclaimed itself the single party by law, 'guided by Marxism–Leninism', but in reality it was still a broad front of different social forces, shot through with contradictions.

Its right wing consisted of the class of retailers (the Dioulas), who had always had an influence on society and were major contributors to party funds. They were linked in turn to the peasantry (whose produce they collected), in an ambiguous relationship of exploitation and service. The SU's left wing recruited state-employed teachers, nurses and civil servants (there were no indigenous senior functionaries in colonial times), and these formed the cadre of their respective trade unions, which were united and quite strong organizations. The PCF had given considerable assistance in their training.

The solidly rooted Sudanese Union had raised the political level of the people, to a degree scarcely thought possible by most experts on African politics. One need only contrast the speeches on serious issues that SU leaders were making at public meetings in 1960 with the addresses that a colonial governor had given thirty years earlier to his Malian 'subjects' (a few sentences in 'pigeon French'; praise for the virtues of the motherland, especially its military strength; exhortations to celebrate the Quatorze Juillet with tom-toms, to drink a lot of wine, and to have many children and bring them up to be good soldiers).

The great mass of the population were small farmers living in tightly organized village communities. Local chieftaincies, sometimes inaccurately called 'feudal', retained a measure of influence that varied greatly from region to region. The colonial administration never succeeded in swallowing up all these chieftaincies, and many of them had been won over by the SU. The peasantry was not the passive mass that outsiders often imagine: it had real autonomy vis-à-vis the chieftains, the retailers and the SU's urban activists. But it did not have a leadership of its own, except for a few nuclei of ex-combatants (those known in the French army as 'Senegalese infantrymen' were in fact mostly from Mali or Upper Volta).

The villagers practised their autonomy with the help of the *komo*, a term often badly translated as 'sorcery' but actually a secret society charged with making order prevail. Its masked members came out at night to punish troublemakers (adulterous wives, for example), handled poison and entered into relations with supernatural forces. In fact, it operated under the tight control of the council of elders, the normal form of political management in societies that did not yet have a state, closely akin to the *shura* in pre-Islamic or post-Islamic Arabia. They did not have the right to introduce innovations but existed only to ensure respect for tribal (or, in the Arab case, tribal and Islamic) tradition. Democracy, however, is defined precisely by the right to innovate, by human rather than divine responsibility for the law, by an affirmation that individuals and society make their own history and do not merely endure it. There is therefore nothing either specific or democratic about the *shura*, and today's Islamists who argue the contrary are merely repeating the claim of 'African socialism', heard so often in those days, to base itself on some traditional village democracy. The *komo* had survived many systems of village rule, whether by precolonial military rulers or by the colonial administration. Indeed, it was said that, although French Sudan was 90 per cent Muslim (because 90 per cent of the population answered 'yes' when asked whether Muhammad had been Allah's Prophet), it was also 90 per cent animist (because 90 per cent of people believed in the supernatural powers of the *komo*). The Sudanese Union made considerable, and not unsuccessful, efforts to uproot the *komo* from people's minds and from reality, so as to create a firm basis for its activists and later its administration to govern the country. The reason it gave was the need to eradicate prejudices and superstitions (though, as we know, one superstition replaces another!), but its real aim was to dismantle the autonomy of the peasantry. In doing this, the SU helped to deepen the process of Islamization, and the price for this is perhaps today's rise of fundamentalist movements.

The Sudanese Union had its intellectuals (left-wing urban activists trained in the school of communism), but it scarcely counted any university graduates in its ranks, for the simple reason that in the late 1950s there had been only one *lycée* in the whole of French Sudan and secondary education was still minimal. The first generation of graduates, who began to return to the country only in 1962–65, had no record of political activity but reaped the benefits of their education by gaining immediate access to quite senior positions within the administration. This tended to favour opportunism, an extravagant verbal nationalism or 'socialism', and often arrogance or pretentiousness. The cadres in question bear a heavy responsibility for the later distortions that led to the debacle of the regime, but they were able to transfer their allegiances to the new regime without facing too many problems of conscience.

What could development and planning mean in these conditions? My opinion on this is the result of deep and constant discussions between the small group of foreign associates (Faure, Molle and myself, later joined by Lobel, plus Bénard during his periods of assignment) and a small group of leaders of the SU Left (the most active being Madeira, Idrissa Diarra and Djim Sylla). This Malian Left was not at all sectarian; it was quite aware that concessions were inevitable, that the chieftains and retailers had great weight in society, and that it was useful to enlist their professional skills behind a progressive social project, 'neutralizing' them (that is, not allowing them to take the leadership) but not treating them as enemies. The conditions really existed for things to move forward; the subsequent failure was not written in the cards from the outset.

We took seriously the declarations that the Party issued with conviction and honesty. Its objectives made eminent sense: to achieve the highest degree of secondary schooling; to carry out mass vaccinations and set up village health centres; to improve the road system and open up remote regions; to double agricultural output per family (leaving scope for discussion and experience to determine the precise role of irrigation, seed improvements, dry equipments, animal traction, etc., as well as of cooperation, pricing, harvest gathering, and so on); to refrain from excessive industrialization, concentrating on a few import-substitutionist light industries and consumption sectors (cement, bricks, textiles, timber, food processing, repair shops) instead of the World Bank's completely senseless preference for export industries; to reform public finances and introduce a fairer and more efficient tax system; to reduce bureaucracy in the civil service; to democratize the life of society, and so on. At this stage, the Party left open the possibility of private–public partnership and various forms of management, and encouraged debate on the role of autonomous women's organizations, trade unions, rural cooperatives and other mass organizations, as part of the process of democratization.

I had special responsibility for the drafting of programmes in these areas, including a quantification of the expected investment and return. It was necessary to ensure that these programmes were coherent at the level of both public and external funding, and to specify what they required by way of credit, wage and price policies (including subsidies, taxes and possible state controls). The idea was not to dream up some spectacular advance on the highway of progress, but to predict the dangers on the winding road ahead. That, in any case, is my definition of planning. Of course, the programmes in view would require our planning unit to be involved in ongoing consultation: both with the technical departments at the relevant ministries and with the National Planning Committee, a hybrid institution that brought together the principal ministers and departmental heads, on the one hand, and the SU political bureau and the leaderships of the mass organizations, on the other.

Instruments had to be devised for the measuring of coherence and efficiency, and it was here that my imagination was supposed to come into play. For there are no planning 'manuals' that provide such formulas. The many 'experts' who think otherwise have probably never really taken responsibility for the implementation of a Plan. The instruments have to be invented for each situation, which is always particular. Planning is not like assembly-line work; it is craft labour (or perhaps artistic labour) which has to deliver a made-to-measure suit, not something off the peg.

I therefore had to work out an ad hoc national accounting framework that built in the deficiencies of information and the nature of the fundamental objectives, in such a way as to highlight the salient effects of the various options. It took perhaps a half of my working time for nearly a full year, but my eventual proposal gained widespread acceptance and won me congratulations at the SEEF and elsewhere. There had been no question of making up for the deficiencies of information by conducting statistical surveys for which we had neither the time nor the money, nor a sufficient number of trained people. Instead, I drew systematically on the extraordinary fund of knowledge that I detected in two individuals. One was the secretary of the Chamber of Commerce (whose name I have unfortunately forgotten), a Frenchman and small employer who played the game honestly enough in the service of the new Malian state. He knew everything about the import trade: not only the statistics – which were rather shaky at the time, since French West Africa had just blown apart and border controls were virtually non-existent – but also the precise quantity of each product category, its price and its markets (public use, private consumption, etc.). The other man was Jean Molle, a former administrator ('Circle Commander') who was a veritable mine of information: he could tell you how many individuals and working days were needed to build a hut, how many years it would last, what quantities of millet and cotton a family could produce in each region of the country, how much fertilizer they would need, what was their food consumption, and so on. When I later started deciphering the Mali archives, I was able to gauge just how seriously certain administrators (the best ones, of course) compiled their reports. I even used them for a kind of economic history of French Sudan between 1920 and 1958.

On the basis of this information – which the three of us discussed again and again, and which I compared with anything I could glean from other sources – I came up with a set of indicators. Each of these was supposed to 'sum up' the situation in a sector corresponding to a possible development objective: for example, the primary education cost indicator per 10,000 inhabitants, the minimal health cost indicator for the same population, the 100-kilometre road cost indicator per 50,000 square kilometres for a population density X, the food consumption indicators (for a similar basket of goods) per rural family, per working-class urban family and per middle-class urban family, the same indicators for housing and related facilities, the trading, transport and tax margin indicators corresponding to each of the foregoing.

By the end I had in my drawer an ad hoc set of tools that could clearly be used to good effect. The objectives of the Plan were immediately expressed in the growth rates specific to each indicator, and from the objective indicators I could deduce by simple rules of three the values of each of the main national accounting categories. By putting these figures in their allotted place in a General Economic Table (GET), I could immediately visualize the likely difficulties, dangers and inconsistencies. This enabled me to submit to the National Committee a 'revised plan' indicating anything problematic in its proposals.

The method made it possible to answer a number of key questions concerning the optimal level and rate of increase of incomes, the relative purchasing power of the main agricultural products, the consumer price index, rates of taxation, and so on. It therefore enabled us to build a social dimension into the Plan: greater or lesser inequality, especially between town and country, a particular hierarchy of wages, a certain level of private profit, and so on. In this way, we could also define which fiscal reforms were desirable, which kinds of import control or rationing, which export levels (and therefore which growth targets for certain key products).

I did not have a computer at my disposal – fortunately, because in my opinion they are not only unnecessary but actually dangerous for the kind of work I had to do. My only equipment was the engineer's slide rule I have used for all my professional and teaching activity. For I think that the great majority of economic calculations needed in Africa boil down to compound interest and rules of three. This does not mean that computers are unnecessary for other situations, as in the construction of SEEF's variable price model to which I alluded earlier.

Some years later, in 1965, I used the method I had developed in Mali to forecast the outcome of various options in Ivory Coast. As I had chosen a twenty-year time frame, this meant that catastrophe – that is, an external debt crisis – would strike in 1985. Ten years later, the World Bank tried to prove me wrong by commissioning a study for millions of dollars – experts flying first class, staying in luxury hotels, and so on, to conclude that everything would be hunky-dory in Ivory Coast by the year 1985. The stupidity was amusing enough, but rather costly. Top civil servants in Ivory Coast who were impressed by the correctness of my forecasts – in fact, a worse crisis in 1985 than I had predicted – invited me to visit the country and eyed me rather in the way in which people consult cowries in Africa. I explained to them that I had not looked into a crystal ball but simply used my political common sense and the rule of three. I don't know if they were convinced.

My detractors will say that the planning method I developed in Mali laid the stress on coherence rather than efficiency. This is not altogether false. But I would say that the extreme emphasis on efficiency in neoliberal discourse is largely illusory and artificial. It is based on the circular argument that markets are self-regulating, which has nothing to do with the real world (where markets are governed by the exigencies of dominant capital) and precludes the placing of the economy at the service of social development. In the Malian case, efficiency consisted of finding ways to run enterprises and government departments in a correct manner. That is already something, quite a lot in fact, and it is not easy to translate into reality. But common sense requires that a start should be made there.

The more or less official Malian plan that resulted from this exercise – I say 'more or less' because it was hedged about with contradictory statements, especially by the main ministers – seemed to me feasible and progressive. Although its implementation was somewhat chaotic, for reasons I shall consider later, it yielded results that were generally positive for Mali and could have provided a solid basis for further advance. The rot set in later. As I said, the plan left scope for discussion of various options important both socially and politically and in terms of economic efficiency. It was here that the deformations began.

I have always liked to discuss my work; I have always believed that collective creativity is richer than the creativity of the isolated individual. In Cairo I had benefited from almost daily discussions with Ismail, and in Paris with Nataf and my other SEEF colleagues. I did the same in Bamako with everyone in our planning unit and, whenever the opportunity arose, with Bénard, Prou and a few others. I can no longer give a proper account of their positive criticisms and suggestions, so closely were they woven into my 'end product'. I owe them a lot, that's for sure.

In Bamako I received visits from a number of 'experts' in the Soviet world, the World Bank and the United Nations, but I must say, without false modesty, that I learned nothing at all from any of them. The Soviets kept churning out the same general 'principles': it's good when the state intervenes, bad when this is not planned – never anything more precise. So, I concluded that they were mediocre bureaucrats who had to stick to such insipid stuff to earn their living. But the World Bank people were, and are, of exactly the same type, and also speak a totally ideological language, even if their basic principle ('it's good whenever the private sector takes charge') is the diametrical opposite. One can easily see this underlying identity if one compares a Soviet propaganda booklet and a World Bank report: the title, in each case, gives away every last detail inside; anything at all proves that the basic idea upheld by the institution is correct and explains everything; facts are ignored or even falsified (the word is not too strong). Thus, for the World Bank, the past successes of South Korea were due to the virtues of the market, while its present difficulties (financial crisis) are due to statism. It's simple – only wrong on both counts. For state intervention played a decisive role in Korea's success, and not by chance the crisis hit when the country joined the OECD and was forced to liberalize the economy. But what does that matter? Neoliberalism is always right, just as 'Soviet Marxism' always used to be. The same dogmatism. Probably the same future.

If I learned many useful things in Bamako, I owe it to a few modest African experts in their fields – agronomists, doctors, veterinary surgeons and one man of genius (René Dumont) – as well as to a number of Chinese experts. With these and Dumont I did a few field trips, which I appreciated not only because I generally like to see the landscape (why not?) but because I think that you always learn most with your own eyes. Of course, you have to be wary of what, in some journalists, turns into straightforward arrogance – the claim to understand everything after a few days in a country whose culture and history are unfamiliar to you. But if you avoid this, the visual experience always adds a great deal. It certainly cannot take the place of hard work – in my case, the serious reading of history, culture, anthropology and economics. But it is an important complement that sometimes quickly increases its impact. With Dumont and the Chinese I came to appreciate the value of agronomists who, in addition to being competent, have a political and social sense. One day in the Delta Mort of the Niger, where we were talking of resettling 30,000 new farmers, I asked the Chinese whether this would really be possible. One of them looked somewhat wistfully at the horizon and the ground and answered: 'Three million with no problem, and it won't cost much.' Underpopulated Africa – I understood what he was saying.

There was virtually no other source for my reflections and my work. I had not heard of ECLA's incipient planning activity, and the French research societies that expanded in Africa in the 1960s and 1970s were still in their infancy. I shall return to these problems below.

Daily life

In Bamako we formed a close little group of friends, both foreign and Malian. There was Marcel Faure, a former colonial administrator, and his wife Solange, who often visited him from France. Marcel had joined the Free French and braved bombs and bullets at Bir Hakeim, in Italy and in France, for which he had received the Compagnon de la Libération award, but all the top positions to which it gave access were closed to him as soon as he joined the Communist Party; he then became a full-timer for the CGT trade union federation. Eventually he retired to the beautiful remote countryside near Marvejols (the town associated with the Beast of Gévaudan[30]) in the Lozère, where he succeeded in re-creating the atmosphere of 'the bush'; when I visited him around 1970, along with Isabelle, my mother and my grandmother, he organized a splendid North African-style barbecue, which convinced me that good European sheep were as good as those of Africa. A big game hunter, with the physique of a warrior, Faure had once been gored by a buffalo and still had a large scar on his shoulder. He certainly missed hunting and, as long as possible, continued to go on African safaris.

Jean Molle was also a former colonial administrator and had always been a supporter of the African Democratic Rally; his wife, Blanche, had been a teacher and then headmistress of a school.

Elie Lobel, an Israeli citizen, had left his country in outrage at the Zionists' behaviour towards the Palestinians, then joined the FLN support networks in Paris and been forced to leave 'in a hurry'. His work at the SEEF had recommended him to us, and we asked him to come and join us. Later, he returned to Paris and was active in the Israeli–Palestinian journal *Khamsin*. He died young, and the PLO representative in Paris – a friend who greatly respected what he had done – attended the funeral.

Not long afterwards, the Portuguese Communist Ruy da Nobrega – who had been forced to escape from South Africa and Mozambique – came to work with us in Bamako, accompanied by his wife Nicole and their children. In fact, Ruy was a banking expert, and his skills were more than useful in setting up an autonomous Malian banking system. After he got a proper passport, to replace the incredibly doctored one on which he had travelled before, he went on a trip to Hong Kong. But the Malians, instead of giving him a vaguely mixed-race identity such as Pereira, had decided to give him a father by the name of Mamadou and a mother called Khadija, together with a purely Malian date of birth and patronymic. So, when the phlegmatic British consul issued the visa, he said to him: 'I've seen some false passports in my time, but this one takes some beating!'

My closest Malian friends were Djim Sylla, a remarkably perceptive man who became a very good manager of the national economy, and his wife Oumou. Intelligence, political nous and a serious attitude to work are indeed often worth more than diplomas. The main leaders of the left within the Sudanese Union were all close friends: 'old man' Madeira Keita at the top, Idrissa Diarra, Ousmane Ba, Mamadou Gologo and the West Indian Henri Corenthin. Political relations also led to friendship with many other members of this current: people like Diarra (dynamic head of the People's Library service), the lawyer Demba Diallo, the pharmacist Samba Diallo (who efficiently organized the distribution of basic medicines across the country), Samba Lamine Traoré (director of the Office du Niger[31]), the mining engineer Bakary Touré and his wife Thérèse, the public finance specialist Oumar Macalou, the radio announcer Gassama (a man not without humour and imagination, who one day found nothing of interest to Malians in the news agency reports and simply announced: 'No news today! Until tomorrow'), and Diakité, the director of a new people's bank.

Then there were the African political refugees: Doudou Guèye[32] and his wife Marie Louise; Oumar Dème (director of the National Printing Works, originally from Ivory Coast) and his companion, the teacher Raymonde Mallebay Vacqueur; and the two beautiful *métis* sisters Jacqueline and Augustine Ancelot. Jacqueline, who married the Senegalese Momar Sakho, told us how, as a young girl, she had had to cross the Niger to go to school in Kayes, at a ford which in parts was so deep that the water came up to her shoulders and forced her to carry her books on her head. It must have made a delightful picture. Augustine, who was still very beautiful despite her numerous pregnancies, went walking with us on Karabane island in Casamance and slept with us in the only travellers' hut there. During the day we had been a little too inquisitive and tried too hard to approach the people in charge of a traditional ceremony, so at night the *komo* (to which I referred earlier) came to pay us a visit. Its agents threw little stones onto the roof of the hut and let out animal cries. Augustine was scared to death, but we explained to her that the *komo* would not do us any harm. 'That may be true for you,' she said, 'because you're *toubabs*[33] and are counted' – by which she meant that our disappearance would be noticed and might cause them trouble. 'But I'm a negro woman, and they may kill me.'

There was also a small group of long-standing French anti-colonial activists, Robert Béart (who died a few years later), and a few 'bushmen' like Molinari and Pierre Gambas – if I remember his name correctly – who had done all kinds of jobs, from hotel work to printing, and were a little too fond of their drink. They often met at Le Berry, a café in the town centre, opposite the main state shop and near the market, and we would sometimes get together with them and some rather similar Malians such as Gassama or Moulaye (a finance director). The new French technical assistants included Bernard Dumont (responsible for the development of social legislation), his teacher wife Geneviève and Claudine Solomon (a science teacher). Among the people from the Eastern bloc were a group of Hungarians, the most open nationality in that part of the world – I especially remember Paller, who represented the Hungarian bus and truck company that supplied Mali.

I took an interest in the training of the new generation. I got to know young people at debates in the embryonic new university: Founeké Keita (whom I first met at Patrice Lumumba University in Moscow, in 1965); the Gakou brothers (Lamine later worked with me at IDEP and the FTM); Denis Traoré, and future lecturers at Bamako university, such as Kari Dembélé and Bernard Cissokho. It was a generation that threw up many leaders of the popular struggle against the Moussa Traoré dictatorship, who were later to be found in the leadership of ADEMA[34] (e.g. Dicko) or the CNID[35] (e.g. Mountaga Tall).

A number of 'missionaries', as they were known, used to pass through Mali: interesting anthropologists such as Claude Meillassoux, and other figures sometimes worthy of mention. For example, there was a teacher from south-west France (I no longer remember his name), an intransigently secular supporter of the Radical Socialists, who was always dressed up to the nines (classical suit and tie, whatever the temperature) and was in Mali for reasons that were not altogether clear. When he had to go to a village, he rubbed his hands and licked his chops in anticipation, thinking that, as in his native south-west, he would be able to indulge in a fine meal. Disappointed by the constant fare of gruel – sweet in the morning, savoury in the evening – he went off and hunted some rabbits, and then, with some shea butter and all the herbs that people pointed out, he prepared a delicious and original dish flambéd in whisky. Good cooks know how to make the most of things.

It was in Bamako that I first became familiar with the Lebanese emigration – an experience followed by others in Dakar and elsewhere in Africa. Harsh judgements are often made about this social group, not without some reason: for it is a stratum of the comprador class, subordinate in those days to colonial capital (which 'imported' it in the first place) and nowadays to the ruling bourgeoisie-cum-bureaucracy of the African states. This is why demagogic politicians often use them as scapegoats. But some traits may also be mentioned in their favour: a natural politeness and helpfulness, a penchant for hard work, but also a liking for 'the good life' (their spending keeps in existence many cafés and restaurants without which daily life would lose many of its charms). My barber in Bamako had come down from the mountains of Lebanon: he spent three months in Beirut to learn his trade and get to know 'the city', then boarded a cargo ship for Abidjan and found a potato lorry for the last stretch to Bamako. The next day he opened his one-room shop, with a chair and a mirror and a pair of scissors. Soon he was a different man: the country bumpkin looked smart, spoke two new languages (Bambara and French) and had learned to read and write. A year later he was sending back home the little capital that his village community had advanced (with nothing in writing), so that another poor individual could take advantage of it. People from the Indian subcontinent serve similar functions in East Africa, and I imagine that their trajectories have often been the same. In both cases, marked social differentiation appears with the second or third generation, as some grow rich or enter the liberal professions, while others become genuine intellectuals, such as my student Charbel in Dakar or people I met in Tanzania and Kenya.

The small left-wing group in the Sudanese Union was so tightly knit that Madeira, the interior minister, invited us all round to his place. He was in the habit of picking up the telephone and saying: 'Seven o'clock at Madeira's', with no further explanation. Once we were there, he used to say through his teeth: 'I've called all the drunks together – and it just might coincide with a political meeting. Yes, we have to drink some whisky: it's a political gesture and you have to get yourselves noticed doing it at public ceremonies. But you don't have to finish the whole bottle.' The guest list naturally included Gologo, author of an autobiographical novel eloquently entitled *The Survivor of Ethylos*.[36] When I mentioned to Madeira that I did not consider myself a drinker, he replied: 'Yes, I know, I was well trained as a policeman. But, as you mix with drinkers a lot, maybe you could give them a talking-to.'

Isabelle was teaching at the main school in the city centre, on Place Maginot. In colonial times the schools had only operated in the morning, but the new regime had introduced French hours that made the afternoons very uncomfortable towards the end of the dry season. The young Africans slept, while the little Europeans cried and complained of the heat. So, Isabelle freshened them all in her way, sprinkling them like flowers or squeezing a wet sponge on their heads. Among these delightful children were the two daughters of Ruy and Nicole and a little Vietnamese girl, Lily Bayoumy, who had been found as a baby in Vietnam beneath her mother's dead body (killed by the war), then adopted by a certain Bayoumy. He was a Moroccan-Senegalese, as they are known in Senegal: in fact, his ancestors had gone from Egypt via Morocco to Senegal, where they had taken part in the Islamization of the country; his wife was a Vietnamese. Bayoumy was a member of the African Democratic Alliance, and soon afterwards he returned to Senegal. Years later, after the death of her adoptive parents, Lily was looking for work; we took her on, and she is now our loyal administrative secretary at the Third World Forum. When she travelled to Egypt in 1997 to attend an Afro-Asian conference, the police officer at the airport asked her: 'Egyptian name, Senegalese passport, Asian appearance – how's that?' 'It's globalization', she replied.

Daily life in Bamako was not monotonous, although our habits soon became fixed. We often dined at one another's houses, especially as some of us (Faure, Molle, Djim Sylla, Lobel, Isabelle and myself) lived in the same neighbourhood in Koulouba. On Sunday evenings we would go in a large group to a pleasant outdoor restaurant on the banks of the river, near the bridge linking Bamako to the south of the country. The place is now known as 'The Three Caymans', but in those days it had a different name which I have forgotten. During the day on Sundays we often went swimming in the Niger, at Sotuba, where the dam had not yet been built. In the middle of the rapids (during the dry season) there were islands of sand, wonderfully fine and clean, washed by the clear current; we used to get there by hopping from stone to stone at the ford, taking with us a picnic and beach umbrellas. One day, when Charles Bettelheim was in Bamako on an assignment, we took him along with us. The Malian children bathing there chose this wise 'grandad' as their playmate and enjoyed jumping on him and splashing him with water. He responded as joyfully as anyone I have ever seen.

Neither Isabelle nor I ever suffered from the climate in Mali. Perhaps we are hot-country creatures. For me there have never been 'temperate' countries, only (warm) human climates and inhuman ones. But Isabelle thinks that I feel neither the heat nor the cold; that all Egyptians have a tough skin, due to the sudden change of temperature, as much as 20 degrees, that the desert climate brings after sunset. In Mali, the thermometer sometimes climbed above 45 degrees, and I remember one occasion on which Isabelle took her own temperature and got a fright. Doctor Hautin, who had spent many years attending to the colonial army, examined her and found nothing special. When we told him about the thermometer, he guffawed and said with a mixture of European and colonial crudeness: 'You put your thermometer in a drawer where it's fifty degrees and it goes bust. Stick it up your arse if you want to keep it cool.'

Here are a few more amusing stories from my time in Bamako. Shortly after my arrival I came to a set of traffic lights at a junction with a completely unobstructed view and merely slowed down instead of stopping. A policeman blew his whistle, 'What do you do at traffic lights?' he asked. 'You slow down, take a good look and if there's nothing you drive on', I replied, with what I thought was a hint of malice. 'No, you stop', he insisted. 'Okay, I'm wrong – I didn't know.' The policeman roared with laughter and got me to repeat: 'I'm wrong.' He then let me go, chuckling that he had just wanted me to say 'I'm wrong'; he had never heard it from a white man before.

When the planning ministry decided to move from Koulouba to the city centre, the orderlies in charge of the operation threw loads of files into a lorry without taking any care. The lorry completed the descent from Koulouba and entered town near the zoo, but then a gust of wind sent some papers flying through the air to the feet of an elephant, which immediately started to tuck in. Among the papers was the original copy of the National Plan. Fortunately there were also some other copies, but when I told the story to the minister I said: 'That's it, all gone. The elephant ate the Plan.'

We often went to see a film in the evening, at an open-air cinema, and sometimes we had to watch it through a sheet of rain. Once they were showing *Last Year in Marienbad*. A couple of ordinary Malians were sitting next to me, one translating from French into Bambara for the other. 'But that's stupid; it makes no sense', the beneficiary of the translation protested – and I shared his opinion. 'I know,' the other said, 'but that's what they're saying.'

The government came up with the idea of launching bottled ginger juice as a 'national drink'. It was not such a bad idea, as this traditional product really is delicious, but unfortunately they decided to use an old soap works, and the tanks, insufficiently cleaned of soda, turned out something more like a 'national purgative' for the next official holiday. The following morning, the president, ministers and other worthies were all absent from their offices, after a long and tragic night. Only Madeira had not wanted to taste the drink, sticking to whisky instead. I saved the country from a *coup d'état*, which would not have been difficult to stage that day.

We often went for long walks, some of which we called 'dumonteries', after the man who used to organize them, Bernard Dumont. Once, when we went to the upper Niger near the frontier with Guinea, to see the gold prospectors at work, Dumont had the crazy idea of bringing along some raw meat to make kebabs. We tried to light a fire to grill them, all very clumsily, and the Malian miners crowded round to watch us. One of them came up to me, took a tin of sardines and a piece of bread from his pocket and said: 'Do you know this? It's very practical.'

We also often went 'hunting' on the Baoulé, a tributary of the River Senegal in western Mali, in beautiful countryside with a forest reserve. But in fact it was a pretext for dawn walks, under the eyes of does and monkeys, or, more rarely, lions. Our camp left a lot to be desired – indeed, we once thought it better to set up beds and mosquito nets outside. This time, however, the lions did not let us sleep but kept growling nearby. 'Don't worry,' said Faure, 'no one's ever seen a lion lift a mosquito net to see what's in the food box.' On another occasion, the Hungarian Paller had fallen behind while we were out walking, and we were beginning to get a little worried when he did not return to the camp. Then he suddenly appeared looking rather pale: he had backtracked along the river, pursued by an iguana. They are quite harmless really, well-known for their curiosity, but people think of them as horrible creatures.

The trips to the Baoulé taught me something I had never previously known about myself: that I am left-handed. Whenever I used a rifle, I would hit a spot some twenty centimetres to the right of the target, yet my hands did not tremble, I took aim calmly, and I am not a hopelessly awkward person. So what was happening? I no longer remember who suggested that I try the other shoulder and shut the other eye. Wham, bull's eye straight away! I was left-handed. Then it occurred to me that I tended to use my left hand to do a lot of common things. So, I had been 'corrected' – and then I recalled that my first primary school teacher, Mademoiselle Masri, had made me hold my pencil in my right hand. I had obeyed, but perhaps the mischievous streak I had for a long time at school was the price they paid for it. I don't think the 'correction' had a serious effect on my intellect or character, although I know that can sometimes happen to people. But nor am I convinced that an American laid-back approach is better, as a kid who takes a pencil in his left hand for the first time is not necessarily left-handed. Judging by the number of Americans who write in the most extravagant – and the least straightforward – positions, one might think that a little more early learning would not have done them any harm.

There were a few memorable evening receptions at the Presidency, not least during the visits by Tito and Nkrumah. I can remember Modibo and Tito seated with their wives at a table for four. The music started as soon as dinner was over: Modibo asked the beautiful Yugoslav woman for a dance, and Tito dutifully did the same with Mrs Keita. It was African cha-cha music, and Tito, who may know how to dance a Danubian waltz, pranced around like a circus bear. Still, the visit earned me a wonderful trip to Yugoslavia, to which I shall return later. As to Nkrumah's visit, the police thought they should keep a close eye on the fairly large numbers of Ghanaian prostitutes in Bamako, who, as a matter of interest, describe their trade as *faire son cul-boutique* ('hawking shop-ass'), an expression also found in Ivory Coast. Some of these ladies, considering themselves fully fledged Nkrumahists, angrily circumvented the police checks and soon found themselves being fêted by the Ghanaian delegation at the Grand Hotel. At the presidential palace one of them recognized the British ambassador – a friend of hers, she claimed, who didn't even bother to say hello. She gave him a piece of her mind and threw up over his dinner jacket, just before the worthy diplomat was due to step forward and shake the president's hand.

Real balance-of-payments difficulties, together with weaknesses in the organization of state commerce, led to frequent stock shortages. One day I whispered in the ear of an assistant I knew at the main state store: 'Do you have any razor blades?' 'No,' she replied, in a low voice, 'but we've got some sardines.' So I left with a few tins of sardines.

Isabelle and I visited many parts of this huge country, either on official business or simply for a holiday. In the land of the Dogon in the central plateau, which all tourists now know, the camp at Bandiagara, the only one in those days, was far from great. We joked on our way there on Christmas Eve that it would be filled with English (from Ghana) – and it was. A beautiful Englishwoman lay sprawled on the only double bed, and it was explained to her that five people could sleep in it. I don't know who ended up sharing it, but the others made do with blankets on the ground. It was unforgettable country: Djenne, Mopti, trips on the Niger, the Sahel road north of the river, the lake shores at Niafunké and Goundam, Gao. We almost got lost in the Sahel, our tyres repeatedly burst on the thorns, we had our work cut out repairing the inner tubes, and so on. There was a memorable ceremony at Timbuktu, where Mahamane Haïdara, chairman of the Assembly, organized a barbecue in my honour. Those present spread out spontaneously in five rows: the first, directly facing the grilled sheep, consisted of Mahamane, the governor, the prefect, myself and a few others; the second of the departmental heads and local notables; the third of ordinary 'free' men; and the last two of lower-class types, 'slaves', beggars, lepers, and so on. The cooks gave us the best pieces, and the rest was passed directly over our heads to the row behind. We could hear the sound of quarrelling in the last rows, which must have been left with nothing but bones. So, while we were enjoying our tasty morsels, Mahamane said to me: 'You know, Samir, we will certainly build socialism.' 'No doubt,' I replied, 'and even equality between everyone.' He looked slightly askance – though he was a fine and sincere man – and said: 'That'll take a long time.' 'Yes,' I concluded, 'but one day you'll have to make a start.' His laughter was loud and frank: 'We will – but the history books will say that it wasn't today.'

I went on another fine trip to the south with Isabelle and her friend Raymonde, who was pregnant and had a 2-year-old girl on her lap plus a 9-year-old son. We drove to Sikasso, then to the western Ivory Coast, Odienné and Man, through that extraordinary equatorial forest. We were caught by one of the storms unique to those parts, complete with a whirlwind, huge lightning-struck trees, and fallen trunks across the road. We thought we would never get through. We wanted to continue to Nzérékoré, in eastern Guinea, but problems at the frontier forced us to turn back.

My responsibilities meant that I was often invited to foreign embassies, but I kept such contacts to a minimum and carefully avoided talking about anything other than generalities. Some kept pressing me, however. One first secretary at the Soviet embassy, probably KGB, asked me one day to explain to him what Mali was. Why not? After all, there was no reason why he should have been familiar with this society and its ways. So I tried to tell him something about its colonial history, its politics and social structure, its economic problems, and so on. 'No,' he said, 'I didn't mean that Marxist stuff. I want to know the truth.' I laughed and said that for me Marxism was a tool to understand the truth. I could see that his truth – realpolitik – consisted of knowing whether X or Y could be corrupted.

The Egyptian embassy had evidently been sent a file on me; the ambassador was visibly embarrassed about it. Modibo, thinking it would be good to 'settle the problem between me and the Egyptian government', suggested that I accompany him on a trip to Cairo. I explained that my problem was not personal, that it was inseparable from the general problem of relations between Nasser and the communists, and that as long as the repression continued against them I couldn't imagine myself strutting around Cairo in a Malian delegation. My comrades would not have understood my attitude. But I have to say that Modino gave me the impression of understanding it, and perhaps even of accepting in his heart of hearts that I was right.

This story reminds me of others that were to some extent its natural sequel. A few years later, in Paris, the wife of an Egyptian embassy official tried to kill herself and her children, and was placed under the care of a psychiatric hospital. Her husband, who was not allowed to see her there, seemed very unhappy, and Moustapha Safouan, to whom he was causing problems in connection with some documents, asked him to explain why he was so troubled. When Safouan, a well-known psychiatrist, learned the reason, he told him not to worry and immediately rang the clinical director at the hospital. 'I know you don't think much of us,' he said, 'but we do have a reputation among the high and the mighty – so please put us down as "dubious types in the VIP or luxury or exceptional category". You can choose which you prefer.' And that's what was done, I think. Later still Naguib Kadri, the talented ambassador in Dakar, who had a good sense of humour, showed me the file in his office. 'I can help you correct the numerous mistakes', I told him. He laughed and said: 'It's not worth the trouble any more. It's classified.'

Missions in Guinea and Ghana

In 1961 the three self-styled socialist countries of West Africa – Ghana, Guinea and Mali – declared their intention of forming a union, to be the core of a pan-African federation such as Nkrumah had long been advocating. It was the time when African countries were divided into two hostile blocs: the Casablanca group (Morocco, FLN Algeria, Egypt, Ghana, Guinea and Mali), which formed a more or less radical wing of national liberation, and the Monrovia group (nearly all the other independent African countries), which maintained that, with independence achieved, there was no longer an imperialist enemy. I have already written of this in the Bandung chapter of my *Re-reading the Postwar Period*, and will say a little more about it below.

Nevertheless, the Guinea–Ghana–Mali Union, though the theme of a song, never went much further. The Malian government commissioned me to gather information about the possibility of economic cooperation among the three countries, and this was the context in which I went once to Conakry and two or three times to Accra.

My mission to Conakry, in late 1962 after the famous 'teachers' plot', immediately gave me a negative impression of the Sékou Touré regime. I stayed at the Hôtel de France (I don't know if its name has since been changed), a fine old colonial establishment in the Boulbinet district, at the end of the peninsula on which Conakry was originally built. The view over the Loos islands was truly magnificent. But the hotel was beginning to decay. There was no longer a kitchen. People 'brought in their own food', as in a Spanish *hostal*. A nearby Lebanese shop sold guests tins of tuna, bread and fruit, which we made into a meal in the prestigious dining room.

I met a few officials and ministers, who refused to say anything more than a few vague generalities probably handed down by Sékou Touré. Finally, after I insisted, they allowed me to see the president himself, who was clearly the only man able to say anything, let alone make a decision. It was an appalling interview. No sooner had I finished politely paying my 'respects' than he flew off into a one-hour monologue, at the end of which he shook my hand and waited for me to make my exit. What had he spoken about? Everything – except for the matter at issue. Just generalities, with so little order that immediately afterwards I could scarcely remember a word.

This one-sided audience confirmed the impression I had gained of Sékou during my student years in Paris: a pure tactician, with no strategic vision and probably not many principles. But a few qualifications do need to be made to this severe judgement. First of all, Guinea was not entirely reducible to Sékou. The PDG (the Parti Démocratique de Guinée, part of the African Democratic Rally) had been a real party, and in the time of the anticolonial struggle Sékou had not called all the shots in it. It was one of the most advanced and best organized parties within the ADR, having been radicalized precisely through the struggle it had had to wage against powerful traditional chiefdoms working hand in glove with the French. Whether these should be called 'fiefdoms' or something more appropriate, whether their fortunate suppression (before the 1958 referendum) should be described as a land reform or, as I would prefer, a political reform, is not really the question. The point is that they were a real adversary, and their defeat opened up a number of real possibilities. But this very defeat made the PDG the de facto single party, with the advantages but also all the dangers that that involves.

Guinea's 'no' to the French plan for the country therefore opened up certain possibilities and generated a lot of enthusiasm across Africa. An impressive number of cadres from the former French colonies – Dahomey and Senegal, in particular, but also Mali and Niger (Abdou Moumouni, for example) – placed themselves at the disposal of the new republic. Independence also allowed the rapid establishment of diplomatic relations with the Eastern bloc, China and other third world countries, opening up new political horizons hitherto unknown to Guineans. Unfortunately, however, these possibilities were soon wasted as the regime became more and more autocratic, for various reasons that I shall not try to summarize here. One of the few people in Conakry to give me a warm welcome was the interior minister Fodeba Keita, founder of the first African ballet company and already a perceptive political activist when I had got to know him in Paris. He ended his days in prison, where the order was given quite simply to starve him to death. Diallo Telli and many other leaders formerly close to Sékou died in the same appalling circumstances; Sayfoullaye Diallo, whom I also knew personally, had the good fortune only to be placed under house arrest. It is to the credit of Modibo and Nkrumah that their regimes did not degenerate in the same way. At Conakry airport there was a portrait of Sékou wearing a red boubou, whose eyes followed you wherever you went and made it clear that there was no escape from his bloody attentions. I blame many progressive intellectuals and politicians who lived through that period in Guinea, or closely followed events there, yet spread the illusion that it was a vanguard country marching ahead despite everything; some even legitimized the repression (whose unspeakable cruelty seemed to give Sékou personal pleasure) or at least tried to tone down the condemnation of it. No doubt one of the reasons for this behaviour was that Guinean foreign policy suited the Soviets. However, the aluminium multinationals – Fria, as it happened – did not suffer from that foreign policy and were able to make the same profits in Guinea that they would have extracted from African countries generally described as neocolonies. The only criterion that should be used to judge the Guinean experience is what it achieved for the Guinean people, and on that score the record was not brilliant, to say the least. To be sure, the regime that replaced Sékou Touré scarcely turned out better, or even fundamentally different. But that is not enough to restore his image. By confusing the noble ideals of socialism with a regime that was in many ways loathsome and in many others ineffectual, one does not serve the cause of liberation and social progress but gets it further stuck in the mire.

When I left Conakry, I was given a large heap of pretty uninteresting documents – the speeches of Sékou on every occasion, which the Great Leader wanted eventually to publish as his 'complete works' in more volumes than Lenin's (perhaps as many as fifty). I gave it all to the customs inspector at Bamako, who probably used it for paper cones to wrap his peanuts. On the way back, the Air Guinée flight made an unscheduled stop at Kankan, where the crew went off for a couple of hours and forced us to leave the stifling hangar to find some shade beneath the trees. I later asked an Egyptian crew member what had happened, and they simply said that everyone had gone off to eat, as there was never anything in the aircraft to satisfy that human need; naturally we could have gone along too if we had asked.

Although I got nothing out of my trip to Conakry, my visits to Accra in 1963–65 were more productive. My old friend Yves Bénot had gone there from Conakry, leaving behind the memory of a well-liked teacher from whom many had learned a great deal (as some of them confirmed to me personally in later years). In Accra, Yves was teaching French but above all putting together a bulletin (*L'Étincelle*) in parallel to the English-language *The Spark*, which was intended to mobilize anti-imperialist forces throughout the continent. I have no doubt that it involved fine team work with brilliant Ghanaians such as Kofi Batsa – who unfortunately ended up a 'businessman' in Nigeria – and francophone Africans such as Damz from Dahomey (who later dropped out of sight).

Accra was a bright and cheerful city. I was never bored during the long evenings spent chatting at the Star Hotel with a host of activists from Ghana and the four corners of the continent, especially from the national liberation movements of southern Africa and the Portuguese colonies.

These influential comrades made it much easier for me to contact the right people, and the top officials who received me (especially J.H. Mensah and Omaboe at the planning ministry) gave an impression of competence.

Ghana was twenty or thirty years ahead of the French colonies and Nigeria in the training of senior managers, but it was 'terribly British' and much more marked than French-speaking countries (except perhaps Senegal) by the culture of the metropolis. Moreover, whereas popular activists in the French-speaking countries had been chiefly trained by the PCF, the only political school open to them, the churches had been the main organization of civil society in the British colonies. This was a major difference, whose effects are still highly visible today.

The great majority of Ghanaians in executive positions were conservative not only by class origin and family connections (the wealthiest planters, in particular) but also, no less seriously, in their culture and ideology picked up from British schools and the churches. They were proud of the colonial achievements they had inherited, the Gold Coast having indeed been opened up for exploitation thirty years before the neighbouring Ivory Coast. They imagined that the colonial model had not exhausted its historical possibilities and could continue indefinitely, and since it had been a form of insertion into world capitalism they were susceptible to all the World Bank nonsense about 'comparative advantages', even though such a strategy has absolutely nothing to offer modern Africa.

As to the matters for which I had come to Accra, they had given them no thought and had nothing to propose. I suggested that, since Ghana and Mali were planning to create some import-substitution industries, they might do well to divide them between the two countries and thereby achieve economies of scale in relation to the world market. But the Ghanaian side greeted this rather banal idea with surprise, especially when I put it within the long-term perspective of West African economic integration, beyond the inherited colonial micro-regions centred on the coast. The construction of such an area, certainly covering a huge area of land (as do the USA and Russia), would require a linked-up railway system, joint development of major rivers, and so on. But, of course, that cuts against the facile 'small is beautiful' discourse popularized by the media, according to which every 'mega-project' is absurd, economically and ecologically unviable, or even 'pharaonic' (as if Egypt does not exist because of the pharaohs' achievements). The truth is that non-development can cause mega-destruction of the environment: unstoppable deforestation, for instance, if agricultural output per hectare is stagnant and local people have no other energy source than charcoal. It would be easy to give many more examples.

My audience with President Nkrumah allowed me to propose again a number of immediate measures (coordination of industrial development, a joint airline, associated banks and insurance companies, etc.) and the creation of a think-tank for both the short term (convergence in economic legislation and tax systems, possible monetary union, etc.) and the long term. Unlike Sékou Touré, Nkrumah accepted the framework for discussion, gave me his point of view and asked me to spell out mine in greater detail. Of course, I know that as a visiting foreigner I may have been treated in a way that he would not have extended to others, especially to Ghanaian politicians. But there is nothing abnormal in that. When Nkrumah was overthrown in 1966 and took refuge in Conakry, I regretted that he had not chosen something better than a life as a guest in debt to Sékou.

It occurred to me that one could learn a lot by systematically comparing Ghana with Ivory Coast, if only because there are important analogies between the two societies, and because the colonial 'development' of Ivory Coast, then in full swing, was reproducing Ghana's earlier experience with all its limits. I followed through on this idea in the next few years.

The authorities in Accra gave me a perfect introduction by inviting me to take part in discussions on the Ghanaian national plan. I then made this the subject of various publications. In my view, the plan's lack of audacity reflected the conservative mentality of those in charge of the economy; it was certainly far from a monument to industrial megalomania, as systematic detractors of black Africa claim without taking the trouble to check their facts. One often hears it said that in 1960 Ghana's per capita income was higher than South Korea's. But could Korea have become what it is today if it had not combined industrial development with more intensive agriculture and management training, at a level that required permanent state intervention across the board? As the World Bank's famous Berg Report eloquently testifies, the systematic detractors are guided by an ultimately racist prejudice that Asians can do what Africans are 'viscerally' incapable of doing.

To be sure, there are special reasons why Ghana did not prosper 'like Korea', but they have to do only with its society, its colonial history and the policies of its liberation movement, as well as the geostrategic and other factors expressing the interaction between the national and global systems. These questions were at the heart of our discussions in Accra, with Yves Bénot, Kofi Batsa and other leaders on the left of the party. I met there a number of young and not so young people whom I would later come across again as leaders of the popular organizations behind the victory of Jerry Rawlings. I shall return to that below.

As always, I liked to supplement my discussions with visits on the ground: Kumasi's forests and cocoa-producing area; Tamale, in the Northern Region, a source of migrant labour; Sekondi-Takoradi, capital of the Western Region, with its modern port and industries, the site of the future Akosombo dam (which I saw later when the lake already existed). On a visit to the market in Accra, I noticed that the 'market women' put up posters that listed the study grants they were funding: an act of genuine patriotism to which they were deeply committed, and which they saw as a token of their success. I asked one of them: 'Who do you give the grants to?' And she gave the expected reply: 'My son, my sister's son, and so on.' 'Only to boys – no girls?' The woman looked at me with barely disguised contempt: 'Of course, never to girls. There'd be no point. Girls are clever and don't need to go to school. But boys are so stupid that they'd be good for nothing without a diploma to open the doors to some office.'

Some remarkable holidays

Each year, during the rainy season in Mali, Isabelle and I went to Europe for our summer holidays. In 1961 we decided to tour Scandinavia for a change, driving from Paris to Copenhagen and Stockholm, then up the magnificent Norwegian coast between Trondheim and the North Cape, and through Swedish and Finnish Lapland. At the time Sweden was not yet the country we know today: there were no foreigners, hardly anyone spoke English, and people were so honest you could leave your wallet on a bench and pick it up an hour later; but, at the same time, Swedes were unusually ignorant of the rest of the world, and there was a general feeling of boredom relieved by a sexual freedom among young people that had no parallel in Europe at that time. (Young people gathered together in town squares would talk quite freely of sleeping together, with no suggestion of a transaction.)

The summer after Tito's visit to Bamako brought us a wonderful trip to Yugoslavia. Tito had offered grants for Malian girls to study carpet-weaving in Skopje, and a group was in fact sent there. But a few months later an SOS came saying that things were happening which threatened to create a serious diplomatic incident between the two countries. The Yugoslav embassy therefore offered Isabelle and me a trip to Yugoslavia, with the task of sorting out the problem of the carpet-weavers (a few of whom we knew personally). In Skopje they greeted us as veritable liberators: they could not get used to the canteen meals and wanted to be given food that they could prepare themselves. The director had been stubbornly refusing to grant this simple demand, but it was not difficult for me to persuade him to change his mind. Meanwhile we had seen quite a lot of the country: we arrived in Zagreb, drove to Rijeka, travelled by boat down the magnificent Dalmatian coast to Dubrovnik, then drove through the mountains of Montenegro and Bosnia to Belgrade and Skopje, where we were put up in the Hotel Makedonia, which, exactly a year later, collapsed in the great earthquake that hit the region. The difference in attitudes between the Croats and Serbs was clear enough. On the boat, the Croat staff behaved in quite a servile manner towards the rather arrogant German tourists, but the scenery changed after Dubrovnik when a tough-looking old Serb took us in hand for the rest of the trip. A veteran of the 1914–18 war, then a partisan during the Second World War, he was obviously a communist but, above all, pro-Russian and pro-French. He was also a very agreeable and cultured person, who made our visits to various places particularly interesting. Yugoslavia was only just breaking out of the isolation to which the Cominform had condemned it, and its relations with the West were still fairly limited. It had launched its grand policy on the international arena, received Nasser at Brioni and taken an active role in the non-alignment initiative.

It never occurred to us that the country might undergo its later dramatic evolution. Once, Nyerere asked Tito: 'Two alphabets, three religions, four languages, five republics and six nationalities – how can it work?' To which Tito replied: 'Yes, but only one Communist Party.' People forget nowadays that Titoism was remarkable in this respect: Yugoslavia was a model of co-existence among different nations, in which each component participated on an equal basis in the life of the country, and a new Yugoslav consciousness, over and above the original nationalities, was making rapid strides.

So, what happened? Alas, it is quite easy to explain – after the event. The opening to the capitalist outside world in the 1970s, together with the persistence of federal structures, certainly made possible an acceleration of economic growth, but in a way that sharpened inequalities between the regions. The World Bank fell over itself praising the 'Yugoslav miracle' and the virtues of the market that supposedly lay behind it. But a cloud of oblivion now surrounds all the 'miracles' that the World Bank popularized at the time, and which led to the catastrophe.

Many Yugoslav communists I met saw the negative aspects of this evolution and the dangers it held for national and social cohesion. They pointed out that self-management, theoretically the best socialist response to the contradiction between market and social ownership, was seriously deteriorating as a result of the less and less controllable opening to world capitalism, and that the workers' stake in it was being eroded by the crystallization of executive interests around a potential bourgeoisie. None of these problems had escaped the attention of my interlocutors.

The crisis of world capitalism in the 1980s put a sudden stop to growth in Yugoslavia, which had become too vulnerable within the system of unequal global interdependence. The ruling class – a communist nomenklatura already worn down by the effects of the 'miracle' in question – was rapidly losing the legitimacy and credibility it had previously enjoyed among the beneficiaries of economic expansion. Increasingly fragmented, this class thought that it might restore the legitimacy of its rule by rallying to neoliberalism – which would enable it to assert itself as an 'ordinary' bourgeoisie – and by exploiting the themes of a chauvinistic nationalism. It is this class, therefore, which carries the responsibility for the dramatic denouement. The strategy of encouraging the break-up of Yugoslavia, pursued by Bonn and backed by the European community, served to add fuel to the flames.

By the time of my frequent visits to Yugoslavia in the 1980s, there were real and growing reasons for concern. But, I must confess, even then it was hard for us to imagine civil war. No doubt it was hoped that a way would be found for less destructive compromises.

During the summer months that Isabelle and I spent in Paris, we got to know better our new friends and their families: Bénard and his delightful wife Sylvie; Prou, his wife Suzanne, who was starting to make a name for herself with her novels (or was that later?), and their daughter Anne Françoise. We also often met Jacques Vergès and other members of the team that was defending the FLN. As soon as the peace treaty was signed and Algeria became independent, Jacques went to live in Algiers with his wife, Djemila Bouhired, whom he had saved from the scaffold.

I should mention here the 'Accra Boys', a group of political activists from the Portuguese colonies who had escaped from imprisonment in Portugal and taken refuge in France. It was necessary to find a way for them to get to Africa, without valid papers. The solution that was devised was to dress them up as a band of 'Negro musicians' and to pack them off in a coach with their instruments and assorted paraphernalia, along with a European guide who did have a proper passport. At the Luxembourg frontier, which was supposed to be the one with the loosest controls, our musicians gave a good imitation of collective drunkenness. The frontier guard looked inside the bus, and the guide said: 'I hope they'll arrive in time for the show, and a bit less drunk.' 'Okay, you'd better get moving.' And from there they flew to Accra. The group included some of my best friends of later years: Mário de Andrade,[37] Elisa de Andrade, and perhaps some others. It was a brilliant plan. Original idea: X. Technical: LR.

The places we went to most in Paris were the Coupole and the Aghion café-boutique. At the Coupole, people from the Bamako group often used to dine together. In those days, it was not yet on the 'must-see' list and did not attract the coach-loads of Japanese and Scandinavians who are now its main clientele. It was still a haunt of real artists and well-known painters, with whom it was always easy and amusing to chat for a while. Our other meeting place was the Aghion gallery, although Raymond Aghion, not being much of a shopkeeper by temperament, would have been bored by the customers if he had not also had frequent visits from friends such as Isabelle and me. During his repeated trips to the café on the corner, it was kept open by Fiametta – an old friend of Yves Bénot's who became, and has remained, our friend too. The beautifully named Fiametta – or *petite flame*, as Yves used to call her – was a perceptive woman who continually made fun of people; she applied herself to making sweet little drawings that decorated L'Opoponax.[38] Another visitor of note to the gallery, with whom Raymond used to play chess, was a Russian painter whose name I have forgotten. He gibbered in a strange way: 'Me, advance queen', and so on. 'Doesn't he speak French?' I asked Aghion. 'No,' he answered, 'he's only been living in Paris for fifty years!'

From drift to debacle

It would not be appropriate here to repeat in detail what I wrote at the time about the vicissitudes of planning in Mali. I will simply mention the six main difficulties that it encountered.

First difficulty: the 'technocrats'. Certain ministers – such as Mamadou Aw at Public Works – had some technical competence but not always a feeling for economics. Their natural tendency was to insist that their projects should take priority, even when they could only be carried out over a long period of time. The 'Kayes seaport' project, for example, required the building of the Manantali dam, and although this has now been done (thirty-five years later) it still does not allow shipping to sail up the Senegal as far as Kayes. Other technocrats were fanatical about breakneck modernization, but did not think that it had to be adapted to the conditions of the country. To take just one example, at the Office du Niger, Lamine Traoré supported immediate heavy mechanization along American or Soviet lines.

Second difficulty: the attraction of expensive prestige projects (sports stadium, presidential palace, grand hotel, an oversized national airline, etc.), which always tickle the fancy of politicians.

Third difficulty: the absolute prioritization of 'politics' over economic calculation. The president certainly had this weakness, which some dignitaries encouraged out of sheer sycophancy. I do believe that politics should be 'in command', but it should be real politics – the kind that defines the social content of a project for the country, not a set of rhetorical flourishes and theatrical gestures. Modibo was in the habit of calling officials together in the early morning (the day began at 7.30 in Bamako, to avoid the midday heat), and on one occasion I was asked to attend. The president said to me: 'Comrade Samir, I've been thinking that it would be a good idea to shut down our rail link with Dakar.' I saw from his face that the idea had probably come to him in a dream. After reflection, wishing both to be deferential and to employ customary usage, I came up with an earthy simile: 'Comrade president, don't you think that would be like a husband cutting off his testicles to spite his wife.' 'Why?' 'Because Mali will bear the brunt of the closure. Senegal will lose some of the profit it gets from through-traffic, but we'll be forced to import goods by road, via Abidjan, and end up paying five times more.' However, I realized that my image had been too strong. I heard later that he had immediately consulted some sycophantic young executives, who had doubtless told him that his idea was a stroke of political genius. The rail link was therefore closed down and replaced with a fleet of three hundred lorries.

Fourth difficulty: retailers who could not easily be integrated into the new 'socialist' environment. This was a real, objective difficulty, and many Malian executives were well aware of it. But it was (or should have been) evident that, if budgetary and trade deficits led to repeated stock shortages and inflation, a space would inevitably appear for retailers to notch up black-market superprofits. The struggle to neutralize this inevitable tendency among retailers demanded strict public management of the economy. This was not always understood, and for some repression was the answer to all problems.

Fifth difficulty: the lack of lower-level operatives, another real, objective difficulty. For example, when the national currency was introduced in July 1962, we drew up a circular explaining in detail, in clear and simple language, what customs inspectors were supposed to do. 'It's a disaster,' Djim Sylla said to me one day, 'they haven't understood anything.' Apparently a patriotic Malian trader in Sikasso had declared wads of CFA francs on returning from a trip to Ivory Coast, and the customs man had seized them, denounced our patriot for using 'imperialist money' and set light to it. There were many similar episodes, which all told us that it was necessary to train operatives with great care at every level of the public service. Many senior executives did not see the point, or did not care two hoots about such matters.

Sixth difficulty: the expectation of students returning from abroad that they would immediately be given the highest possible jobs. The harmful effects of the 'diploma rent' did not take long to make themselves felt. For they refused to admit their lack of experience – a quite normal lack, since an apprenticeship is always necessary – and substituted pompous phrases for serious thought and hard work. Not having had a militant past – again, not their fault – they were inclined to toady to state dignitaries. There were some exceptions, of course, but not many. And, on the whole, the new intake of executives played a very negative role and accelerated the downward drift.

The upshot was that, within the space of a few months, the Plan disintegrated into a collection of disparate, poorly designed projects, adding every day to the jumble of ad hoc decisions and faits accomplis. I tried to sound the alarm whenever Bénard dropped by. I drew up one projection after another, especially for public and external finances, so that people would understand that the problems would be insoluble in two or three years' time. But I don't think these notes were ever read in high places. They were given to 'young patriotic cadres', who must have dismissed them as reactionary twaddle and passed on to something else.

The drift was becoming a headlong flight. Our prediction of worsening deficits in the state budget and the balance of trade inevitably came true, but the authorities thought they could use the printing press to solve the former and foreign loans to address the latter. I had not been opposed in principle to the creation of a national currency and the nationalization of the banking system. But I had not foreseen the uses to which they would be put – on the contrary, I had suggested that they become the instruments of a stricter, more tightly controlled management of the economy.

The *fuite en avant* spurred the degeneration of the Party. The planning ministry had asked Party leaders to organize great debates about a few clearly defined basic issues, such as rural cooperation, ways of modernizing agriculture, the structuring of the retail trade and enterprise management. However, none of the debates was seriously organized, and ordinary Party members were kept on the sidelines. Instead, ad hoc commissions – in which young cadres fought hard to outshine one another – packaged a number of ill-conceived proposals in hastily written reports, full of flattery for the leaders for whom 'nothing is impossible'.

The Sudanese Union thus changed from a real people's party into the collective organization of the new class. Its social base shrank, despite the almost obligatory distribution of membership cards and the holding of national conferences at which debate was replaced with orchestrated applause. Thus, as with other parties of this ilk, it just quietly disappeared when a new dictator came along and banned it by decree (in November 1968), absorbing the core of the class that had been in control. It is true that the Sudanese Union made a comeback, as one of the forces opposed to the dictatorship, but that happened only later, thanks to the steadfastness of a few historical leaders of the left wing of the party, including Madeira and Gologo. Meanwhile, Modibo was murdered in prison by a doctor whom he had asked for an injection. (The doctor later committed suicide, out of remorse for his cowardly compliance with orders.) Modibo's death transformed his historical figure into an emblem for resistance to the dictatorship, while his share of responsibility for the disaster was forgotten. That is a common phenomenon in history.

The degeneration of the Party brought with it a compensatory stepping up of rhetoric and gestures. Instead of being offered debates and education, the young were dragooned into 'militias' whose task it was to check the movement of cars at night. This was supposed to give them a way of expressing their revolt against 'the rich', but the whole operation was objectively grotesque. Police commissioners soon tired of being woken up every night by the haul of imaginary spies and saboteurs. Once, even Isabelle and I found ourselves under arrest because we had left our papers at home. We gave them a choice: either we go together to our house and you check our papers, or we go to the police station and wake up the authorities. I also mentioned the name 'Madeira', thinking that I would be able to make him see the absurdity of the whole thing. Anyway, the young militiamen became hesitant and frightened and eventually let us go on our way.

It seemed impossible to halt the slide. Seydou Badian Kouyaté, the first planning minister (until September 1962), bears a heavy responsibility for this. He was one of the few Malians – they could probably have been counted on the fingers of one hand – who had completed a university education before independence. As a doctor, he immediately qualified as a candidate for high office, even though he did not have a record of political activity; this made him particularly prone to make up for political shortcomings by turning up the rhetoric, which in turn pushed him closer to the 'young wolves' among whom he drew his clientele. The minister was not interested in planning and never seemed to grasp what it meant. His attention was focused on various hobby horses, mostly absurd little projects of one kind or another. For example, he wanted to set up a pasta factory, although there was no way in which that should have been a priority in a country that produced no wheat. My functions allowed me to hear many such stories, not all of them connected with Kouyaté's hobby horses. Ministers in Africa (and elsewhere, I suppose) are visited by hordes of small businessmen (and big sharks), smooth talkers who try to sell them anything.

None of this would have mattered if Kouyaté had done what Bénard and our think-tank in Bamako expected of him: that is, to present and defend the Plan before the highest decision-making bodies, and to report back on their criticisms and suggestions. But he did neither. The explanation I heard a thousand times, from people at the top as well as further down, was that Kouyaté, being from the caste of griots, behaved 'naturally' as a professional flatterer. (Another griot – Diabaté, the richest trader in African *objets d'art*, a pleasant man without complexes, whose shop we often visited – once said to me: 'There are two griots who've made it in this country: Kouyaté the minister, and me the rich merchant.') I did not accept this explanation, however, nor do I today. Castes are a taboo subject in African societies where they exist: one is not supposed to discuss the issue, but only repeat a few clichés or display one's encyclopaedic knowledge without discrimination. Of course, virtues and defects are not passed on in the blood but only through education, which can (or could) transform the relations in question, or even do away with them altogether. In any event, caste/class relations change as they adapt to modern economies and societies; they no longer have anything in common with what they represented in the original village society. Nevertheless, for a number of reasons, caste prejudices continue to operate in many societies, where it is hard to imagine that the president or chief of staff does not belong to a noble caste, whereas the information or police minister may well come from a 'lower' caste. Is this because such ministers perform the services of a domestic servant or someone specialized in inferior tasks: propaganda, espionage, torture? The planning ministry is therefore often entrusted to people who are expected to behave according to the schema, thereby confirming the idea of the Plan as a propaganda document that should not be taken too seriously. This, I believe, was the case in Mali.

On the positive side of the balance, Kouyaté paid dear for his devotion to the ruling group in the Sudanese Union; he was not one of those who turned coat on the day of its downfall. He spent long years in Kidal prison, in appalling conditions, together with Modibo, Madeira, Ousmane Ba and other leaders of the Sudanese Union left, even though he was not really on the same wavelength as them despite his period of leftist rhetoric. This needs to be said, to give honour where honour is due.

My hopes rose a little in September 1962, when a government reshuffle placed the planning ministry in the hands of Jean-Marie Koné. I interpreted this as a recognition that the planning ministry had to regain its authority if the downward drift was to be halted. Koné did not belong to the left of the Sudanese Union, but to the group of moderates. But I did not think it an unfortunate choice in the circumstances, as it was necessary to bend the stick a little in the other direction, and Koné had a certain authority as a historical leader of the movement. For me, the year of his reign was most agreeable. He asked questions – the real ones – and listened attentively to our analyses, comments and even proposals. But I think it was all too late; the die was already cast. None of the positions that he probably defended was followed through in practice.

My analysis of the degeneration placed a lot of the blame on the Malian leaders, but also, behind them, on the objective conditions of Malian society. Those conditions should not, however, be reduced to the historical legacy of colonization and the national liberation struggle. The international conjuncture of the 1960s, the main features of which I outlined above, also played a role that should not be underestimated.

At the time there was a political dispute between Mali and France, which was settled through low-key talks or unilateral decisions on Mali's part that Paris and neighbouring African countries appeared to accept – though not without reservations, manoeuvres and stratagems that created additional problems for the Malian project.

France had a military base at Kati, some 20 kilometres from Bamako, but Mali's support for the non-aligned cause led it to terminate the agreement under which the base existed. This caused some gnashing of teeth in Paris, as the Algerian war was only just nearing its end and there was perhaps still some idea of splitting the Sahara from Algeria to form an oil-producing client state. It is hardly necessary to add that Mali and Niger – which shared with Algeria that part of the Sahara and its basically Tuareg population – had every reason to feel uncomfortable about France's intentions.

Mali's decision to create a national currency in July 1962 was not regarded well in Paris; nor, for different reasons, in Dakar and Abidjan. Paris was eager to promote a single currency within the Franc Zone, and the 'pro-French' demonstration of retailers in Bamako against exchange controls had clearly been manipulated from outside. France stuck to its guns until 1994, when the IMF (that is, the United States) imposed without preparation a devaluation that opened a period of uncertainty in relations between France (and the post-Maastricht EU) and the associated African countries.[39] In these countries, the alternative model proposed by Mali – first monetary independence, to create an African payments system or even monetary and economic integration – could find a positive echo. This vision, which the Guinea–Ghana–Mali union theoretically embraced, was not only the property of extreme nationalists; the ECA (the UN Economic Commission for Africa) developed similar themes, which English-speaking countries in Africa supported, at least in theory. To be sure, the appalling management of the Malian franc soon wiped out this potential and paved the way for the capitulation of 1967, when the Modibo regime itself begged to be readmitted to the Franc Zone. But that was a long way off in 1962, and the well-known position we advocated at the planning ministry – using the currency not to encourage sloppiness but to impose tighter discipline – could still have won through.

As early as 1961 we were discussing the creation of a national university in Bamako. The French voluntary workers proposed the classical model then in force everywhere, in France as in French-speaking Africa, and rejected any other framework for cooperation. But Bamako rejected this approach, quite rightly in my view. Mali – and the planning ministry played a role in the business – suggested creating a number of *grandes écoles*: one for public administration and economic management (with departments specializing in law and justice, the civil service, public finances and economics, and enterprise management); one for the training of middle-level agricultural managers (first academic cycle) and agronomists (second cycle); a polytechnic (civil engineering, construction, mechanical engineering); a medical school (with a short first cycle); and a college for the training of secondary-school teachers. This was a far superior approach, which, if properly implemented, would have made it possible to avoid the shortcomings of the classical university. This is more or less what happened, and the weaknesses observable today do not reduce the strength of the arguments in its favour. The weaknesses have to do with other factors. Besides, classical-style universities suffer from the same problems and have by no means shown themselves to be better.

France was not the only external partner to have certain attitudes capable of hindering a positive outcome for the Malian project. The eastern bloc countries also bore some responsibility by bending the stick too far in the other direction. My view is that these countries, headed by the USSR, were only really interested in the diplomatic side of the choices made by Mali and like-minded regimes in Africa. It is true that they made a significant contribution to development, funding major projects and helping to correct balance-of-payments deficits. But their representatives were never prepared to discuss this contribution, only to negotiate the technical details of how it should be carried out. Their argument was that – unlike the EEC and the West in general, or the IMF with its restrictive conditions – they fully respected the independence of the countries they supported. Whether honest or specious, this justification encouraged the downward slide in Mali and other countries.

The slide was heading towards a full-scale disaster. I therefore saw less and less point in remaining in Bamako and finally left in October 1963. But my heart was (and is) still sufficiently attached to Mali for me to contemplate further missions there, in the hope that in the end they might help to put things back on an even keel.

There were three such missions between 1963 and 1966, each with the aim of analysing the chaotic Treasury accounts and proposing some short- to medium-term solutions. I had already had some experience of this in Cairo. In Mali we were facing a classical situation: an incredible interweaving of debts and claims between the Treasury and public enterprises, between different public enterprises, between public enterprises and the local private sector, and between all these and foreign debtors and creditors. The central bank was supposed to take responsibility for such matters, but it was failing to do so. I don't know whether this was because its president – Louis Nègre – was more an administrator than an economist, or whether other reasons were involved. In any event, they called on me to sort things out, and I did it willingly. Once the Treasury and public sector accounts were legible again, my recommendations were little more than common sense: to cancel mutual debts immediately and to consolidate outstanding balances on the best possible terms, with a view to taking the minimum steps in the next few years to wipe out non-structural deficits, and effecting a more basic reorientation that would allow Mali to correct its structural imbalances.

In the course of these missions, it became quite clear to me that the slide was turning into a debacle. All the deficits had grown worse by the year, and the headlong dash at the political level had accentuated a purely repressive response to the problems. I remember one painful evening that threw a sharp light on the reality of the situation. At a dinner organized by some friends of his, Louis Nègre, president of the central bank, complained of an orderly who had failed to greet him, and whom he had put in 'the clink' for his lack of politeness. Isabelle immediately remarked that the man's behaviour had perhaps indicated the people's attitude towards the dignitaries of the regime, and that it was up to them – the leaders – to ask themselves whether this was so. The answer from everyone, including Macalou (whose slide to the right I had already had cause to regret), was: 'No, the whip, the whip: these people are worth nothing, they've got to be beaten for them to do things right.' Shortly afterwards the *coup d'état* put an end to the regime. And what did we see? Nearly every top cadre of the old regime, with the exception of the real left, changed sides in the twinkling of an eye and placed itself at the service of Moussa Traoré. Not only does that say a lot about the sincerity of their personal convictions; it also testifies to the objective fact that, despite a few demagogic gestures commonplace after a coup, the new regime inherited the legacy of the old and rested on the same shrivelled social base. It therefore continued to use the whip.

The rebirth of a popular movement, though difficult, was predictable. This has sometimes been attributed to the intrinsic qualities of the Malian people – combativeness, courage, and so on. But the reborn movement, which waged a glorious struggle in the face of mounting repression and eventually brought down the dictatorship, was largely a result of the history of the left: both that of the old Sudanese Union and that of the new generation that we had seen beginning to take shape. This may be the best aspect of the conditions that Modibism created, intentionally or otherwise.

Marxism–Leninism as such is certainly not responsible for the degeneration in Mali. Its teachings, though scholastic and somewhat fundamentalist, actually helped young people to become aware of the distance between theoretical principles and the reality of the regime. It therefore made a contribution to the rebirth of the Malian left. Its fundamentalism, at least in Mali, proved incomparably less negative than the neoliberal or Islamic fundamentalism that is today being offered to young people in distress.

Some time in 1962, I agreed to join a UN team to work on setting up an African 'Planning and Development Institute'. I therefore went to Addis Ababa (for the first time in my life) and spent a month there exchanging ideas with other members of the team. I have to say that I was not impressed by how things looked. The majority – African bureaucrats and foreign 'experts' – knew what was a 'good development policy' and 'good teaching of planning and management techniques'; everything had been written up in expert reports and put in the heads of all good teachers. This demonstrated either incredible naivety or mindless conceit. My minority position had the support of some key people outside the team, both in New York (Philippe de Seynes) and in Addis (a few senior top African diplomats, some Ethiopian civil servants well above the average for the continent), and of the Englishman Arthur Ewing, who was temporarily in charge of the UN Economic Commission for Africa (UNECA) until the arrival of Robert Gardiner (who also soon showed an inclination to take our side). It was therefore worth remaining involved in the project, and in October 1963 Isabelle and I left Bamako for Dakar, the base of the new African Institute for Economic Planning and Development (IDEP).

SIX

Professor of Political Economy, 1963–70

After my university studies, I had decided not to pursue an academic career, but to prefer positions (in Cairo and Bamako) that were more directly linked to economic and social activity. This does not mean that I thought university life uninteresting: on the contrary, I felt that I would really enjoy teaching if I were to choose to do it, both because of the organized relations with young people that it offered, and because oral exposition, with its pedagogic constraints and associated discussion, is an excellent way of forcing yourself to be precise and rigorous in your thinking. So, I like teaching – as long as it is not just a question of passing on more or less frozen pieces of knowledge. I find it meaningful only if it is linked to ongoing research, preferably not in stuffy libraries but in a close and living relationship to action. The job offered me at IDEP fitted very well into this conception.

Professor at IDEP–Dakar (1963–67)

After Isabelle and I arrived in Dakar in October 1963, we spent the first month at the Hôtel de la Paix, before we were allocated a three-room flat on the sixth floor of the Immeuble Bourgi, on the avenue de la République.

IDEP soon brought home to me the advantages of UN work – doing something new, in a multinational spirit – but also the extreme weaknesses of the system, buffeted as it was by two centrifugal forces which, for reasons bound up with its international character, were impossible to reconcile. The rapid turnover of directors in the 1960s – once a year for the first four years of its existence, when there should have been maximum continuity – was one clear expression of these weaknesses. Although the preparatory committee had produced a document defining the Institute's aims, mode of operation and funding, as well as an outline of its teaching programme (plus a purely formal reference to research), it was a document in the diplomatic and ambiguous style of UN 'resolutions'. The director and the team in charge of implementing the document therefore had considerable autonomy if they wished to use it.

I do not know how it happened, but for the first year the directorship was entrusted to two men with poorly defined functions: Christian Vieyra (a legal expert from Benin, or, as it was then called, Dahomey) and John Mars (an economics professor from Britain, of Austrian origin). Each shouted aloud that he was the director, one in French, the other in English, as both were resistant to bilingualism and communicated with (or, more often, insulted) each other through the offices of a rather embarrassed interpreter. Vieyra was close to the most moderate politicians in French-speaking Africa, especially Dahomey, who were highly sensitive to the views of the French 'Coopération' service (the former colonial ministry, quickly rebaptized without a change of location or, for the most part, personnel). Mars was a mainstream economics professor, who had no experience of the 'third world' and had given little thought to its problems. He was also totally naive politically, and used to stand on his balcony (one floor above ours) to applaud some public figure or folklore troupe as they passed by in the street. He probably had some character problems too: we used to hear him grousing alone at night, or hurling his shoes across the room.

There were originally five people on the teaching staff: Mohamed Mahmoud El Imam, an Egyptian econometrist, who, when he went back to Egypt a few years later, made a career in the Nasserite system and became a minister (he has remained a personal friend of mine, and still has unshakably Nasserite convictions); David Carney, an economist from Sierra Leone, who had studied under Robert Gardiner at Fourah Bay (the oldest British colonial college for West Africa); the statistician Bastiani; the development sociologist Jacques Bugnicourt (whom I had got to know at *Sciences-Po* in Paris); and lastly myself. The team of interpreters included a pleasant and cultured Englishwoman, Jean Hughes, who had started out as a translator between the Free French and London during the war.

Later, others joined the team: the Egyptian Gamal Eleish, who had overspecialized in input–output techniques and made excessive use of them, without first considering the nature of a problem or whether the solution did not require a structured political and social vision; the legal expert Naguib Hedayat from the Egyptian Council of State (an institution modelled on a similar one in France, responsible for the consistency of administrative orders), whose naturally active and savvy wife Wahiba, with a beautiful face reminiscent of Nefertiti, soon made contact with Senegalese officials and found a job at the planning ministry in Dakar; the anthropologist Claude Meillassoux, who only stayed there for a year; and Elie Lobel, who used to come on an assignment from time to time.

Senegal had placed at IDEP's disposal a building behind the National Assembly that had been occupied by the embryonic Faculty of Sciences before the completion of the university campus. (IDEP is still in these premises.) Later, when I was appointed director, I had a prefabricated building set up in the Institute's garden, giving students the kind of small individual studies for which no allowance was made in the French university tradition.

In 1964 Robert Gardiner, the director of UNECA, got rid of the Vieyra–Mars duo and appointed a Dane, Boserup. I have a lot of respect for that man, who, despite his somewhat Prussian stiffness, was open-minded and eager to learn. His wife, Ester, was an extremely sharp woman, whose work on demography and agrarian technological change (overturning all the prejudices about the evolution of work in so-called primitive societies) is a classic in its field. We became friends, and many years later I met up with Boserup again in Copenhagen. In the period I am talking about, however, his task was to find an African director to succeed him at the Institute within the space of one year. He kept his promise, but in my opinion he made an unfortunate choice. The Senegalese–Mauritian Mamodou Touré did not have the right preparation for the job – although this did not prevent him from later making a career at the IMF (whose zealous servant he was in Zaire) and as finance minister in Dakar. Joseph Stiglitz recently wrote that the recruitment of bogus economists served the function of turning them into executors of a policy decided elsewhere, but his critical spirit was not much in evidence during his days as a servant of the World Bank. In fact, he was timid in the extreme and tried to avoid any research that might displease one government or another, one minister or another. For my part, I did not think it possible to teach without doing research, and I used the time available to us to work on Ivory Coast and Mali, as well as on the three countries of the Maghreb. My conclusions terrified Touré, who would have liked to put my 'reports' under lock and key and prohibit their use or dissemination. I began to think of leaving IDEP if Touré kept this position. And, when I left in October 1967, he was still director – although soon after he would be recruited by the IMF. His successor was David Carney, whom I myself succeeded in 1970.

In resigning from IDEP, I thought it best to explain my reasons in a letter to U Thant, then secretary-general of the UN, without mentioning anything personal regarding either myself or my colleagues and the director. I simply said that, in my opinion, IDEP's role should not be that of a technical college poorly placed in the competition with African and other universities; that the Institute should aim to become one of the main centres for critical reflection and teaching about the theory and practice of development in Africa. It was this letter which made people think of me for the job of director, when a UNDP task force under Vu Van Thai was set up in 1969 to propose solutions to the failure of the Institute to take off.

IDEP was not working well as a team: it had numerous meetings, but the successive directors tried to block any serious discussion on the role of the Institute, its teaching and research choices, and so on, preferring instead endless chit-chat that left everyone, or nearly everyone, feeling bored. Things had functioned well at an everyday level, thanks to Dulphy, a simple and effective French administrator who loved messing around with boats and all the things that make a person likeable to me. Carney forced him to leave.

There was not complete clarity about who was ultimately in charge of IDEP. Was it UNECA in Addis Ababa, on the other side of the continent? Or the UNDP (which funded the Institute) and UN Secretariat in New York? Fortunately, so long as Robert Gardiner was executive secretary at UNECA, a solution was easily found to various problems. Firm but gentlemanly, conservative but democratic and respectful of other people's opinions, Gardiner could not fail to get on well with someone like Philippe de Seynes, a man of principle, brilliant, shrewd and diplomatic, who was under-secretary-general in New York. Later, when I took over as director of IDEP, the three of us never had the slightest difficulty in reaching agreement. This ceased to be the case when Adebayo Adedeji succeeded Gardiner. But I am beginning to run ahead.

My original job at IDEP was to teach national accounting and African techniques (and experiences) of planning. The first problem I faced was that the students had very different levels of education, and in economics never more than an ordinary degree. There should have been a stricter selection procedure, but in those days the directors were mainly concerned to push up total numbers. The second problem was that some of the students were English-speaking and others French-speaking, so it was necessary to resort to simultaneous translation. Although our interpreters were top-quality professionals, I think the job was harder than they realized – especially when the lecture, as it should be, was not read out but given 'live'. Besides, interpretation always loses some of the meaning, because it eliminates the element of direct communication without which private reading is a perfect substitute for lectures. As I am able to teach in both languages, I therefore alternated my lectures and took care to repeat some of the content; I also used the relevant language during the time for discussion. Two other teachers, Meillassoux and Lobel, were also bilingual, but I do not know how they actually operated. The others could speak only French or English.

In my course on national accounting, I taught both the French system and the Anglo-American one (which had been adopted by the UN with a few refinements), and tried to show that it was possible to 'translate' accounts between the two. Nevertheless, I have always believed that the French accounting system is to the English what the metric system is to English weights and measures: the former obeys a single rigorous logic imbued with the spirit of Cartesianism; the latter conforms to different empirical logics. Interestingly enough, both the countries of the Maghreb as well as Egypt and the Middle East have opted for Cartesian rigour in this respect. Will they maintain the choice? I have started to hear talk of 'Islamic' accounting, alongside other such stupidities. It may be that terrestrial accounts (for households, firms, government departments, financial intermediaries, and so on) could have a parallel column listing obligations to the divinity. Indeed, the 'Islamic' finance company Rayan in Egypt might well require such an extrapolation, having first swindled hundreds of thousands of believers and then organized a fraudulent bankruptcy. When the victims complained to the state and demanded compensation, a Central Bank official not without Egyptian humour explained that they had signed a contract expressing their trust in divine justice in the event of problems here below, and that the modest Egyptian state was not equipped to predict what Allah's judgement would be. He therefore urged the protesters to be patient, since the right solution would one day certainly be found.

As to my course on planning, I taught input–output techniques (which were relatively easy to handle and provided a minimum of mathematical training, even for students who felt hopeless in the subject), but I repeat what I said before: they should not become a way of avoiding the necessity of prior social and political choices. I also gave my students a warning about project analysis: either it is nothing more than a rationalization for capitalist calculations of profitability, and should be studied to understand how the real (capitalist) world functions; or a claim is made to extrapolate the logic of such calculation, giving it a social dimension that is alien to it. In the latter case, national decision-makers are offered instruments that are unusable, because they conflict with the type of decision that real economic agents operate. Such 'planning' – which the World Bank prefers, to the exclusion of all others – therefore comes down to throwing dust in people's eyes; it expresses a refusal to plan. After all, if the market is self-regulating, what is the point of intervention? And, if development is simply the spontaneous result of 'market forces', it becomes synonymous with the expansion of capitalism, whereas the whole specificity of the concept of development is precisely that it expresses a project containing identifiable social and political objectives.

The French *Coopération* service had produced a number of pedagogically excellent manuals on input–output techniques and the various kinds of project analysis, and I myself used these in my courses. For the more advanced students, to whom I gave additional classes, I also used the materials of the Centre d'Études et de Programmation Économique (the Paris college established by the SEEF). But there were no real planning manuals. It would have been dangerous to try to produce one, because it would have frozen into a set of dogmas what should be a theory and practice adapted to the special conditions of various countries. The *Coopération* people tried to do this, with unfortunate results.

I therefore spent two-thirds or more of my teaching time on analyses of the macroeconomic coherence of planning projections. I had noticed that the problem in Africa – from Egypt through the Maghreb to Mali and Ghana, and probably elsewhere – was a lack of macroeconomic coherence among all the projects adding up to 'the Plan', invariably expressed in budget and trade deficits that doomed it to failure. In my view, therefore, the first task was to teach future planning officials how to identify such inconsistencies, to understand the mechanism through which they came about, and to propose ways of correcting them. What I had learned to do in Cairo and Bamako, and at the SEEF in Paris, was indispensable here. I set about teaching through a series of exercises, which I first did in class and then gave to the students to do by themselves. I devised a simplified General Economic Table (GET). I defined a 'Plan' in the terms in which plans are usually defined (investment volume, external funding, etc.), and used it as the basis for long-term (say, five-year) projections of the principal macroeconomic quantities. This made it possible to establish the crucial links between these quantities (propensity to import, coefficients of capital, recurrent charges, etc.) and then, by placing these quantities within a projected General Economic Table, to identify the inconsistencies. The tools: compound interest tables and the slide rule.

So, this is how I understood my job as a teacher. I would say that, for the third of students who had a minimum of education (albeit very general) or intellectual capacities and a will to work, the results were not bad. I met many of these students again in later years, in their respective countries, and I could see that their work was appreciated there.

The *agrégation* in political economy

I am not very docile. I have never found acceptable, for myself, the compromises that 'making a career' often involves. I certainly do not look down on those whom life obliges to follow certain well-worn tracks, whether they accept or criticize them. But, perhaps because of my temperament, it has been very difficult for me to act in this way, and I have waged one battle after another to be allowed to make independent choices. No doubt I am very lucky to have won the decisive battles that allowed me to live as I wished, without having to suffer for my intransigence. I have reached retirement without ever experiencing either the agonies of capitulation or acute material want.

So, if IDEP was not going to satisfy me, what was I to do? One day Bénard said that maybe I should sit the competitive *agrégation* for a professorship in political economy; it would give me a much freer life. Why not? The main hurdle was that rival candidates would have been preparing hard for a long time (since childhood, some said ironically of certain sons and daughters of professors) and have accumulated encyclopaedic knowledge in every area of mainstream economics, whereas I had never been interested in that and regarded most of the literature as stupid. I was not going to change now, and even a few weeks of preparation seemed to me a major sacrifice.

Fortunately I discovered a miraculous solution. Raymond Barre – yes, the future French prime minister – had generously produced a manual to help *agrégation* candidates: a book of some thousand pages, summarizing the fifty volumes of an encyclopedia that one would be expected to have at one's fingertips. On the basis of three lines and two paragraphs, accompanied with footnote references on every conceivable subject, would it be possible to keep writing for 45 minutes without exposing one's ignorance? Yes, I said to myself, it would. And, if I did it with success, it was thanks to all the past reading that had given me the critical capacity to go to the root of things, to put wrong answers in their proper place. Without that, the only way of overcoming the difficulties of the exam is to bow slavishly to its rules: to learn everything, however pointless and stupid it may be.

I sat the written exam in May 1966, I think, and was due to give the 'lecture' that formed the oral part in September. The rules of the game are well known: you are given the subject 24 hours in advance, then prepare the lecture with the help of some teamwork. I turned to a small group of friends: Eliane Mossé, Eli Lobel, Suzanne de Brunhof and Monique Florenzano. We met at my place, in Paris, and divided the working day into three: first, having consulted the 'Barre', I gave an outline of my proposed lecture, which was followed by discussion; then each person went into a corner (or the group continued to discuss in my absence) – I had specifically asked them to find two or three shaky sentences in the Barre, at least open to dispute or even particularly idiotic; finally, I delivered the 45-minute lecture to my team and noted down their observations and suggestions. We had supper together – without mentioning the subject again, except when one of us had a 'brilliant idea' that could be succinctly formulated. Then I went to bed normally (unlike most candidates, who went on working until morning). The next day, I delivered my lecture in the required 'French style' to which I was already accustomed – with no more notes than could be fitted on a visiting card, but, above all, in three sections of exactly 15 minutes each (not 14 or 16). One of the panel members, Taddei, told me afterwards that he had wondered whether I was poking a little fun at the system, by carrying to perfection the 'recommended' formal rules. He also said that, once the panel had checked the curious quotation for which I had nonchalantly given the page reference, they knew that I had not been trying to pull the wool over their eyes.

I therefore passed at the first attempt, with an acceptable grade. I had asked for nothing more. I don't think I would have gone through the whole thing a second time.

Professor in Poitiers, Paris and Dakar

The *agrégation* led in December 1966 to the usual initial appointment in a provincial university – at Poitiers, as it happened. I say usual, but as a foreign *agrégé* I had no automatic entitlement to a post. In fact, I was very lucky to receive the offer I did, especially as Bénard was already teaching there and Gabillard, who became a personal friend, was a very understanding dean. At my request, he grouped my lectures in such a way that I could continue teaching at the University of Dakar for three successive university years (1966–67, 1967–68 and 1968–69). Meanwhile, as everyone knows, there was the great upheaval of 1968, and the new university of Paris VIII was established, first at Vincennes and considerably later at Saint-Denis. I secured a transfer from Poitiers to Vincennes for the 1969–70 academic year, still sharing my time with Dakar.

The French university kept its traditional structures until 1968. Certain principles, which happily survived, still seem to me the best (or the least bad): for example, the refusal of the principle of limited tenure. In the United States, where universities generally offer only a limited contract, intelligent young academics seeking to get this renewed have to compete with one another to produce a steady stream of texts – and, in order to get these published, they have to be in step with the dominant fashion, perhaps to the detriment of serious critical work. There is a tendency today in France, especially among neoliberals, to hail this American model inspired by the private sector as the last word on education, so that when Régis Debray ventured to defend 'French education' the postmodernists, headed by Annette Wieworka, naturally treated him as a dinosaur. It is true that, in offering complete security of tenure, the French model protects not only the freedom or right to take one's time for reflection, but also simple mediocrity. Who has not known at least one recently qualified *agrégé* who writes the lecture he will dictate for 'the whole of his career'? It is a real abomination – and promises nothing but boredom, for the author as much as his unfortunate audience. I even met one such person on a train from Poitiers to Paris, perhaps a pathological extreme case, who used indelible ink to ensure that the text of his lecture would still be legible in twenty years or more. But that kind of caricature is only one element in the academic world – and perhaps no worse than those besotted with the latest US fashion. Most of the rest know how to use their freedom to work better and more creatively, as the SEEF experience, among others, demonstrated to me. Anyway, in the old days, the mediocrities needed formal respect for the conventions of tradition. Without a gown and a raised platform, how could they have got their students to swallow the repetitive reading out of 'original' lectures? I have seen such specimens literally in tears when they were forced to allow their students a few minutes for questions after a lecture.

Traditionally, university teachers were able to live in Paris and spend only a block of two days a week in their provincial institution. This was the case for me, Bénard and others. My modest hotel room in central Poitiers, within walking distance of the faculty, thus came to be known as 'the professorial transit room', used on Monday night by Amin, Tuesday night by Bénard, and so on. But fortunately there were also the serious mainstays, like Gabillard in Poitiers, who enjoyed their provincial life.

On 'my' day, I always had lunch at the same restaurant, where all the places were strictly allocated to clients who were likely to be there for life. There were serviette rings, and so on – a scene straight out of Balzac.

The luck of the timetable meant that I used to return from Poitiers on the same train as a pleasant colleague, Madame Blondel, whose husband came to fetch her at the Gare d'Austerlitz and dropped me off at my place nearby in the 13th arrondissement. I became aware that, beneath her posh exterior, this lady lacked neither a sense of humour nor a critical social spirit. When the Poitiers notables invited us both to one of their series of annual soirées for worthy professors, on the evening of 'our' day at the university, I saw no one but her with whom I could carry on a conversation. May '68 would show that she was capable of joining the most radical camp.

By another stroke of chance, my course in Poitiers started at the beginning of May '68. I left Dakar on the eve of a First of May that went down in the history of Senegal, and arrived in Poitiers in time to go on strike before commencing work. Bénard drove me back to Paris, on 12 or 13 May if I remember correctly, as no trains were running. I'm not sure of the exact date of my return to Poitiers, some time at the height of the movement, when students and teachers had discussed and hammered out proposals for radical reforms. There was a meeting with the dean, a man named Janot, whom everyone called Jeannot the Rabbit because of his remarkable timidity. It was explained to him that all he had to do was 'resign', to demonstrate his support for the proposals of the elected assemblies. But Janot was not willing either to resign (what if the Whites win and blame me for giving up?) or not to resign (unless I do, the Reds will shoot me if they win). In the end, the solution that occurred to him was to run away. How? By going to the toilet and escaping through a skylight on to the rooftops. The old medieval building had high ceilings, and when we got worried and went to look for him in the toilets we were amazed that such a stocky little man, not used to physical exercise, had managed to haul himself up by the biceps. Fear can certainly work wonders. Anyway, once on the roof, Janot was not sure where to go next. Some students waiting for the outcome of the meeting spotted him and shouted out: Janot's up there. The fire brigade was called in to bring down the unlucky fugitive. And the conclave resumed...

Nevertheless, the Poitiers teaching programmes were, if not revolutionary, no longer the same as the ones I had known in my youth. There had been some reforms here and there: for example, economics had become more autonomous, no longer requiring a prior degree in law. I therefore taught planning and economic–financial policy to fourth-year students and for the Diplôme d'Études Supérieures (DES).

In Dakar, too, 1968 had had its effects. In fact, as we shall see, things had begun there well before Paris and incubated for at least two years, echoing to some extent the Cultural Revolution in China. At the level of university reform, however, the advances were more timid and the authorities appeared sufficiently strong to keep them within bounds. The resulting ossification is largely the reason for the subsequent decline of the university, the marginal role of its students in the life of the country and their withdrawal into egotistic demands. The reform commissions dragged their heels, sabotaged by a French rector whose intellectual mediocrity went together with limitless pretension. He could not see any problems with the nineteenth-century French university: it was the model of perfection, valid in all times and places. Most of my colleagues (not friends!) had been brought in from France to nod everything through. Some of them later made a career for themselves in a provincial university by posing as 'Africa specialists', always happy to legitimize the official position (on the CFA and the Franc Zone, for instance) and a week later to back a change of line (e.g. the IMF-imposed devaluation). My Senegalese colleagues (and friends), feeling that the die was already cast, grumbled but did not dare to make a move. Only Fougeyrollas, a member of the reform commission, laid into the rector at every opportunity, with the gift of the gab that characterizes people in the south-west. Naturally we soon became good friends.

So, neither the teaching programmes nor the pedagogic methods had really changed. For myself I chose some specialized DES courses (in economic theory, for example, which allowed me to engage in root-and-branch criticisms of economics), but above all I wanted to have the general economics course for first-year and second-year students. No problem: none of the other lecturers wanted the super-crowded lecture halls and the mass failure at examinations. My view was that that was where a teacher had to start. Students would arrive from secondary school not really knowing how to read; they had often not been taught to make the effort to understand what they were reading. So, what was to be done? Most of my colleagues just got on with dictating their lectures, some with a false-hearted glee, others with a guilty conscience. It was a way of operating that systematically failed 80 per cent of the students, especially those from the least privileged classes.

My first principle was to teach students how to read, and to develop, through reading, their capacity for reflection and critical analysis. I worked out quite an original teaching method with which, I have to admit, I feel rather pleased. I divided the year into two semesters. The first involved parallel reading of two famous economics manuals: Samuelson (the glory of American universities and mainstream economists) and Popov (the glory of the Soviet academy); I indicated in advance of each class the pages in the two manuals that dealt with more or less the same topic. Then I began the class with a number of oral questions, singling out some good students (most of them girls, as here too they tended to be sharper and more serious than boys) and some average to poor students. I asked: what are they saying? How would you express it in your own way? I introduced, as a corrective element, an explanation of the texts, of certain words, and of the structure of the argument. During the second semester, when the students had more or less acquired a capacity for reading, I reconstructed the course around the question: what is economics? Why does it ask the questions it does? How do mainstream economists and dogmatic Marxists answer them? In what way do their answers differ? In what way do they converge? Judging by what students told me later in life, I think that most of them had a good memory of the course. In any event, the results of the examinations – which we marked together as a group – were much better than in the past.

My colleague at the faculty, Abdoulaye Wade, was the first Senegalese *agrégé*. I wanted him to assume the official functions of head of department, but he opposed this for the respectable reason that his first priority was national political activity. Although I was formal head of department, I used to consult him before raising any matter in our work group or having any dealings with the rector's office. Abdoulaye Wade conducted himself with perfect rectitude. We became close friends and tried to strengthen the department by creating a research centre, to which we planned to recruit the best two students from each class; they would be given the funding to spend most of their time on a well-structured thesis, in return for light duties as assistant lecturers. We thought that this strategy would make it possible to 'Senegalize' the teaching body in the best possible conditions, and to found in Dakar an academic tradition in the full sense of the term. Unfortunately, for reasons that I do not know, the project was not systematically followed through by our successors, and the best elements eventually tended to take up more attractive offers in the civil service or the private sector.

Vincennes, by contrast, was at the highest point of innovation, perhaps the highest anywhere in the world. Michel Beaud – who, as far as I remember, had more or less coordinated the endless debates in a commission that I occasionally attended – ran the department with unfailing patience, as anyone in his position would have needed to. Later, we were joined by Kostas Vergopoulos, who also became a good friend of mine. The dominant trend in Vincennes was fundamental theoretical analysis, the weapon of radical social critique. I, of course, had nothing but sympathy for this, but I soon saw that there was a danger in offering nothing else: not all the students – and we wanted there to be many, for anti-elitist reasons – were cut out to become theoreticians and leaders of movements. Nearly all would have to earn a living in one way or another. So, why not divide their education into two parts: half the time for efficient professional training (accountancy, management, etc.), the other half for cultural criticism? With various ups and downs that I was not always able to follow, this is the formula that has continued to assure Paris VIII of its success.

For my part, the freedom to design courses meant that I could concentrate on 'the political economy of capitalism': that is, the history of capitalism (very different from the traditionally impoverished subject of 'economic history'), the stress falling as appropriate on distant roots or the recent past, with special attention to France and/or third world countries. This seemed to me the best preparation for serious debate on the question of questions: What is capitalism? What is the significance and scope of the (Soviet or Maoist) attempts to go beyond it? After 1968 young people were quite rightly fixated on this question. It was necessary to get them to discuss it in a fundamental manner, without concessions, but also calmly and non-polemically, tackling as seriously as possible the whys and the wherefores. I tried to mobilize all my capacities to this end.

Vincennes became one of the main centres of French social theory; its advantage was that it completely ignored the stupid compartmentalization of disciplines that was often the rule elsewhere. Economists, sociologists, political scientists, philosophers, psychologists, historians and geographers conducted together the research and teaching programmes, and discussion of them was always rewarding for everyone concerned. An impressive number of those who later became famous – François Chatelet, Derrida, Deleuze, Foucault, and many others – took an active part in these debates. Along with Nanterre – which had Henri Lefebvre, Georges Labica, Alain Touraine and the review *L'Homme et la Société* – Vincennes thus formed the core of post-1968 French theory, which later developed for better or worse in different directions, including into that postmodernism whose success across the Atlantic could scarcely have been imagined at the time.

SEVEN

The Political Context, 1960–98

A political animal like myself cannot write his memoirs without spelling out how he saw the political events and developments in the times through which he lived. I have suggested above a reading of these during my younger years and stressed the importance for me of the Bandung challenge to the strategy that had previously guided our revolutionary activity. Bandung inaugurated a new period, marked by the spread of a national-populist project for societies throughout the Third World. Here I shall merely summarize what I said about this in greater detail in my *Re-reading the Postwar Period: An Intellectual Itinerary*.

Of course, the four decades considered in this chapter, which contain the years of my maturity (30 to 68), were also marked by the watershed of 1968 – and not only, as it is too often thought, in France and the West. As I see it, 1968 is a date in world history. It was when new lefts separated themselves from Soviet Marxism, developed in parallel with Maoist critiques in China and, as if by ricochet or association, spread to the third world and the capitalist heartlands. I still find it difficult to say whether this page in history has turned or not, given that the triumph of neoliberalism seems to me so illusory and fragile.

Other dates in this period were also especially important to me: above all, the defeat of Egypt and the Arab world in the war of 1967, which heralded the inevitable demise of Nasserism. This was the context in which my activities unfolded at IDEP in the 1970s and the Third World Forum after 1980.

Deployment and erosion of the Bandung project

The Bandung conference of 1955 seemed to place a question mark over our guiding ideas of the post-war years: that the socialist revolution, through an uninterrupted process of stages, was on the agenda everywhere in Asia and Africa; that there was no longer room for a bourgeois-led national liberation; that the bourgeoisie, everywhere compradorized, could act only as an intermediary for a new-style imperialist domination, under the thumb of the United States. Now, suddenly, in addition to China, Vietnam and North Korea, there were independent regimes in Asia that had managed to stabilize themselves, whereas the various guerrilla campaigns had run out of steam. The India of Nehru's Congress Party, the Egypt of Nasser and the Indonesia of Sukarno were taking new initiatives both internally and in relation to imperialism as well as the USSR and China. These unexpected developments seemed to show that the bourgeoisie had not exhausted its historical role.

The central issue for debate throughout the period after 1955 was whether a capitalist solution was possible in the third world. What could capitalism really achieve there, and what were its limits? Should we be preparing for socialism to go beyond it? The ebb and flow of the national-bourgeois project in the third world was linked to the general evolution of capitalism in the West, to the USSR's entry into the international arena and the division of world politics into two military camps, and to the conflicts opposing Sovietism to Maoism and the USSR to China.

I give a central place to China's evolution because, after 1960, the perspective it offered seemed to break from the rut of Sovietism, which Maoism accused of taking a road that would lead to capitalism. The political regime in China drew important conclusions from this, both for revolutionary strategy in the third world (seen as the 'storm zone') and for analysis of the international situation and of the strategies of imperialism and (Soviet) 'social imperialism'. I should add that from 1957 to 1980 I almost fully shared the positions of the Chinese Communist Party, whereas after 1980 I had a more critical view of the Chinese openings to capitalism.

The Korean war (1950–53) and the first Vietnam war (1945–54) had already shown the limits to the power of the Western imperialist bloc; the second Vietnam war (1965–75) and the war in Cambodia (1970–75) clearly demonstrated that national liberation could take a radical form and even wear down the armies of the United States. In Africa, the collapse of Portuguese colonialism in 1974 also illustrated the dividend to be gained from a protracted armed struggle. But the Algerian war (1954–62) had eventually ended in a radical nationalist regime (Boumédienne), which we saw as in no way more promising than Nasserism.

History did not stop either with the Chinese Cultural Revolution or with the Vietnamese victory in 1975. In any event, the ebb and flow of socialist forces in China, Korea and Vietnam seemed to us the product of internal social conflict, not at all of external factors. I have not changed my mind about that since. Liberation, when sufficiently advanced, reduces the weight of the external factor (which is obviously always unfavourable) and fully reinstates the decisive role of the internal class struggle. This is not to say, however, that the external factor disappears. In parallel with the ebb of socialist forces in East Asia, the region embarked upon phenomenal capitalist development that we had never expected (any more than the rest of the world had).

For Egypt the golden years of the Bandung project were 1955 to 1967, yet even then there were plenty of weaknesses. The failure of the union with Syria (1958–61), the persistent anticommunism, the toleration of traditionalist Islamic discourse, the elements of degeneration expressed in corruption: all these contributed to the eventual defeat. Subsequently, I was happy to see the fairly large section of socialist-minded youth attack the 'new class'. But I have to say that I was worried when the regime, far from adopting the strategic perspectives of those young people, opted for a policy of concessions. After Nasser's death (1970) and Sadat's dramatic break with the left wing of Nasserism (May 1971), this policy became the so-called Infitah – an open-door compradorization which, still disguised until the 1973 war, took full and explicit shape at both regional and international levels, when Sadat joined the American camp, visited Jerusalem and signed the Camp David accords (1977). The Infitah, then, appeared to me not the 'counter-revolution' that Egyptian Communists less critical of Nasserism held it to be, but rather the acceleration of a tendency that had been part of Nasserism itself. Twenty years later, I analysed in a similar way the open restoration of capitalism in the ex-USSR.

Whatever my own reservations, the peoples of the Arab world certainly saw Nasserism as liberatory and progressive. How often did I hear this said, and how often was I reproached for my own attitude, during those two decades! In my view, Nasserism shared with Baathism and the Algerian regime a number of negative features: a bourgeois vision of the future, a deep-rooted hostility to democracy, a second-rate pragmatic philosophy, an overestimation of Soviet support (rightly seen as mainly military), and a cheap cynicism that made them think they could 'play the American card' if the circumstances required it.

I placed greater hope in the poorer fringes of the Arab world (Sudan, South Yemen) and in the Palestinian struggle. In 1964 the Palestinian people finally created an organization of its own that took its distance from the Arab regimes. Its radicalism chimed with that of many popular movements of the time, and we expected a lot of it. But the slide of some Palestinian groups towards terrorism, as well as their behaviour in host countries (Jordan and later Lebanon), made it easier for local reactionary forces and imperialism to mount a counter-attack. That was how things remained until 1988, when the Palestinian intifada opened up a new perspective by waging the struggle directly in the occupied territories.

The years I spent in Bamako (1960–63) corresponded to the first wave of radicalization in Africa. The Guinean 'No' and Ghana's independence in 1958, followed by the Malian choice of direction in September 1960, were the chief manifestations of this trend, but they were not the only ones. Lumumbism was carrying the day in Congo, and between 1960 and 1963 there was reason to expect a similar radicalization in Congo–Léopoldville. In 1963, moreover, a popular uprising in Brazzaville put an end to the neocolonial regime of Fulbert Yulu.

Still, I did not share the (in my view, infantile) optimism of those who saw 'African socialisms' as a new, almost radiant path; rather, there was for me an obvious analogy with Nasserism. But a battle is never lost if it is not begun. It was therefore necessary to begin the battle. If it was eventually lost, this was for the same reasons: immaturity of the vanguards, illusions maintained by the Soviet 'friend', imperialist interventions, and the appetites of a new embryonic bourgeoisie rooted in the state. The fact remains, however, that the first radical wave in Africa was followed by another: in 1964 Zanzibar carried out its revolution and got rid of the Sultan; and in 1967 Nyerere opted for socialism, as expressed in the Arusha Charter. It was necessary to wait until 1983 in Burkina Faso, where a new wave took shape around Thomas Sankara that drew the lessons from previous failures and emphasized more popular and democratic forms of action. In 1974 the Ethiopian military overthrew Emperor Haile Selassie, in a country where the revolutionary forces seemed to be powerful, although they were divided into mutually hostile groups (rather like the ones I had known in Egypt) and paralysed by the military dictatorship. They were also bogged down in a war in Eritrea, which the imperialist powers and their clients – or, at other times, nationalist regimes – kept completely ambiguous, and which the Soviet Union and Cuba sometimes muscled into, as in the Ogaden conflict of 1978, when Syad Barre changed sides. In these conditions, the revolutionary forces, though exceptionally courageous, were unable to prevent the disintegration of their country. Meanwhile, in Madagascar, the same wave led to the fall of Tsiranana (1972), the attempted radicalization under the short-lived Ratsimandrava government (1973) and the consolidation of the system when Ratsiraka took the reins of power (1975).

Other developments, though less promising, indicated that neocolonialism was incapable of overcoming its permanent crisis: for example, the successive coups in Congo and Benin (where Kérékou came to power in 1972), or the sliding of Kaunda's regime in Zambia towards a 'socialist' statism. By the late 1980s the crisis of neocolonialism was becoming general, as democratic demands either took on a genuinely popular dimension or remained more limited and susceptible to imperialist manipulation.

The long war of liberation in the Portuguese colonies naturally led to a radicalization of the movement, at least in terms of ideological formulations, although personally I had some reservations about Amilcar Cabral's theory that it could induce the petty bourgeoisie 'to commit suicide as a class'. Any such possibility greatly diminished when the sudden collapse of the Portuguese system in 1974 speeded up the achievement of independence.

The hard core of colonization lay in South Africa, and the Rhodesian whites thought they could hitch their wagon to it through a unilateral declaration of independence (in 1965). In fact, they were supported by the British mother country, and what unfolded was a comedy involving the usual hypocrisy. Here too the liberation struggle was finally victorious, and an independent Zimbabwe came into being in 1980. But at what price? By signing the Lancaster House Agreement, which stifled any serious attempt at agrarian and other social reforms, the Patriotic Front went down a road that naturally led to schizophrenia: it maintained a (doubtless sincere) left-wing discourse, while the structural adjustment programme it had to swallow brought a constant worsening of the social crisis.

Does the same fate lie ahead for South Africa? In my analysis of that country, I emphasize two characteristics that are too often overlooked. First, the project to make South Africa a modern industrial power by reducing the black workforce to semi-servitude – which was started by English settlers more than a century ago and developed under the forty-year apartheid regime – has ended in failure. South African industry is uncompetitive, and therefore, by the key criterion for the global capitalist economy, the RSA counts for no more than the few other 'industrialized' countries of Africa and the Middle East. The failure is certainly due to the resistance of the black working class, from Sharpeville (1960) to Soweto (1976), and the general civil insurgency that led De Klerk to agree to talks in 1990. But it is also due to the incredible waste bound up with a 'white' minority that consumes as in the West without the same productivity. Second, South Africa is a kind of microcosm of the world capitalist system: a minority of first world consumers, a large active army of 'township' labour concentrated in the mines, industry and colonial-style agriculture, and a no less sizeable reserve army in the Bantustans and the informal sector surrounding the cities. Under these conditions, what will become of the compromise associated with the end of apartheid? External forces hold out the prospect of an 'advantage' that the black majority will inherit from the 'fine industrial infrastructure', so long as it helps the country to become 'competitive' in line with the spirit of the age. In other words, the working majority is being asked to pay more to achieve what capital, with global financial, economic and political support, has failed to achieve.

In Asia, the Bandung project can claim less fragile achievements, especially in East Asia (to which I shall return below).

There can be no doubt that the conventional view of Congress-ruled India, with its spotlight on parliamentary democracy and competitive industrialization, is too favourable. The Indian left rightly tempers such overhasty judgements. Even in the days of Nehru (who died in 1964), the Indian industrial bourgeoisie, allied to the large northern property owners and the state technocracy, never saw its project as conflicting with transnational capital. It pays the price for this, in so far as its control of technology and finance is today more apparent than real. Parliamentary democracy, the only reasonable way of managing in this vast country the set of regionally differentiated hegemonic social alliances, has not prevented – indeed, rests upon – the social marginalization of the poor. The exhaustion of the project, which looked so nationalist when it first got off the ground, is today evident enough.

The Shah's dictatorship, restored after the fall of Mossadegh in 1953, launched Iran on a state-led modernizing programme which, though conservative in its social dimension, had some major achievements to its credit. Its Achilles heel was the anti-democratic spirit in which it unfolded, made worse by an unqualified opting for Western culture. But the Islamic Revolution of 1978–79, which put an end to this experiment with a right-wing

Bandung, is incapable of coming up with a real alternative that goes beyond religious rhetoric.

If Iran is no longer a threat to the dominant capitalism, could Afghanistan have become one? The small-scale revolution that replaced the Daud regime with a modernizing populist government would undoubtedly have come up against its natural limits; the para-communist ideology in which the modernizing intellectuals expressed themselves would, in my view, have gradually been adjusted. But the Soviet intervention of 1979, by playing off the 'parties' of the intelligentsia against one another, provided an unexpected opportunity for the United States to mire the Soviet armies in the region and to nip Afghan modernization projects in the bud. In supporting the Islamists – who, after their victory in 1992, predictably plunged the country into an endless war even more appalling than the last – the Western powers again displayed the cynicism with which they treat the peoples of the region and the hypocrisy of their democratic discourse.

Latin America was not present at Bandung and never planned to join the non-aligned group. There were at least three reasons for this: the fact that the countries in the region have been independent since the nineteenth century; the dominance of European culture; and the long-standing influence of the United States and its acceptance by the local ruling classes. Nevertheless, after the Second World War, Latin America underwent a parallel evolution to that which took place in Africa and Asia under the banner of Bandung, essentially because of the objectively analogous position of its peripheral capitalism in relation to the world system. Three experiences here deserve to be grouped in the category of radical third world experiences.

The first is that of Cuba, which managed to liberate itself in 1959. Washington soon realized that Castroism was a real danger, as its attempt to reconquer the country in 1961 (the Bay of Pigs invasion) amply demonstrates. The US threat weighed heavily on the island and (given the economic boycott by the United States and its European allies) intensified its dependence on the USSR. The episode of the missiles in 1962, which Khrushchev and Castro skilfully negotiated, helped to send Castroism veering towards the Soviet model, to the detriment of its potential to develop in a more democratic and less artificial direction.

The second experience was the democratic (in the traditional parliamentary sense of the term) strategy attempted by the Allende regime in Chile, between 1970 and 1973. Chilean democracy found itself paralysed as a result and succumbed to the blows organized by Washington. The compradorization promoted by the bloody Pinochet dictatorship, with the help of the United States and Europe, has become a model to inspire the neocapitalists from Warsaw to Moscow. But has it really been such a success? That is certainly not my view, both because the social price of 'adjustment' has been exorbitant, and because, within the very logic of globalized capitalism, Chile's place will remain that of a producer amenable to the 'putting out' operations of dominant capital and its local allies. It holds no prospect of an acceptable future for Chile's popular classes.

The third experience followed the overthrow of Somoza in Nicaragua, in 1979. Drawing some lessons from history, the Sandinista movement tried to avoid the excesses of a statism confused with socialism, to practise a more genuine democracy, and to preserve a broad range of external relations. This did not spare it the hostility of the United States, which supported the Contra war, nor the rallying of a faint-hearted Europe to the views of Washington. In these circumstances the Sandinista withdrawal from government, following the elections of 1989, was an honourable result that could allow the popular forces to remain intact for other battles in the future.

The call by third world countries for a 'New International Economic Order' (1975) marked the end of Bandung as an active project, since a second wind for the national-bourgeois project required the North to 'adjust' to demands for globalized capitalist expansion under acceptable conditions. The proposed reform of the international order fitted into this line of thinking. But its rejection by the Western powers drove it home that national-bourgeois construction on the periphery of the system is a utopian project. What followed was therefore a unilateral adjustment by the periphery to the requirements of globally dominant capital – that is, to a new wave of compradorization.

It may appear extreme to make the national-bourgeois project in the three peripheral continents central to the history of the period. I would insist, however, that throughout the post-war period the huge political and social transformations in those continents (where the great majority of the world's population lives) were the main axis around which the world order was organized. They were major qualitative transformations, incomparably greater in their long-term impact than the calmer tendencies operating in the societies of the capitalist core – although in some respects the latter did play an important role in the evolution of the world system.

Is not the truth of this statement implicitly accepted by those who maintain the exaggerated, but no less significant, view that East Asia is becoming the 'centre' of a new world? Whether a miracle or not, the capitalist development of Korea and Taiwan in exceptional geostrategic circumstances (expressed in concessions never granted elsewhere, and in agrarian and other reforms made obligatory by the competition of the communist world) spread in different ways to South Asia and the vast expanse of China. Whereas, for South Asia, the model appears to be one of dependent comprador capitalism largely dominated by the transnationals, the experiences of Korea and China cannot be reduced to that. Are we talking there of forms of national capitalist development? Has history, contrary to what was said above, proved that such forms are possible? Are they capable of gradually closing the gap between centre and periphery – that is, of creating new capitalist centres? Or, despite the successes, has the polarization been taking new forms, so that these regions will become the true peripheries of tomorrow's globalized capitalism, while the rest are simply marginalized?

Later developments in the region – above all, the financial crisis of Southeast Asia and Korea – are in my view the harbinger of a protracted war. Taking the opportunity of Korea's ultimately minor financial crisis (France and Britain have known a number of greater severity since the war), the United States tried to force Seoul to dismantle its national oligopolies and to open up the country to foreign capital. The most specious arguments were mobilized for this purpose. Can one imagine the IMF declaring that the solution to the US financial crisis (a twenty-year external deficit higher than Korea's in per capita terms) is the forced selling-off of Boeing to its European rival, Airbus? It is clear what is at stake. Will Korea be able to achieve the status of a major capitalist centre? Or will it assume a subaltern place in the new global polarization that lies ahead? The subaltern-comprador fate can hardly be doubted in most of the new third world (Southeast Asia and Latin America), but the war is only just beginning over Korea, China and perhaps India. A counteroffensive against American aggression may be shaping up, initially centred on the control of speculative movements of capital. History remains open.

In any event, these transformations in the third world, and especially its uneven industrialization, are not simply the result of the unilateral expansionist logic of the dominant sections of capital, but also correspond to the struggles which third world societies, in varying measure, have waged against that logic. Bandung was not a uniform phenomenon. According to the social and political conditions in each country and the play of global and regional forces, we saw four sets of changes gradually work themselves out during the postwar cycle.

1. Clear-cut capitalist development, accompanied by a so-called 'liberal' ideology but often strongly marked by resolutely modernist state intervention, open to the world system but concerned to control any opening, always anti-democratic in its practices. South Korea, Taiwan, Mexico, Brazil and the Shah's Iran are typical of this model.
2. Various populist experiments, highly statist, never democratic, ambiguous about their relationship to globalization, usually calling themselves 'socialist', often supported by the USSR. Depending on their historical legacy, some of these experiments went further than others along the path of industrialization.
3. The self-styled 'Marxist' experiences of China, North Korea and Cuba, originating, like the Soviet experience, in a radical revolution inspired by the doctrines of the Third International. Their present orientation, explicit in the case of China, is now towards a capitalism that claims to control its relations with the dominant world system.

4. Experiences that never went beyond a banal neocolonial framework, so that their growth (Ivory Coast, Kenya, etc.) or persistent stagnation (the Sahel countries, etc.) was passively dependent on external stimuli.

As a whole, these huge transformations have left us with situations quite different from those that prevailed in 1945. The analytic key here is the criterion of globalized capitalism itself: the existence, or absence, of segments of the local productive system that are 'competitive' in global terms, or capable of becoming so without too much difficulty. Accordingly, we are now talking of a 'third' *and* a 'fourth' world.

The new third world consists of countries that have achieved sufficient 'modernization' in terms of global competitiveness: roughly speaking, all the larger countries of Latin America, the countries of East Asia (China, the two Koreas, Taiwan), Eastern Europe and the former USSR. This, for me, is tomorrow's real periphery. The new fourth world consists of all the other countries, essentially Africa and the Arab–Islamic world. This too seems to cover quite a large range: some have completed a few stages in the industrialization process but failed to become competitive (Egypt and South Africa, for example), while others have not even embarked upon the industrial revolution (the whole of sub-Saharan Africa, Pakistan, Bangladesh, Indonesia); some are financially 'rich' (mainly the oil-producing countries with a small population), while others are to a greater or lesser extent financially 'poor' (from Ivory Coast to Somalia). My criterion here in not per capita income but a capacity for productive insertion into the world system. There are also countries which, in varying degrees, combine these characteristics. India is a case in point.

All the popular classes of this third and fourth world face the same challenge, but the conditions of their struggle are different. The challenge is simply that peripheral capitalism offers them nothing acceptable at a social or political level. Yet third world social formations contain both a large active army of labour and a reserve army that cannot be absorbed into the labour force. The objective conditions exist there for a strong popular alliance to crystallize through struggles over management of the productive system and political and social democratization. Of course, a number of real obstacles stand in the way of such an alliance, not the least of which is the ideological obstacle bequeathed by Sovietism and the historical limits of Maoism. This is especially apparent in the countries of the old eastern bloc. Will its peoples manage to shake off their illusions in capitalism and avoid sinking into chauvinistic nationalism? China also apparently belongs to this group. Will its vanguard know how to renew Maoism and build into it a democratic component in the real sense of the term, by developing the autonomous organization of the popular classes as a counterweight to the concessions made to capitalism? As to the 'fourth world' social formations, whether 'rich' or 'poor', unindustrialized or very weakly industrialized and under threat from neo-compradorization, they are virtually reducible to an ill-defined 'people' on the one hand, lacking roots in a viable productive system, and 'the powers that be' on the other hand. Consequently, the shifting of conflicts to the spheres of the imagination is a real, and no doubt disastrous, aspect of the problem facing these societies. In the Arab and Islamic world, the marriage of oil money with an outdated programmatic discourse – which, despite its 'fundamentalist' pretensions, is fundamentally traditionalist – represents the best guarantee of success for the imperialist programme of regional compradorization. In sub-Saharan Africa, the flight into mythology sometimes takes different forms, such as eruptions of ethnicism that may lead to a total break-up of the country.

Given the collapse of the Bandung project, were we not right to maintain in the 1945–55 period that the national bourgeoisie had exhausted its historical role, that the project of national capitalist development was obsolete and utopian? Was it not light-minded to accuse of 'ultra-leftism' those who argued that the Bandung project would reach a dead end because of its bourgeois character and that the pseudo-concept of a non-capitalist path was fundamentally opportunist? When I reread what I wrote at the time, I remain convinced that the general line of those analyses was correct. And, although it may seem lacking in modesty, I would even go so far as to say that some of them were quite perspicacious. Here are a few examples:

- The near-premonition (in 1960) that the 'natural' end of Nasserism would be the forms that came to be known as Infitah.
- The warning against a possible neo-comprador solution in the Middle East, which would include building Israel into an overall regional picture.
- My analysis in 1965 of the Ivory Coast 'miracle', in opposition to the World Bank forecasts that were later belied by the facts.
- My view in 1975 that the best solution in Angola would be to continue stubbornly working for a coalition government of all the liberation movements. I am not convinced that such efforts would have succeeded, but nor am I sure that everything was done to achieve that end. Today, after seventeen years of pointless war, this solution will perhaps impose itself, but in a form bordering on farce.
- The fears I expressed in 1972–74 that a compromise solution was on the cards in Zimbabwe and South Africa – which eventually went by the name of Lancaster House in Zimbabwe and a 'federal solution' in post-apartheid South Africa.

1968 and its aftermath

I must confess that May '68 took me by surprise. I felt that young people in the West were depoliticized and that the successes of the welfare state had anaesthetized the working class for many years to come. I remember one occasion in summer 1967, on a café terrace in the Latin Quarter, when Abdou Moumouni and I were lamenting the narrow horizons of a youth that was only interested in its hairstyles. Isabelle did not agree with us at all: she argued that this apparent lack of interest concealed a deep rejection of the consumer society model on offer to young people; the whole thing would blow up, and a lot faster than we thought. Isabelle had a better flair for politics, and Gabillard in Poitiers was speaking much the same language. He told me that his daughter, a school student, spent long evenings in smoky cafés heatedly discussing how to build a movement to the left of the Communist Party (which, it has to be said, was pretty sclerotic by that time).

We also knew the scale of the new 'hippy' movement on American campuses and its opposition to the war in Vietnam. But we did not fail to note how different it was from the opposition that had shaken France during the first Vietnam war, based on principles of internationalism and peoples' rights, not on a 'rejection of war' as such. The contrast was all the more striking because the French had not sent national servicemen to Indochina but had relied on professional armed forces who were presumably willing to wage the war, whereas the opposition of American conscripts was largely motivated by a refusal to go and be killed, rather than by active solidarity with the Vietnamese cause. Hippy ideology itself expressed these limits of the movement, inspiring a kind of hedonistic individualism that would later become the backbone of postmodernism.

In my view, Maoist critiques of the Soviet system played a more decisive role in the origins of 1968. I had associated myself with those critiques from the beginning, when I was still in Egypt, and they had an obvious echo in many third world countries, especially after the onset of the Cultural Revolution in 1966. Moreover, the Cultural Revolution began to arouse the hopes and enthusiasm of young people in the West: Godard's film *La Chinoise* is a perfect illustration of this point, which has often been forgotten – or passed over in silence. It was the enthusiasm that lay behind the later 'third worldism' of young people in the West.

As the luck of the calendar would have it, I was able to witness – and to participate in – the French May until it seemingly ran its course (July 1968), while Isabelle was experiencing the events in Dakar, to which I shall return.

I shall not say anything here about the demonstrations, declarations, party lines and general strike that punctuated May in France, nor about de Gaulle's flight to Baden-Baden, the sea of red flags that covered Paris, or the counter-demonstration on the Champs Elysées at which the red, white and blue tricolour came out on display. An abundant literature has described these things better than I could do. A few serious works (though not serious enough for my taste) have offered retrospective analyses of the main currents of thought and action, as well as of their later evolution and the profound social changes that they induced.

My experience of 1968 in Paris taught me a lot about left-wing intellectuals in France. As we know, they were constantly in the news from the 1930s to the 1970s, more than anywhere else in the West. Throughout the nineteenth century, French intellectuals were the children of the Revolution, both those on the left (Jacobin Republicans) and most of those on the right (moderate liberals and some supporters of English-style monarchy, to the exclusion of people descended from the Ancien Régime, for the most part lifeless clerics). This general rallying to the spirit of 1789 proved an obstacle to the penetration of Marxism – as Marx himself noted. The Dreyfus Affair initiated a split between right and left, which grew deeper in the interwar period as the left sided with the Russian Revolution and the right inclined towards fascism. The defeat of Nazi Germany forced the discredited right to leave the scene, although it never really disappeared, any more than it did in post-war Italy (where fascist opinion lay hidden). The left, pro-Soviet in varying degrees, monopolized the intellectual stage.

May '68 and its aftermath were perhaps the last important moment when this weight of the intellectual left made itself felt. The sizeable academic right appeared to have no presence in 1968, nor was there much sign of all the opportunists whom the victorious left seemed to draw in its wake. All kinds of 'committees' were set up, and hundreds of academics took part in them to speak of everything under the sun. But when the situation grew tougher, their participation suddenly diminished. 'Brave but not foolhardy', the cowards ran off to breathe the country air. I remember, for example, how we laughed at Jacques Attali's vanishing trick right the way through until October, when it was all over. And how many others there were!

The ground was thus laid for the subsequent ending of the left's monopoly among intellectuals. The old liberal or openly reactionary right (the 'new right', the open or shame-faced 'Lepenists' of the future) made their reappearance. The new 'liberalism', having recycled what it could from 1968, became the dominant ideology and among intellectuals took the form of postmodernism, once time had been called on the hollow booming phrases of the *nouveaux philosophes*. A 'return to the Belle Époque' is how I described it. Its ravages have been truly appalling: the elimination of political economy from teaching programmes; universities that turn out mere copies of the graduates of wretched American business schools; or 'researchers' bogged down in the strict formalism of 'pure economics' and game theory. By the late 1990s, however, a reaction seemed to be developing against the calls for personal resignation, submission to supernatural 'market forces' and abolition of the inventive power of the human imagination.

To return to the 1960s: in 1963 I joined the monthly review *Révolution*, which published thirteen numbers between September of that year and December 1964. Run by Jacques Vergès, it drew on the active support of M.A. Babu (Zanzibar), Viriato da Cruz (Angola), Mamadou Gologo (Mali), Samba Ndiaye (Senegal), Rabah Bitat (Algeria), Carlos Franqui (Cuba), Cheddi Jagan (Guyana), Martin Legassick (South Africa), Hamza Alavi (Pakistan), N. Kien (Vietnam), H. Riad (Egypt). The last of these was none other than myself; I had already used the name to publish my book *Nasser's Egypt*. The review was also published in English, in London, incorporating *African Revolution*.

The review had an attractive form (thanks to financial support from China) and luxurious offices on avenue François Premier and later (or earlier, I don't remember) on rue Galande. Vergès always had a liking for luxury. Kien, who looked after the administration, got his fingers burnt and suffered for a long time because of some advances that were never reimbursed. As to content, the review was an out-and-out success because of the high quality of its analysis; it was in the vanguard of left-wing critiques of the Soviet system, serving as a counterweight to the right-wing critiques, from Khrushchev through Gorbachev to the final demise. Nor did its analyses simply reflect what the Chinese were publishing – far from it. They were the original products of critical thinking within the radical left in the third world, as one can tell from the above list of names and those of other contributors. What we may not have suspected at the time was the depth of their influence on young French readers.

This general influence of Maoism manifested itself in various, and divergent, forms in 1968. Five major movements claiming to be to the left of the Communist Party occupied the centre of the stage. There were still the Trotskyists, of course, who had been marginalized by the PCF and were no more than a *groupuscule*. In my view, they grasped the opportunity of 1968 rather poorly: the traditional Trotskyists, if I may call them that, were capable only of rehearsing the polemics of the 1920s and 1930s and the master's analysis of Soviet society at that time – a bureaucratically degenerated workers' state; others did try to respond to new challenges, giving rise to a current of renewal that continues to have some success, even electorally.

The *maos*, as they came to be known, were divided among three organizations. There were the 'regulars', so to speak, who had split from the Communist Party and especially its youth movement, and who published *L'Humanité Rouge*; they were thought of as the 'pro-Chinese wing' of the pro-China movement, being as attached to texts from Beijing as many in the PCF were to those from Moscow. Next, there were those who combined the French anarchist tradition with a Maoism that they trumpeted without much interest in analysis: the eloquently titled *Vive la Révolution* was their paper. Finally, there were the so-called Mao-sponties, who hailed the spontaneity of the masses as if they were revolutionary by instinct. They gave rise to the Gauche Prolétarienne (GP), which came to the fore after 1968 as the other currents receded.

The history of this movement is becoming better known, thanks especially to a few texts by Jean and Olivier Rolin (the latter a former GP leader) and a few analyses produced on the basis of its documents. Isabelle, who had to spend extended periods in Paris for health reasons between 1970 and 1972, got to know its active members better than I did. We used to see regularly Jean Baby and his wife Renée Bourdon, Benny Lévy (the ideologue of the organization, whom we first met through his brother Adel Rifaat), Jean Rolin, Alain Geismar and many other young people who got together at Renée Bourdon's. They were our source of information, which had the advantage that it was based on lived experience.

Some figures in the movement chose to 'establish' themselves as proletarians, so that they could operate directly among factory workers. Between 1970 and 1973, the year when the government banned the Gauche Prolétarienne, a number of prominent benefactors gave it vocal support – the best-known being Jean-Paul Sartre, who sold in public copies of its banned paper *La Cause du Peuple*. Then the movement gradually withered and its militants went their different ways. Many have remained good personal friends, ageing like the rest of us but still fundamentally honest and progressive. Some of the GP's leading lights, however, did not turn out well. Benny Lévy, who became Sartre's private secretary and got mixed up in his refusal of the Nobel Prize and the disputed *Temps Modernes* legacy, has been accused of abusing the generosity of the ageing philosopher and is now a mystic of Judaism.[40] There is nothing surprising in that. One often sees over-intellectualist theoreticians like Benny Lévy pass unproblematically from one extreme to the other – not, or anyway not necessarily, out of ruthless ambition, but because they have a basically religious temperament that makes it easy for them to switch beliefs in their endless quest for the absolute. Roger Garaudy is a good example of this species. I remember one day when, speaking of his wartime youth in the Resistance, he suddenly said: 'That's when I converted to Marxism' (he had been a Christian). I was immediately struck by the way in which the word 'converted' had slipped out. And, in later life, the conversions started again – to Buddhism, to Islam. There is no reason to be alarmed by the existence of such human types, even when they join movements in favour of progressive action. But one should try to avoid letting them rise to leading positions, for the movement has nothing to gain, and everything to lose, from the sectarian attitudes that are part of their nature.

Of course, the '68 movement may have been at its most flamboyant in Paris, but it was no less striking in other parts of Europe. It certainly lasted longest in Italy, if we mean by that the 'creeping May' which stretched right through the 1970s. No doubt certain objective features of Italian society explain why *operaismo*, in its various forms, managed to link up the workers' movement with a theoretical critique of Sovietism (and the Italian

Communist Party); the rapid spread of Fordism in the industrial cities of the North was based on the massive immigration of unskilled workers from the South, who enjoyed full citizenship status (unlike the Arabs, Turks or Africans who go to work in France or Germany). The fact remains, however, that this link-up produced a dazzling display of powerful mass movements and brilliant theorizations, one of the strongest being the Manifesto group launched by Rossana Rossanda, Luciana Castellina, Lucio Magri, Valentino Parlato and others. The way in which the movement gradually exhausted itself was therefore very different from the process that occurred in France. Through a combination of fatigue in the workers' movement and repression manipulated (with PCI complicity) in the grand Florentine tradition, sections of Italian leftism veered towards terrorism and linked up with the anarchist tradition still alive in the country, while the middle classes again dared to express old fascist sympathies that they had buried in their subconscious for many years after the war. The declining attraction of both Christian Democracy and the PCI, together with the slide of the Socialists into political racketeering, contributed to the deep political crisis that Italy underwent in the 1990s.

In other countries 1968 did not manage to break out of the ghetto. In Germany and Japan it produced little more than a rapid slide towards the sectarianism of groups that the authorities and the surrounding society – partly on the basis of real facts, partly through deliberate manipulation – described as 'terrorist'. There were also some European countries – Britain, for example – where 1968 passed virtually without incident.

The 1970s witnessed the gradual exhaustion of the welfare state model built in the West after 1945. There were two major axes along which the neoliberal turn of the 1980s was being prepared. On the one hand, the post-Fordist dissociation between the (global) space of the reproduction of capital and the fragmented (national) space of the political-social management of the conditions of its reproduction – a dissociation which represents the main challenge for Europe in the twenty-first century – was undermining the effectiveness of the national policies on which the construction of the social-democratic welfare state had rested. On the other hand, the gap between the United States and the other centres of world capitalism (Europe and Japan) was closing so fast that many saw evidence of a 'decline of America'. Did this mean that the construction of the European Union, originally conceived as a subsystem of an open, globalized capitalism, was destined to become a rival centre to the United States and Japan? I had my doubts, considering that the Western bloc had never shown a crack in relation to the South (or the East), despite de Gaulle's hopes in a Euro-Soviet rapprochement and his withdrawal from the NATO military command. And the Soviets failed in their strategy of breaking up the Atlantic bloc, either with smiles (Khrushchev, Gorbachev) or by wielding the big stick (Brezhnev).

The crisis that began in 1971 with the end of the gold convertibility of the dollar unfolded against this backdrop. Productive investment plummeted and has never fully recovered. The huge growth in American military expenditure and financial speculation has filled the vacuum, but despite the wild fluctuations in the value of the dollar the solidarity of the centres has remained intact, no doubt because the interpenetration of capital there has made the old national solutions ineffective.

For a solution to this structural crisis of capitalism to make any headway, new socialist forces would have to take shape in the West, operating on a continental basis in the case of Europe and replacing the failing nation-state with a supranational state capable of managing the new social compromise. There seemed to be some prospect of this in the 1970s, after the great ideological upheaval of the late 1960s. In 1969 Willy Brandt was elected German chancellor, in 1974 Labour returned to power in Britain, in 1974–5 Spanish and Portuguese fascism collapsed, in 1974 Greece shook off the military dictatorship it had had since 1967, and in 1981 Mitterrand was elected president of France. Nevertheless, all the hopes went up in smoke, as the Western left wasted the opportunity to renew itself. A few years later, when the systems in Eastern Europe and the USSR collapsed (1989–92), nothing was in place to begin the reconstruction of Europe on the basis of progressive social compromises. On the contrary, the dominant forces of the right saw an opportunity to create 'their' Latin America in

Eastern Europe. Unified Germany, from its newly dominant position within the perspective of capitalist polarization, tacitly pulled back from the European project and fell out of step in the new stage supposedly opened by the Maastricht treaty (1992).

The chaos resulting from the short-termism of capital, with no counterweight on the left, now affects the European continent itself (as we can see in the former Yugoslavia). It is also the occasion for the United States to resume the offensive, by setting itself up as gendarme of the capitalist world. The utopian vision of a world run by the market will thus, in reality, call for powerful military interventions, and it is to be feared that these will become increasingly frequent as the disastrous social consequences lead to uncontrollable explosions.

My personal thinking, and my political options, make sense only within this context.

In 1970, the journal *L'Homme et la Société*[41] organized a conference in Cabris that directly posed the question of post-'68: what is to be done? (Cabris is a marvellous place in the wooded hills near Grasse: the wife of an industrialist from northern France, who was shot by the Germans, had bequeathed its little castle and magnificent park to *Les Lettres françaises*.[42]) The conference was attended mainly by French intellectuals, including Jonas and Jean Pronteau, Henri Lefebvre and a number of younger people such as André Gauron,[43] but there were also some Italians from the Manifesto group (most notably Rossana Rossanda, a perfect combination of intelligence and gentleness, and the dazzling Luciana Castellina). The weather was so fine that we had the wonderful idea of meeting beneath a large tree (a 'council tree', as they would have said in Africa) instead of a stuffy room heated by the midday sun. The event marked for me the beginning of a period of close collaboration with *L'Homme et la Société*, edited by the two Pronteaus, and with their publishing house, Anthropos.

My major preoccupation in all this was the fate of the USSR and the attempts of the Stalinist system to reform itself. The analysis that I developed was that the right-wing critique of the system, initiated by Khrushchev and later by Gorbachev, conformed to the bourgeois aspirations of the dominant class, and that the eventual collapse was less a 'counter-revolution' than a speeding-up of the evolution of the system. The failure of the reform initiatives was anyway already evident by 1985, when Gorbachev undertook the perestroika that would lead to the final demise.

On the other hand, the USSR had broken out of its isolation after 1955 and strengthened its hand through a strategic alliance with third world regimes and liberation movements in conflict with imperialism. This alliance was a positive development, whatever judgement one may have of the Soviet system itself, for it forced the imperialists to moderate the violence of their interventions in the third world. The Gulf war of 1991, and the terrorist methods of destruction employed immediately after the disappearance of the USSR, illustrate the natural violence of imperialist behaviour when it is not subject to such constraints.

Soviet intervention in the third world did, however, have serious negative aspects. It is not that Moscow ever tried to 'spread socialism' by subjugating geographically distant allies, but it always sought to legitimize its intervention through an ideological discourse consistent with the one it used in the Soviet Union: the discourse of 'socialism'. It did not present the alliance with national bourgeoisies for what it was, but described it as support for 'progressive forces' capable of 'evolving towards socialism'. Woolly theories of a 'non-capitalist path' were invented for this purpose. And, when this kind of discourse was taken up by the radical left of liberation movements or even by the principal Marxist currents, it underlined the confusion and left the popular classes ill prepared to face the erosion and collapse of the Bandung project.

In these conditions, it was important to analyse as seriously and scientifically as possible the nature and objectives of Soviet foreign policy. Was it always fundamentally defensive, so that even apparently aggressive initiatives were designed only to exert pressure on the Western powers? This was the view I mainly supported: Moscow's strategic aim was to splinter the Atlantic bloc, not in order to 'Finlandize' Europe but to open up the contradiction between the USA and Europe, or even to pave the way for a Soviet–European rapprochement, within a joint capitalist (or neo-capitalist) perspective. At the same time, I did not rule out the possibility of backsliding in the direction of 'social imperialism', as in Afghanistan.

These were also major preoccupations for the Yugoslav communists, who, in the 1980s, expanded on the Cabris formula by organizing a much larger annual symposium at Cavtat, near Dubrovnik, on the future of Marxism and socialism, to which they invited Marxists from all countries (East and West, as well as South) and every imaginable tendency (Soviet and Chinese, Trotskyist and left-socialist). Isabelle and I (sometimes I alone) went there as often as possible. We met a number of old friends – Henri Lefebvre, Harry Magdoff and Paul Sweezy, Anouar Abdel Malek, Luciana Castellina (sometimes accompanied by her charming mother) – and made new friends such as the Yugoslav Milos Nikolic and the Lebanese Fahima Charaffedine. Milos, whom Isabelle thought resembled an Orthodox priest, used to ring a bell to summon back participants from their coffee break. He is now a leader of the anti-chauvinist Serbian left opposition. Fahima later organized one of the most active groups in the Third World Forum, where I often encountered Sana Abu Chakra, Adib Noema and others.

Cavtat has an exceptionally beautiful location, on a cape beneath which we used to go on coastal walks and find each year the same small cafés and familiar cats. Sometimes the return flight did not leave for one reason or another, especially as late September/early October was the season of mists in the Danube valley; we then had to drive from Dubrovnik to Belgrade through Bosnia, where we became familiar with the bridge at Mostar, the Turkish mosques and Sarajevo's labyrinthine bazaar. Isabelle and I made one of these trips with the wife of the man, a Macedonian, who that year held the rotating federal presidency of Yugoslavia. In Belgrade all the hotels happened to be full, but we found a place at the top Hotel Metropole, thanks to the intervention of the still all-powerful Central Committee.

The debates at Cavtat went round in circles, although the topics were always important and the contributions strong. Clearly there were two blocs: everyone was critical of 'actually existing socialism' and wanted to move beyond it, some on the right, others on the left. The division ran through nearly all the national groups – the Yugoslavs and East Europeans, as well as participants from the West and the South – and between the two sides it was a dialogue of the deaf. In the real world, the right-wingers were everywhere in control, but their strategies were everywhere leading to catastrophic results. Their arguments against 'ultra-leftism' must appear pretty unconvincing today.

Cavtat was an opportunity to observe political Yugoslavia at close quarters. It was disturbing. Cynicism was making visible headway – and alcohol abuse made people open up. Isabelle and I have clear memories of some pretty unedifying evenings in this respect. The Chinese, on the other hand, did not put in much of an appearance: one delegation, which listened more than it spoke. The reason for this was probably the road on which China had embarked in the 1980s, so that Maoists, ex-Maoists and anti-Maoists all felt rather uncomfortable at an occasion like Cavtat.

Back in Paris the atmosphere was very different. During the 1970s the main task was to end the long succession of right-wing governments since 1947, but an election victory for the PCF – which the left had traditionally seen as the way forward – was no longer a realistic prospect. The point, then, was to 'rebuild' a credible Socialist Party (the old SFIO being as frozen in its right-wing course as the PCF was attached to increasingly hollow dogmas) and to forge a union of the left. Some wanted this to be open to the legacy of 1968 and its 'new lefts', in the hope that the long-term dynamic would be favourable. I myself shared this view and still cannot see that anything else would have been both possible and defensible. This drew me closer to Pronteau, who was one of the (fortunately many) architects of renewal. We became firm friends and saw a lot of each other, until his death sadly ended our long discussions.

I remember one incident during the 1974 election campaign (when Mitterrand ran against Giscard d'Estaing for the presidency), which taught me a lot about Mitterrand's political personality. The whole of the post-'68 left was represented in the great auditorium of the Cité Universitaire, both in the audience and among the twenty speakers on the platform. The star turn was Mitterrand himself, who happened to be seated next to me. Each speaker said his piece, attracting applause from supporters and boos from the rest. Mitterrand listened attentively and took notes, then stood up to give the final address – and managed to win nothing but applause. How did he do it? By saying things that pleased now some, now others, without ever really displeasing anyone. It was a fine speech, which, if it had been written down, would have revealed all its inconsistency. But I remembered it as the product of a truly great politician, as smart as anyone else I could think of. Mitterrand forged the union of the left, with words and nothing but words. It was possible to hold this against him – as a theorist would certainly have done – but I think that the union of the left, however fragile, should be viewed positively.

Since neoliberalism triumphed in the 1980s – openly under Thatcher and Reagan, more stealthily with Mitterrand's change of tack in 1983 – should we conclude that 1968 ended in a historic defeat? I think that would be too one-sided a judgement.

The events of 1968, like all the great moments of history, placed society on an irreversible path; nothing could ever be the same as before. Of course, history sometimes advances backwards. And all great revolutions have in a way been defeated, as their moments of paroxysm have subsided and given way to anti-revolutionary tendencies. But they have also been victorious, in the sense of producing something that (passing) periods of counter-revolution could not reverse.

I did not for a moment think that 1968 could have accomplished the task that one has a right to expect from a 'great revolution': that is, the overthrow of the dominant mode of production and the social relations associated with it. I did not think it even when Paris was covered with red flags and a young, previously apolitical worker gave me a lift and suddenly said: 'We've got to get rid of the bosses once and for all. Otherwise we won't be able to have the kind of interesting work we want; we'll go on being slaves to mindless routine.' So, '*Boulot, metro, dodo*' (Job, metro, sleep) was not a slogan invented by refugee intellectuals in a romantic reverie. Large numbers of factory and service workers felt the truth of it in their innermost being. But, I repeat, not even in May–June '68 did I think that socialist revolution was on the agenda but had been betrayed by the PCF, the CGT or even various 'ultra-leftists'.

We were a long way, a very long way, from such a possibility. The reason for this seems to me fairly easy to understand. The legacy of the Third International was perhaps moribund, but it was not dead; it continued to weigh heavily on society. The USSR continued to have a double-edged effect of attraction and repulsion. It had offered the alternative: socialism. And, despite all the restrictions implied in 'actually existing socialism', despite a widespread awareness of the autocratic nature of the regime and its dogmatic rhetoric, it was in the end the product of 1917. The Maoist critique itself was only partial, limited both by the same tradition going back to Bolshevism and by China's historical legacy and present-day challenges. Neither in the developed West nor in the third world had Maoism come up with an alternative vision sufficiently coherent to be effective. Hence the easily understandable tendency towards verbal incantation ('we want everything, now!'), the choice of symbols (capturing the Odeon theatre, not police headquarters). Lack of real power rather than betrayal.

But, although 1968 could not be the 'big night', it was still a big moment in history and, in its way, a revolution. I have no wish to trivialize the concept by applying it to anything that moves, as people do when they speak of 'technological revolution', 'moral revolution', 'demographic revolution', 'revolution in ideas', and so on. But there is a problem that 'the' social revolution always presents many aspects – qualitative transformation of the modes of production and work, a new way of organizing political life, sweeping changes in morals and culture – and nothing says that these must all be simultaneous or reach completion in a brief historical time. We must give up any such simple, or simplistic, vision of historical change. In this connection, I have tried to stress the concept of 'underdetermination', which leaves open the possibility of evolution in different directions and suggests that we cannot know in advance where the great moments of history will lead. This is not incompatible with the historical materialism that Marx only began to theorize, although historical Marxism shifted it away from his field of reflection and the actions that it inspired.

Sixty-eight was a cultural revolution – and not by chance am I using the same term as the Maoists in China. It inaugurated major changes in every area of the life of society, or speeded up tendencies of change that had already been present for a long time, albeit unevenly and embryonically. However, the transformations were and remain ambiguous, since the cultural dimension is only one of the facets of social reality. Many authors and commentators have rightly, if a little lazily, used the idea of a subsequent '*récupération*' or hijacking of the culture of '68. The question is: how can such advances be protected from hijacking?

It is difficult to say any more – for me, in any case. But the blossoming of social and philosophical thought in 1968 has not exhausted its potential. The discovery of the 'Frankfurt School' critique (begun in the 1930s and continued in the United States during and after the war) was the point of departure. By coincidence, the French edition of Marcuse's *One Dimensional Man* was published in April 1968 by my friend Jérôme Lindon. With characteristic humour he said to me: 'I'd have sold a thousand copies to the members of a sect of specialist philosophers, but the educated public didn't even know of the school's existence and would have mistaken it for a school of choreography. Then May came along. I've sold 30,000 in eight days. It's a must-have in every bourgeois bookcase – even for people who'll never read it.'

'Back to Marx!' declared *Il Manifesto* in Italy. But which Marx? The debate has been open ever since, and we should be glad that this is so. It cannot be contained within the invective of the Stalin–Trotsky dispute, or the inadequate framework of the conflict between Sovietism and Maoism.

Sixty-eight also breathed new life into anti-authoritarian theories of every kind, both positive and not so positive. Some of the directions this took gradually led to the ground of hedonistic individualism, one of the foundations of bourgeois ideology and culture, and then – by an easily understandable deflection – to postmodernist nihilism. I am convinced that this was a real 'hijacking', and I have written elsewhere that this postmodernism is a perfect accompaniment, and an effective support, for neoliberal management of the real world.

No less important was the impact of 1968 on social movements. At a trivial level, the generation of hippy 'sixty-eighters' chose to lead a life far from the stress of organized obligations. More seriously, relations between men and women underwent a profound shift towards greater equality. Of course, feminism did not have to wait for 1968 to exist (it is as old as women, as old as humanity) or to make some headway in favourable circumstances. But 1968 gave an impulse to movements throughout the world which, though sometimes mixing steps back with steps forward, helped to spread a sense that feminist demands were both legitimate and necessary. This is indeed an essential dimension of the socialist future, without which the project of world socialism is unthinkable. Not long ago, the main currents of historical socialism were not convinced of that. The combination of this change with what is known as 'sexual liberation' – that is, the revolution in family and personal relations – is a much more complicated matter than pioneers such as Wilhelm Reich thought in their time.

With regard to political action, 1968 saw the beginning of what came to be known as 'third worldism'. Disappointed that the European proletariat had proven less spontaneously revolutionary than they had imagined, many young people naively, though with noble motivations, transferred their messianic expectations to the peasants of the Andes, India or Africa. Third world activists, for their part, have never been 'third worldist'. Many could be nationalist and little more, but others were critical of the national-bourgeois project, even of the populist variant thrown up by a strong and popular liberation struggle. Third worldism was a strictly Western movement, whose militants were not usually very critical of the left wing of national liberation – that is, of the very populism in which they had invested their hopes. Moreover, this tendency to populism later induced many of them to take up in a rather undiscriminating way the defence of ethnic, religious and other 'communitarian' rights. Aligned at this level with postmodernism, third worldists often ended their career in the service of humanitarian organizations and NGOs, easily manipulated by the strategies of imperialism and neoliberalism. Yet Western third worldism did also have a positive side, in so far as it had the potential to strengthen an internationalist awareness that what happens in the countries of the periphery – which contain three-quarters of the world's population – is important for the future of humanity as a whole, whether it is a question of the effects of capitalist expansion or of social struggles against its devastating consequences. In this way, third worldism helped to correct the principal deformation generated by imperialism: that is, the idea that only what happens in advanced capitalist societies is relevant for the shaping of the future.

EIGHT

Director of the Institute for Economic Planning and Development, 1970–80

The UN assessment to which I referred earlier had reached the conclusion that IDEP's main role in Africa should be to analyse planning and development strategies and experiences, and to gear its education programme to this specific knowledge. This was exactly the position I had upheld in the commission responsible for setting up the institute, and which I had recalled in my letter of resignation. So, when my letter was found in the UN 'briefing' folder, it was normal that the assessment team should think of me as a suitable person to take over. Philippe de Seynes, whom I had not yet met, was given the job of contacting me.

I hesitated at first, unsure whether I could really implement the necessary changes in view of all the weaknesses of the UN system that I was beginning to know from experience. But I was in a strong negotiating position, so why not give it a try? I met Philippe de Seynes in New York for an interview, and found a charming man with all the qualities I described above. We were able to discuss frankly and cordially, and from that day we became good friends. I reminded him that I had certain views which I would never give up, that I would continue to express them in writing, and that this would probably not be to everyone's liking. 'It doesn't matter,' he said. 'Someone without opinions cannot play the role expected of him in a position like that. Look at the Economic Commission for Latin America

(ECLA): Raúl Prebisch doesn't think twice about surrounding himself with intellectuals who are in opposition to their governments, some of them even political refugees, like the Brazilians Celso Furtado and Fernando Henrique Cardoso. ECLA's success is due to them, and to the academic freedom inside it.'

So, I agreed in principle to take the job, although I feared that the 'joke' – the word I actually used – would only last a few months. First I had to convene the IDEP board of governors, which was chaired by the executive secretary of the UN Economic Commission for Africa (ECA), and submit to them my proposals. I did not think they would accept them, and I had no intention of wangling some kind of half-hearted agreement. 'I won't try to blackmail them,' I said. 'And I won't let them think I'll resign if the meeting doesn't go my way. We'll see. So, Monsieur de Seynes, please agree not to be surprised if you receive my resignation letter in three months' time.' 'I'll take the risk,' he replied, 'but you'll see it's not much of one.' 'They'll have my hide in the end, though.' 'It'll take a long time, much longer than you think.' And history proved him right.

It was also necessary, for the United Nations, that Senegal should accept my appointment. President Senghor was therefore duly informed of it. I was not sure whether Senghor – who is reputed to have a good memory for people – actually remembered me. Probably not, as I had been only one of the many students he had received in Paris. He might have been told of the things I was teaching at Dakar University. But by whom? And what had they said? In any event, Senghor clearly expressed his support. At the time – it must have been May–June 1970 – I was in Paris for the exam season at Vincennes. Senghor therefore called in Isabelle, who was just finishing the school year in Dakar, and told her he just wanted her to persuade me to take the job. 'Women,' he said, 'always have a decisive influence on what their husbands decide. And Samir Amin meets all the necessary conditions for this post.' I found out later that Senghor knew exactly who I was. He is a cultured man who reads, and properly argued ideas did not frighten him, even when he did not agree with them. So, in August 1970 I returned to Dakar and reported for work to the Institute.

The spread of IDEP's influence in Africa

Soon after my arrival, I rang Gardiner and said I would like to meet him to tell him of my intentions. 'I know what they are, you've already expressed them', he replied. 'Okay,' I went on, 'you know the principles, but the ways of implementing them also have to be spelled out, and I'd appreciate your views as we have to hear what the board of governors has to say.' It was a polite exchange, but not enough to tell me whether Gardiner had been sincere in backing my nomination in New York.

I made a tour of the Institute and got to know the staff. Kwame Amoa had been recruited after my departure and was already thinking of leaving, but I immediately realized that he had some great qualities. Behind a phlegmatic, English-style appearance, this young Ghanaian was intelligent, sharp, thoughtful and progressive in his immediate reactions. I therefore at once thought of a first innovation in the work of the Institute: namely, the creation of a post of deputy director that he would occupy. I Egyptian and officially French-speaking, he West African and English-speaking: it would be good for balance and representativeness at IDEP. It would also ensure a degree of continuity, since each of us would have to travel that much less frequently. Finally, I could see that he had considerable organizational abilities – more than abilities, in fact, the temperament of a high-quality diplomat, who knew to perfection how to draft proposals, to negotiate, to get the gist of something, and to identify which concessions it would be worth making. We became very close friends, and I said of him that he could have been the foreign minister of a major power. None of the directors before me had imagined having a deputy; they had thought like good little autocrats, seeing their colleagues only as rivals eager to take their place.

I did not know the members of the board of governors, which was elected by a 'Conference of African Planners' that met every two years at ECA headquarters in Addis Ababa. Although the relevant ministers were supposed to attend this conference, it was in reality a gathering of development administrators, varying from insignificant nobodies to high-quality civil servants. It was not necessarily the best who were chosen for the IDEP board, and the rule requiring linguistic balance and representation of all four regions of Africa (North, West, Central and East–Southern) complicated matters and created considerable scope for manipulation. Gardiner, probably by temperament, baulked at that kind of thing, but later Adedeji was not so loath to get involved in it. Anyway, I lost no time worrying about it, having decided on principle not to try 'cultivating friends' among the board of governors. Boards in my experience have had a heterogeneous composition, in the image of administrations in Africa and elsewhere. They generally contain some open-minded and competent members, with whom it is possible to argue, but also some eternal 'daily allowance hunters' who get elected so that they can have an opportunity to travel. I even remember one Libyan who came to Dakar only to drink in three days what he had been deprived of for a year in Tripoli. He was drunk from the moment he arrived to the moment he left.

In the end, Gardiner supported my proposals without reservations, but perhaps also without enthusiasm. The board of governors passed them without a problem.

With the governors' approval, I introduced the idea of a 'consultative academic board'. I thought it not only useful but necessary to be able to draw on the views of well-informed people; that is the kind of temperament I have. But the board of governors could not serve that function, and so I submitted a list of names to Gardiner. He approved this, but added that they were too important and would never come. They all came, however: people like Dudley Seers, director of the Institute of Development Studies at the new and modern University of Sussex; Celso Furtado, who gave us the benefit of the knowledge he had accumulated in Latin America and at ECLA; the Nigerian Onitiri, one of the longest-serving academics in Africa; Ismail Abdallah; and Charles Prou, director of the French Centre for the Study of Economic Programmes (CEPE). Do I need to add that the last two, though friends of mine, were not cut out to be anyone's accomplices? Their opinions, criticisms and suggestions were as free as anyone else's.

The basic choice was to make IDEP a front-ranking centre for African theory and reflection; to take away from foreign 'technical assistance' or 'cooperation' agencies the monopoly of thinking about Africa. This meant emphasizing research and creating special teaching programmes to relay and continue debates.

There were various formulas to achieve this. We offered quite long courses (one or two years), which could tackle issues in depth and associate students as apprentices in research projects, enabling them to acquire the tools of the trade. One of the main innovations was the holding of a 4–6 week programme of seminars outside Dakar. This had a number of advantages: in particular, each seminar could be attended by as many as 50 to 100 students at relatively little expense (the seminars were monolingual and most participants were already living in the country in question); and the operation helped to build closer links with the local universities that shared the responsibility for the seminars, and with the government departments in charge of development. IDEP thus frequently played the role of catalyser and shock absorber between mutually dismissive academics and civil servants, and between different political forces and theoretical currents who otherwise had very little contact with each other.

More than thirty of these seminar courses were organized during the 1970s, in a total of twenty-five African capitals, thus giving the Institute a continent-wide reputation. Each of these operations was a real event in the country concerned, long remembered and discussed by those who took part in it. As for myself, I have a sufficiently clear memory of ten (those held in Algiers, Bamako, Cotonou, Ibadan, Douala, Brazzaville, Kinshasa, Mogadishu, Dar es Salaam and Tananarive) to be able to speak about them in greater detail.

To fulfil these tasks, we naturally had to recruit the minimum staff at the necessary level of competence. We did more or less manage to attract enough intellectuals known by their published writings for there to be no need to present them here. The team gradually fleshed out and, at one moment or another, included: Norman Girvan (Jamaica), Oscar Braun (Argentina), Héctor Silva Michelena (Venezuela), Fawzy Mansour, Naguib Hedayat and Hassan Khalil (Egypt), Samba Sow (Senegal), Jacques Bugnicourt and Duhamel (France), Bernard Founou (Cameroon), Cadman

Atta Mills (Ghana), Jagdish Saigal (India), Marc Franco (Belgium: with a fine career later in the EU), Anthony Obeng (Ghana) and Joseph van den Reysen (Congo). Hassan Khalil – who was the spitting image of Nasser: tall, brown-skinned, wide nose, booming laughter – later turned to literature and wrote some interesting memoirs. We also managed to strengthen the team with a number of 'missionaries', either funded by the French *Coopération* (e.g. Pierre Philippe Rey, Catherine Coquery-Vidrovitch, André Farhi, Francine Kane) or invited by us as a result of one of our seminars. When we had the funds we allocated some of the latter to special research programmes: for example, the two Guineans Baldé and Kouyaté, the Malian Lamine Gakou, the Sudanese Hamid Gariballah, the two Senegalese Abdousalam Kane and Alioune Sall, the Kenyan Abdalla Bujra and the Malawian Thandika Mkandawire. A young American, Barbara Stuckey, who came with a grant from Los Angeles University and was highly critical of the education system and society in the United States, proved able to give us a helping hand. Despite our duties, Amoa and I did not give up teaching; I would never have accepted the idea that one can 'run' an institute without direct knowledge of the problems: that is, without living contact with students and active involvement in research teams.

As I had learned at the SEEF in France, the best research programmes are those which the people in charge of them freely define and carry out. The team therefore served as a structure in which proposals and voluntary commitments could be discussed, and debates could be organized at various stages of the work in progress. If a few individuals may possibly have used this as a way of shirking responsibility, it probably produced better results than any authoritarian division of tasks. The evidence is the number of papers written – more than four hundred, some of book length – and the launch of a publication series with Anthropos in French and the University of Dar es Salaam in English.

The growing influence of IDEP led to a greater demand for consultative visits to the Institute, both from governments and from African regional institutions or transnational third world organizations (the Group of 77, the non-aligned countries). Unfortunately, we could respond to only a small fraction of even the most serious requests; neither our finances nor our human resources enabled us to do more without unbalancing IDEP's activity, which we wanted to be as well integrated as possible. Yet some of these missions were too important politically for us to turn them down, as they allowed us to hope that we could make a little real impact on political forces that had chosen in principle a progressive path. I shall return to these points later.

I had always thought that one of the main priorities was to break the isolation in which colonialism had encircled Africa. With this in mind, we organized the first two major encounters between intellectuals from Africa and Latin America (Dakar, 1972) and from Africa and Asia (Tananarive, 1974). For many participants, it was the first opportunity they had had to debate the big issues facing the third world; at most, a few had caught a glimpse of one another at international gatherings not necessarily focused on their own concerns. Moreover, many of the Latin Americans and Asians were making their first trip to Africa. I will spare the reader a list of all the names, most of them well known. The Latin American *dependentista* school was represented by its leading figures: Fernando Henrique Cardoso, Ruy Mário Marini, Theotônio dos Santos, Pablo González Casanova, André Gunder Frank, Aníbal Quijano, Gérard Pierre-Charles. Cardoso had never before set foot on the continent, which after all is not unimportant for the country whose president he became, Brazil. It was the first time anyone had invited him. He arrived in Dakar on a flight from Morocco, suffering from ferocious indigestion brought on by dates (a fruit whose great nutritional value he had never realized before). I don't think he will ever forget that indigestion, which we nevertheless managed to treat. After the symposium, we went with his wife to see the vestiges of the old colonial settlement at Saint-Louis, and to admire the birds in Le Juch.

In Tananarive, the Southeast Asians – especially the Indonesians and Malaysians – were surprised to find themselves almost at home, whereas the Africans heard for the first time a panoply of the best names in Indian social science.

The expanding activities of IDEP required more than the regulation budget funded by African states and the UNDP. We managed to collect more than 50 per cent of the sums promised by African governments – a little over $600,000. This was a higher percentage than for financial commitments to the UN itself, and much higher than for African official undertakings to any other African or international organization. But this did not prevent certain unsavoury types – Doo Kingue (whom the Americans propelled to the head of the UNDP), Bertin Borna (resident UN representative in Dakar) and a few others like Paul Kaya – from waxing demagogic over the 'mere 50 per cent'. When I left IDEP these critics were able to call the shots, and the percentage fell close to zero.

At the same time, Philippe de Seynes and Gardiner gave me carte blanche to seek out extra sources of funding, and I managed to collect almost enough to double the IDEP budget. The French *Coopération* people were really disappointing and have not changed since: their narrow regulations and pretty chauvinistic vision meant that they never went beyond the funding of French teachers and researchers. It is hard to tell which gains more from that kind of overseas aid: the institution on the receiving end of French expertise or France itself, which thereby increases its stock of knowledge about foreign countries. I had better luck with the Italians (who agreed to fund a research programme set up by Baldé and Kouyaté) and especially the Swedes, whose recently founded International Development Cooperation Agency subsequently displayed exemplary generosity in relation to our projects.

The IDEP administration supported our efforts with an efficiency for which I am sincerely grateful. UN institutions in the third world paid salaries considerably higher than the going rate in the local civil service and private sector, which enabled them to recruit high-quality local staff often relatively more competent than the managerial personnel. This was the case at IDEP, where I discovered that the best were 'banished to the basement floor', as I often told them. Marcelle Huchard, a first-class administrative assistant who could have answered most of my mail without even consulting me, or composed a draft on the basis of a couple of dictated sentences, found herself doing nothing but typing. No doubt the 'bosses' were afraid of intelligence, as a colleague with such talents would have understood what they were up to. And, when Marcelle Huchard left IDEP, she had no difficulty finding a job in Geneva that allowed her to go further in her career. Her successor, Geneviève Colin, had similar qualities, and I could say the same about many of the IDEP support services. The Algerian Madani, who was in charge of organizing travel, ran his section outstandingly well and kept costs down without ever having to be pressed.

The administrative expenditure was certainly high, largely because UN pay scales, bilingual translation and interpretation requirements and my insistence on a well-stocked library meant that there was little objective scope for cost-cutting. I thought that there could have been economies in some areas, however. The unwieldy UN hierarchy keeps multiplying the number of administrative and financial jobs, and its accounting system is one of the most pointlessly complicated one could imagine: this does not exactly make it easier to carry out the indispensable work of auditing, but it does fuel bureaucratic guerrilla warfare when the circumstances are right! I therefore asked Gustave Massiah, whom I knew to be hugely competent in these matters, to look into the way IDEP was organized. I did not implement the sensible proposals that he put to me, however, as I immediately realized that I would be leaving myself open to attack on ground favourable to the enemy. It was not the ground on which I had chosen to force my opponents to fight.

For the same reasons, I soon gave up my desire to democratize the management. Absences were common in the purely female typing pool, often justifiably because of problems to do with family, children or health. So, one day I called them together and said: 'There is no need for me to sign you off. Anyway, I have no objective way of telling how serious a request for absence is. You are better placed than me to establish free collective discipline among yourselves. All I ask is that the work is done. It's up to you to share it out.' A fortnight later, the women collectively asked me to reintroduce the hierarchy and all the permissions and monitoring paperwork.

I did not imagine that IDEP alone could serve all the functions of a major research centre. It was therefore necessary to take initiatives and to create more specialized, complementary institutions. The IDEP director was in a good position to do this, and I branched out in three directions.

In 1972 I was invited to the conference in Stockholm that really began to raise awareness about global environmental problems. I immediately grasped their importance and in 1974, having negotiated for the Swedes to support a first trial programme for Africa, made Jacques Bugnicourt responsible for its implementation in Dakar. It was he who had the idea of calling the programme Environment for Development in Africa (ENDA), and with his good connections in the French *Coopération* establishment he secured funding for a core support team (Mataillet, Guibert, Melle Mottin, Langley and, later, Mhlanga) who soon got the project up and running. In keeping with my temperament, I gave Bugnicourt carte blanche to negotiate the ways and means of implementing his programme. Legally, however, the ENDA programme came under IDEP until 1977, when, as I had originally intended, it became an independent institution.

It was the same story for CODESRIA, the Council for the Development of Social Science Research in Africa. The original idea was to create something along the lines of CLACSO in Latin America, whose outstanding executive secretary, the Argentinean Enrique Oteiza, had become a personal friend of mine. I used the opportunities provided by IDEP's activities, especially our national seminars, to bring together the founding nucleus of the institution. But a minimal secretariat was required, and there was no money to support one. I therefore accepted the responsibility of executive secretary for the five difficult years when the operation was getting under way. I recruited two African intellectuals to help us: Abdalla Bujra, a Kenyan sociologist I had met in Dar es Salaam, and Thandika Mkandawire, a bright young Malawian student I had met in Sweden. They coped with things perfectly. Bujra and then Mkandawire were the two executive secretaries who put CODESRIA on the rails and won it the confidence of high-quality African researchers. Twenty years later, CODESRIA awarded me the 'golden baobab' – which adorns my office at the Third

World Forum – in recognition of my role as founder of the institution. I am very appreciative of this recognition. At the same time, I helped Bujra and the chairman of the CODESRIA management committee (the Ghanaian professor Tshumbariba) to negotiate an agreement with Senegal for the institution to be located in Dakar. It was not a straightforward matter, as other countries were in the running. President Senghor asked his prime minister of the time, Abdou Diouf, to meet with us and give a favourable response to our application.

I will say more in the next chapter about the creation of the Third World Forum. For the moment, I will just point out that I took the initiative together with colleagues and public figures from Asia, Africa and Latin America; we managed to get Salvador Allende to invite us to Santiago to finalize the project (barely three months before the Pinochet coup). The founding congress of the Forum took place in 1975 in Karachi, where one of our members had obtained funding from the National Bank of Pakistan. I will also come back to the audience I had with Olof Palme (in the same year, I think) and to the invaluable financial support from Sweden's International Cooperation Development Agency.

The 1970s were the high point for IDEP: I can say, without false modesty, that its name was known and respected all over Africa. For that very reason, however, I knew that things could not last.

The US administration was fundamentally opposed to us, as it was – and is – to all liberation forces in the third world. However minor an institution like IDEP might be on the global chessboard, it had to be destroyed. For American strategy never neglects to do what needs to be done, on every front major or minor.

The third-party positional warfare began in 1972, through mediocre or (corrupt) African bureaucrats prepared to play the CIA tune for the sake of their UN career. My counter-strategy – to get African governments on our side – was an application of the Chinese formula: 'states seek independence, nations liberation, and peoples revolution'. The idea, then, was a struggle to win respect for the independence of African governments. Once this had been defined as the battlefield (which meant giving up the secondary terrains I mentioned earlier), my strategy was simple: to keep governments in the picture. This did not mean reporting in detail all the enemy's intrigues, but, on the contrary, treating them with contempt and making our own activities as transparent as possible to the top authorities, including heads of state, that we knew to be sensitive to the independence argument and capable of understanding the positive significance of what we were doing.

But then the enemy was given an opportunity to intensify the offensive. Gardiner left the ECA secretariat, and his successor, Adebayo Adedeji, was an autocratic and greedy young wolf. He immediately stepped up the guerrilla warfare, using the 'head of administration' (whose career depended on him) to undermine our work and flood us with 'memos'. I refused to fight on this terrain and did not even reply to the 'memos', thereby forcing Adedeji to come into the open. In 1978 he had the supervision of IDEP transferred from the UN to the ECA – that is, to himself – then set about manipulating the Conference of African Planners and the administrative board of the Institute so that they adopted two disastrous resolutions. The first did away with the national seminars and kept only the course in Dakar, supposedly in order to make it stronger. As a result, the amount of teaching at the Institute, measured in student/months – which had nearly doubled between 1970 and 1977 – fell back to its initial level by 1979, the year I gave up the directorship, and (as far as I am aware) has never risen above it again. The second resolution eliminated all the supplementary budgets under special funding agreements, and transferred responsibility for the negotiation of agreements from the IDEP director to the ECA. Of course, the ECA did not negotiate anything after that, or anyway never obtained any funding. I did save something from the wreckage: ENDA, CODESRIA and the Third World Forum could be detached from IDEP and had the means to establish their autonomy. I and (to Adedeji's surprise) Amoa resigned in May 1980.

The three-month 'joke' had lasted ten years. Adedeji's subsequent careeer was not brilliant: when he was forced to leave the ECA secretariat, he tried to find a position in a major UN agency such as the Industrial

Development Organization. But he got nothing. Then he rediscovered his African patriotic language. When I came across him years later, I put it to him directly: 'Okay, so you didn't want me around. But why did you choose Essam Montasser, a fellow-Egyptian, to succeed me? Anyone could see from a mile off that he was stupid and had an unstable character. You're smart enough to realize that. So, in choosing him, you killed off IDEP. Why?' And Adedeji sadly confessed: 'I got a couple of phone calls that forced me into it: one from the US embassy in Cairo, giving me an order beyond any discussion; and one from President Sadat's office begging me to do it.' 'So,' I said, 'the Americans make the decisions and the Egyptians or Nigerians carry them out – that's what we should conclude.' Adedeji remained silent.

The ten years as IDEP director were important for me as much as for IDEP. This fifth stage in my professional life – after the Mwasasa in Cairo, the SEEF in Paris, the Malian planning department and my years of teaching – may not have changed my personality very much, but it did provide an opportunity for it to unfurl. I am certainly an active person by nature, resolute, wilful, even stubborn by character. Isabelle, Amoa and my colleagues have all noticed this, and many of the errors of judgement I may have made are attributable to this tendency. The people close to me have certainly helped me to avoid worse mistakes. This said, however, I think that on balance my personality had some effect in serving the cause we wanted to defend through IDEP. This is the general view in Africa: IDEP's influence was great throughout the 1970s and altogether disappeared after 1980. Fortunately the Third World Forum picked up the baton. We had been consciously preparing for this.

I conducted IDEP's affairs as one wages a war. The strategic objective must be clearly defined, and that is always a political question. For us the objective was to create an independent centre in Africa for critical thought. It was then necessary to choose the field of battle, and to force the enemy to fight there rather than on ground of his own choosing. We therefore had to identify the main enemy: not the 'UN system', far from it, but the hegemonist diplomacy through which the United States sought to make the UN bow to its own objectives. Both inside and outside the system, the

Americans certainly had a number of allies, but above all people prepared to do their bidding – more incidental than fundamental enemies, as far as we were concerned. Our task was to strengthen the barriers against the enemy offensive, to build effective alliances with anyone whose interests were being harmed by the Americans. In other circumstances, I might well have been a military person. I like reading about the art of war. And as a young man I was very fond of chess, although I never found the time (which I would have considered wasted) to try to excel at it.

It may be that warfare develops authoritarian forms of behaviour. But I was protected against the worst such dangers, not only by my ideological and theoretical options but also by my personal temperament. I like equality, I like to be surrounded by friends and colleagues in whom I can place all my trust, I like to hear other people's points of view and to discuss them. All those who have worked with me – especially employees of the institutions for which I have been responsible – can testify that I have never resorted to even mildly repressive methods. The whole idea disgusts me. I am not able to do that, even if it means that things don't go as well as they might. Moreover, perhaps it is due to a certain optimism in my view of human nature, but I think that democratic tolerance generally pays; it makes things work better, or at least no worse.

For these reasons, the prototype of the institutional autocrat – to which real people all too often conform, not only in Africa but just as much elsewhere – inspires in me total contempt. A pathological attachment to the external manifestations of power – prestigious office, large car, and so on – has never tempted me in any way. I see such things more as a bothersome constraint.

During the 1970s President Senghor granted me an annual audience. It was not to talk about IDEP, which only featured once in our conversation: 'How's IDEP?' – 'It's going well, *monsieur le president*.' Senghor usually wanted to talk about political matters. What do you think of the situation in the Middle East (after 1973 or after 1977)? I gave him my analysis, and he did not conceal the points on which he disagreed. Sometimes we had a conversation about culture, which for him was an important, decisive dimension

– perhaps too much so for a politician. But sometimes there were also funny things that testified to a mischievous mind at work. One day, pointing at the safe in his room, he asked me what I thought was inside. 'State secrets', I said. 'No, money: piles of banknotes. This is what I use them for. When certain people come here, I casually open the safe and measure their greed by the intensity with which they look at it.' Another time he told me that when Asian ambassadors had something to say, whether pleasant or not, they usually came straight out with it, whereas most African ambassadors (and Arabs were no better) said only what they thought he wanted to hear. 'If I then remain impassive, they get into a flap and can't find their words.' I laughed and told Senghor that, though he was certainly right, the real explanation was that the Asians represented real political forces of one kind or another, whereas the African ambassadors represented nothing at all. 'No,' he retorted. 'That's Marxism; I know that's what you think. For me, Africans and Arabs are chronic waverers; it's our cultural weakness.' On another occasion, when my audience followed one with some Nigerians accompanied by Alioune Diop,[44] Senghor said to me: 'Do you know who those were before you?' 'Yes, they were obviously the committee in charge of preparing the Negro Arts Festival in Lagos.' 'Right, and do you know what they've done? They collected $100 million in the USA for the festival and put it all in their own pockets; then they came to me and begged for some more. I told them: look, the festival may cost 10 million (the one in Dakar cost less, even with all the waste). You could have taken 90 and left 10 for the festival! No one would have said a thing.'

The story of the safe reminds me of another. I had inherited an office safe from the previous administration at IDEP, whose director I imagine to have been the type who considers each of his letters 'confidential'. The Egyptian ambassador Naguib Kadri dropped by from time to time 'to drink a bad coffee with you' (in fact, a Nescafé), so one day I repeated what Senghor had told me about his safe and added: 'My safe has no secrets and no money inside, but it does have one important use as it allows me to check every morning that my memory is still functioning. The combination is a complicated business, and I have jotted it down on a piece of paper in an unlocked drawer of my desk. That might make a spy's task easier one day. Anyway, every morning I open the safe without looking at the piece of paper. And, to have a serious reason for opening it, I've put the tin of Nescafé in the safe. There's nothing else.'

My work at IDEP also led me to develop my organizational capacities. I am an orderly person by nature, almost to the point of mania. I like to classify things, logically, so that I can find everything at once and put it back in its proper place: whether one of the books that cover our apartment walls in Paris (not a patch on Maxime Rodinson, by the way, who had bookshelves running down the middle of his rooms) or an office file. But, if you want to work quickly and efficiently as the director of an institution, you have to devise the most suitable way of organizing things. No one can do it for you. Various organizational 'techniques' are not worth much, although they make up a large chunk of fashionable American-style training systems.

Another thing that IDEP made me more familiar with was the UN system, a not insignificant dimension of contemporary international life.

The UN machine

The modern world is made up of interdependent nations, in a context of inequality that has been growing constantly worse for the last two centuries. To devise and achieve a different organization and a different interdependence of societies, one which removes the polarization inherent in the expansion of global capitalism, is one of the major tasks of human civilization, if its body and soul are not to perish in the material and moral devastation that capitalist polarization inevitably produces.

The victory over fascism at the end of the Second World War and the rise of national liberation movements in Asia and Africa were the background to the creation of the United Nations, the first attempt in human history to organize international relations on a global level (although it would take another fifteen years for virtually the whole planet to be covered). The founding of the UN was thus a positive historical development;

the United Nations is necessary, and if it did not exist it would be necessary to invent it.

My vision of the UN is therefore essentially political, unlike that of most who have operated under its banner and seen it as a kind of 'pool of expertise' that certain nations place at the disposal of others. That vision, corresponding to the 'global village' discourse, has always struck me as simply ridiculous, because it ignores the crucial dimension of polarization generated by the logic of the system.

Globalization is not a new phenomenon, and I was doubtless not the first to take an interest in the issue before it started to capture the headlines. But this dimension was already present in my earliest analysis of actually existing capitalism (my 1957 thesis). I have always thought that the most important unit for analysis was the world system, not the sub-systems that make it up. Anyone who remains confined to the framework of a single country – whether the USA or Belgium, China or Somalia – will not really be able to grasp the dynamics of change even at the level of his or her own society.

To be sure, this problem will not be solved tomorrow, for it implies fundamental changes in every aspect of social existence, in every part of the world, which can only be described as 'socialism on a world scale'. Such changes will necessarily entail, at some point, a supranational perspective that goes beyond mere relations among nations; nor is it impossible that this requirement will first make itself felt at the level of large regions, as the construction of Europe might illustrate. But, as things stand today, the United Nations does not provide even the embryo of a worldwide supranational framework. It is still a strictly inter-national organization. If it remains this indefinitely, there is a danger that its founding project will disappear from view: that is, the organization of the world within a humanist perspective. The UN can help the world develop in that necessary and desirable direction only if its components – the various nations – pave the way by transforming themselves.

There are many obstacles to such an evolution, both locally and at the level of the world system. The main immediate obstacle, however, is United

States hegemonism, which is no longer based on overwhelming economic and technological superiority – as it was in the period after 1945 – but rather on military strength backed up by the effects of neoliberal globalization and a vulgar 'culture' of capitalism expressed in Anglo-American jargon.

In my view, then, the UN is not a useless, contemptible institution which, because of its generality, interferes with the real relations (of force) among nations. But nor is it the kernel of a 'global village', that naive idea popular in some circles that skates over the reality of the mechanisms of polarization. The main enemy, American hegemonism, exerts all its might to subjugate every country in the world, in varying degrees and by suitably adjusted means, and to organize the international order as it sees fit. This involves instrumentalizing the United Nations, and the struggle to defend that organization and its mission in the world is therefore synonymous with the struggle against American hegemonism. If I have dwelt a little here on these general points, it is because they constitute the lesson I drew from IDEP's extremely modest battle away from the central arena. The US administration, for its part, does not overlook a single detail in its unrelenting struggle for hegemony.

On my travels, at separate times and places, my path crossed with those of two fairly high-ranking black American civil servants. Probably without knowing what the other had done, each insisted on striking up a conversation with me. I was distrustful in principle and decided to remain almost silent. Then I realized that it was they who wanted to talk, with the most nonchalant of airs, about how the CIA was infiltrating the UN and monitoring its activities. As black people, they were evidently filled with remorse at serving an openly racist state – whose top officials concealed neither their contempt of Africans nor their admiration for apartheid – and each felt some sympathy for IDEP's activity.

The CIA has intelligence agents in every department of the UN and in the mission of every country where it operates. These agents are required to file reports at frequent intervals, which are centralized in the huge US mission at the United Nations in New York. It is a typically American system, imposing heavy quantitative norms similar to the number of pages that an academic has to publish every year. For my part, I think that too much information – inevitably including a lot of trivia – has a negative impact on efficiency. But, well, that is not my problem. The people in charge of the US mission use the information they receive to formulate instructions for 'friendly' non-American officials at the UN. The system therefore requires the deployment of quite a dense network of 'friends', whom I would prefer to call executive agents. One can imagine that the incompetence or even corruption of such agents is a significant quality when it comes to their CIA-backed promotion. I have no illusions on this score concerning a large number of African careerists, particularly those in positions of command (and there is no reason why this should not be true of people from other parts of the world).

I am not revealing anything that is not already known by every ambassador to the UN, with the possible exception of a few congenital idiots. So, why are there not scandals and protests from other governments? An answer requires us to analyse the attitude of various governments to American hegemonism.

The majority of developed capitalist countries have accepted US leadership and are therefore quite happy about the activities of the CIA. Britain made this historic choice in 1945, and no major political force there questions it. The same is true of the other countries with British roots – Canada (now an external province of the United States in many respects), Australia and New Zealand. Germany and Japan have taken long-term strategic decisions that point in the same direction, limiting themselves to US-tolerated regional expansionism (towards Eastern and Southern Europe in the case of Germany, and Southeast Asia in that of Japan) and otherwise, on global issues, steering in Washington's wake. Tokyo, in particular, considers its dependence on the USA an unavoidable fact of life, since it would otherwise be disarmed in relation to China and even Korea.

The situation has consistently allowed Washington to instrumentalize the United Nations, not without a certain arrogance in such matters as its late payment of UN dues. Things are even worse today, especially as Western diplomats have joined in the US-orchestrated campaign to denigrate the international organization in favour of NATO.

France is probably the only Western country that sometimes kicks over the traces. The 'cultural' sensitivity of French speakers is not a satisfactory explanation for this, even if the 'anti-French' media try to make their job easier by claiming otherwise. Up to now, however, this contradiction has remained secondary, in the sense that the solidarity of the triad (US + EU + Japan) vis-à-vis the third world is still decisive. Hence the irresolution of French foreign policy, further complicated by the constraints of the European Union.

It may be said that, apart from these medium-sized powers, other developed countries have been active within the UN system: the Scandinavians, among others. In terms of financial contributions and positions of responsibility, the weight of these countries within the UN system is indeed great. Do they exploit its potential to the full? The answer to this question is simple. I have often heard it said that top officials from these countries are 'naive' and tend to indulge in 'wishful thinking' about the role of the UN; or else that their Protestant culture makes them inclined to side with the hegemonist policies of the central American power. In my view, such explanations are at best highly superficial, but also largely false and misleading. Sweden, in particular, has taken courageous positions in support of third world struggles, sometimes in frontal opposition to the United States. It welcomed American deserters during the Vietnam war (as no other Western country dared to do); it supported the liberation struggles in the Portuguese colonies, at a time when no member of the Atlantic alliance was prepared to do it. I rather think, therefore, that some of the countries in question have made a strategic decision in principle to back the United Nations, perhaps because, given their modest size, they feel most vulnerable in a situation of international chaos. This decision of theirs seems to me correct and positive. It does not mean that the positions they derive from it are necessarily effective, nor that they are making the most of their presence within the UN system.

Third world countries were very active within the UN system throughout the Bandung period, and especially between 1960 and 1975. Who does not remember those meetings of the General Assembly in September–October of every year, when leading statesmen and famous journalists used to gather in the lobby of the UN building in New York? Nowadays, the only people one sees there are minor officials and insignificant reporters. The diplomacy of the non-aligned countries and the Group of 77 used to force discussion of all the real issues of our time, from the nature of the international economic order (and the creation of UNCTAD in 1964) to the political intervention of the major powers in the affairs of the third world. I had the opportunity to attend several of these General Assembly sessions, as an adviser to some of the most active non-aligned states. I learned a lot there from well-briefed officials and experts, and I made a lot of new friends. The weight of third world diplomacy in those days helped to temper Washington's ambitions, despite the presence of its African and other agents within the UN apparatus.

There were a few amusing episodes during my visits to New York. Once, I had gone to see Philippe de Seynes and left Isabelle waiting for me in one of the foyers. We had not noticed that in fact it was the antechamber of the Security Council, nor that the Security Council was in session for a debate on Palestinian terrorism. Isabelle was wearing quite a bulky overcoat. Suddenly six policemen touting at least fifteen guns and other devices advanced on her, with a plain clothes cop in the rear. 'Hands up! Name?' 'Amin,' she said. 'Are you an Arab?' 'No, but my husband is.' 'Don't move!' Obviously they were convinced she had a bomb beneath her overcoat, perhaps to throw at Golda Meir. With her kohl make-up, henna-dyed hair and dark complexion, she certainly looked the part of a Palestinian terrorist. 'What are you doing here?' 'Waiting for my husband.' 'Where is he?' 'He's gone to see de Seynes.' The plain clothes cop stepped to one side and rang Philippe's secretary: 'Does Mr Amin have a wife?' To which she replied that she had no idea. 'Ah, ha!' 'Please check again', Isabelle calmly insisted, her hands still in the air. So the secretary got in a panic and burst into the room where de Seynes and I were chatting. 'Are you married?' she asked me. 'That's a strange question. Yes, I am. Why?' And the story ended happily enough, as they did not shoot Isabelle. You never know with those anti-terrorist squads. They're not always so intelligent.

Another time, I found myself attending a session of a UN international body that was being addressed by a succession of speakers. The 'distinguished delegate' (as the chairman put it) from New Zealand thought it a smart idea to speak of the 'new nations' of Asia and Africa. In the panoply of Chinese, Indians, Egyptians, Iranians and others among whom I was sitting, we exchanged a number of smiles. The speaker did not understand why, I am sure. The story seems almost too good to be true, but what it reveals is not only the arrogance of Westerners, and especially their overseas offspring, but also the stupidity of 'old' Europeans in relation to the new worlds (the United States and its copies in Australia and New Zealand). Who has not heard a declaration to the effect that America shows the future to Europe, that it is the beacon illuminating the path of progress? Who dares to think that, on the contrary, it is more likely to be the Americans who eventually Europeanize themselves, as their relatively new country matures?

Whatever the value of third world diplomacy at the time, its role in the running of the UN was largely cancelled by the activities of the Americans and their 'friends'. The latter, whose position in the executive hierarchy seemed to depend on their mediocrity, or on what the CIA had on them in its files, never had a function other than the one assigned to them by their bosses. There is no point in naming names: what I said earlier should immediately suggest a few. Many of them certainly looked the part.

I am referring to their crudeness, of course, which I personally experienced at a few of the functions to celebrate someone's passing visit: boorishness, raucous laughter, grovelling formulations ('the King's cabinet has decided', 'the President has determined…' – apropos some decision whose only significance was to advance A's career). 'What else can I do?' they asked in turn – not that the idea of thinking or acting differently ever entered their head. 'I do my job and explain to B that he is a victim of the decision favouring A' – even though the actual decision was taken by a brilliant 'senior official' of the UN, not by the king or president in question. 'Next time I'll try to make it up to him.' In other words, it was not the cynicism of a decadent prince, but the spinelessness of a lackey – not even puffed up enough to be arrogant, as any half-intelligent British graduate would be. Dull, completely dull and coarse. And often horribly ugly – not the ugliness that nature distributes at random, but a physical ugliness corresponding, as it were, to the individual's soul. Truly dreadful. Back in the nineteenth century, poor old Cesare Lombroso used to seek in vain to isolate the characteristics of the 'born criminal'. The type I am talking about is much less noble: the petty crook, a mixture of complete cretinism and cowardice; the slicked-back hair of a Moroccan who opens his big mouth to fulminate against 'the West' while grovelling before its local lackeys; the piggishness of a guy from Cameroon proud of his 'king size'; or the sagging potbelly of a Congolese who cannot take his whisky, his eyes showing that he cannot understand any idea beyond 'how much it pays'. There is no need to attach names to these portraits: they are recognizable from the moment you set eyes on them.

The trouble is that, behind these 'friends' of the Americans and the many others in the West who accept their strategy, one has always been able to glimpse cohorts of 'experts' and sometimes even 'intellectuals'. They are not sufficiently strong to assert their 'irreplaceability' (besides, as de Gaulle once said, 'the cemeteries are full of irreplaceable people'); nor are they sufficiently courageous to avoid the temptation of 'making a career'. And, once that choice has been made, the rot soon sets in. Some even sink into alcoholism – no doubt in order to drown their sense of remorse.

Here I have simply tried to sketch the human context in which IDEP and many others had to struggle in those days.

NINE

The Third World Forum

Genesis of the institution

I have already said that, as director of IDEP, I played a role in the creation of other institutions for research and discussion: CODESRIA, ENDA and the Third World Forum. As far as the Forum was concerned, we straightaway thought it necessary to operate at the level of the third world, breaking out of the isolation in which the colonial period had confined Africa.

In 1958, the Non-Aligned Movement (NAM) had founded an Afro-Asian Peoples' Solidarity Organization (AAPSO), with its headquarters in Cairo. In 1997 this organization tried to shake itself out of its lethargy by organizing a major conference together with the Third World Forum. I say lethargy because it had not managed, or perhaps even tried, to assert its independence vis-à-vis the most active governments in the NAM: Nasser's Egypt, Indonesia (until the fall of Sukarno in 1966) and a few others. Their financial support had made its life too comfortable, so that it represented the various 'peoples' only via the single parties that were supposed to be their emanation. Moreover, AAPSO's credibility had been reduced by its extreme 'pro-Soviet' option, and it did not embrace Latin America (except Cuba) on the grounds that the continent remained outside the NAM.

In the late 1960s the Cubans had set up the 'Tricontinental', which presented itself as the organization representing the 'peoples' of the three continents. Once again, it was a question of grasp all, lose all. How to represent 'the peoples'? The only two ways I know are the election of a representative assembly and formation of political parties. But, although elected assemblies may sometimes be credible within certain limits, there is no assembly of assemblies operating at a regional or global level. The European Parliament itself is not such an institution, as there is no European government accountable to it. Political forces have sometimes created an 'International' together with ideologically 'fraternal' parties: for example, the Socialist International or the Communist International. As to the Tricontinental, it was little more than a gathering of national liberation movements and the (usually single) political parties that came out of them; history would prove just how eclectic was this group of third world 'parties'. Moreover, the orientations of the Tricontinental were more or less those of the Cuban state. What we had in mind was something more modest: an association of third world intellectuals. But, of course, it was necessary to define the objectives and then the selection criteria.

We were certainly not alone in considering this need for a more intense cross-frontier exchange of views among intellectuals; the Western powers were also giving it serious thought. The World Bank had taken the initiative of establishing a 'Society for International Development' (SID), based in Rome, whose aim was to bring together public figures from the North and South with an interest in the 'development problem'. The strictly reactionary vision of the founders, for whom development was synonymous with the expansion of capitalism, never allowed the SID to depart from the tracks marked out for it by the World Bank, so that it soon degenerated into a caricature of a club dominated by the Anglo-Saxon establishments, with no other culture than the one taught by the mainstream economics of market liberalism. It was hard to believe in the occasional minor role offered to a third world figure not completely in agreement with Washington. Could we create a different SID, to bring together intellectuals who were critical of conventional concepts of development? This was the idea behind the Forum. The Trilateral Commission – the think-tank of the American, European and Japanese establishments – had certainly fulfilled more important functions than the SID in the days of the Cold War, operating half-underground as an instrument of ideological mobilization against the Soviet Union and Communism. But in the 1990s its time seemed to have passed. The flame was being taken up by neoliberal fundamentalists, who now stepped out of the shadows as the wind turned in their favour. They were behind the annual gatherings at Davos, a kind of fair for billionaires enjoying life in the era of globalization.

The idea of strengthening exchanges in each continent among third world academics and intellectuals with an interest in development had also come of age. Not surprisingly it had first appeared in Latin America. There were several reasons for this. The most fundamental was that, thanks to the activity of Raúl Prebisch, a 'developmentalist' theory or ideology had taken shape around the analyses, studies and debates at ECLA. By the mid-1960s this had led in turn to a counter-theory, associated with the 'dependency school', which won massive support among intellectuals critical both of the 'dependent capitalism' on offer in their countries and of the orthodox dogmas of Latin American Communist parties signed up to the official Soviet line. This gave birth to the Latin American Council for the Social Sciences (CLACSO), a project all the easier to realize because Latin American intellectuals traditionally moved from one university to another, often because of political exile, taking advantage of the shared Spanish language or, in the case of Brazilians, the similarities between Spanish and Portuguese. I thought that a similar kind of institution in Africa could overcome the stupid opposition between 'French-speakers' and 'English-speakers', North Africa and sub-Saharan Africa, West, Central and Eastern-Southern Africa; the idea of CODESRIA emerged against this background. The situation was different in Asia, where some countries (above all, China and India) are already of gigantic proportions, and where political and cultural traditions are more diverse than elsewhere. Communist China situated the debate on development issues entirely within the framework of Marxism. India, the bastion of the Non-Aligned Movement, promoted a national-bourgeois social project tinged with populism, which was opposed by three Marxist currents otherwise at loggerheads with one another: the original Communist Party of India, the Communist Party (Marxist) and the Communist Party (Marxist–Leninist). For their part, the Southeast Asian and West Asian countries both felt alien to these Chinese and Indian orientations, although there the violent autocracy of the state was (and is) a further factor making it impossible to create independent regional institutions along the lines of CLACSO or CODESRIA.

An analysis of this situation convinced me that there was a huge lacuna which a Third World Forum might be able to fill. The major African/Latin American and Afro-Asian conferences that IDEP organized at this time began the early work of building the Forum. The vision was initially what I would call 'third world nationalist' (not 'third-worldist'). Yes, I admit it. The first aim was to give critical third world thinkers the means to begin correcting the fundamental imbalance within all international bodies, where the world is always seen from the North. A different perspective had to be opened up, and a pluralist critique developed of 'Eurocentrism' (now centred more on young North America than on old Europe). Marxist currents obviously had their place within this, but so did other approaches. The main thing to avoid was imprisonment in any orthodoxy; our ambition was to become not one school among others but a centre for critical debate.

I therefore had in mind the formation of a group to propose objectives and a mode of operation for the Third World Forum, a group sufficiently small to start work on the initial stages, and sufficiently open to avoid the many pitfalls that would appear in its path. I discussed a lot with a few friends who I thought would share my idea and be prepared to make a commitment to it. In the end, external circumstances played as much of a role as deliberate choices in the formation of this first informal group. As far as Latin America was concerned, we were spoiled for choice: all the leading lights of the *dependentista* current could have had a place in the group, and in the end it was Celso Furtado (its most senior figure), Fernando Henrique Cardoso, Enrique Oteiza (who had leadership experience in CLACSO behind him) and Pablo González Casanova who were the most active in the preliminary exchange of views. For Africa we had the IDEP team, in which we could have frank daily discussions, as well as the contributions of the political scientist Claude Ake (Nigeria), Justinian Rweyemamu (Tanzania), Ismail Abdallah (Egypt) and the group of Algerians around the Applied Economics Research Centre (CREA). As to Asia, those who had shown interest in the project included a number of Indians (Paresh Chattopadhay, Amiya Bagchi, Ramkrishna Mukerjee), Thais active in Southeast Asia as well as their own country (Kien Theeravit and Suthy Prasartset), the Sri Lankan Ponna Wignaraja, a Chinese well known in Beijing but then living in Canada (Paul Lin), and later the Filipino George Asniero (who at the time was still in his youth).

We thought it useful to strengthen this initial team by consulting some third world figures with important posts in the UN, on condition, of course, that they had expressed and defended trustworthy positions within the system. History has shown whether our choices were good or bad. But, in my view, Enrique Iglesias (who had succeeded Raúl Prebisch at ECLA), the Chilean Juan Somavía and the Sri Lankan Gamani Corea (who headed the important UNCTAD) played an active and positive role in the enterprise. The choice of Mabbub ul-Haq, who later became a minister in Pakistan and passed into the service of the World Bank, was certainly a mistake, although he did make it possible for the Forum's founding congress to be held in Karachi, with financial support from the National Bank of Pakistan. Mabbub ul-Haq did not think it worth his while to continue any visible activity for the Forum: his attempt at 'entrism' was a failure.

In April 1973, the Allende government in Chile invited us to organize a meeting in Santiago. I remember this as the date when the Forum really saw the light of day, although it was eight months later, in Karachi, that it officially adopted its founding documents. In Santiago a number of decisions were taken in principle that would define the subsequent evolution of the Forum.

First, the Forum was not a club of 'development officials' operating either at national level (planning technocrats and others) or in the international institutions of the UN. There could be no question of creating a Southern imitation of the Society for International Development. The point of the Forum was to bring together 'thinkers'. The term may sound a little grand, or even pretentious, but not every academic automatically had a place in the Forum; it was not meant to overlap with the international (or African, Arab, Indian and other) associations of academic economists, sociologists or historians, worthy of respect as these are in their way. We wanted something different, something that went outside the requirements, conventions and limitations of the academic world.

Second, the 'thinkers' in question would not be definable in terms of one scientific discipline (economists, sociologists or political scientists) but would always be 'cross-disciplinary'. They could be academics, officials or people holding positions of responsibility in political or social organizations, but such functions, often temporary, would not 'entitle' anyone to be a member of the Forum. If the Forum was to deserve its name – that is, to be a centre for debate and not for academic research – its participants had to have the necessary qualities to bring it to life.

Third, the thinkers should be critical: that is, 'organic intellectuals'. After a long exchange of views, we agreed that this should involve two dimensions. One of the axes of critique was the idea that the world system was not per se favourable to development – in other words, that development was not synonymous with insertion into the natural expansion of the system, driven by its own logic. In my language, this meant that development was not synonymous with capitalist expansion and therefore implied conflict with its one-sided logic. But nothing was defined beyond this general critical position; everyone was free to judge the most effective ways of transforming the system and to debate them at the Forum. The other axis of critique was that the fundamental goal of development should be to solve problems facing the whole of the population, not only a minority. In other words, development had a meaning only if it was 'popular', only if it was of benefit to the people. We did not think that such development could be the natural and spontaneous outcome of an extraneous logic – for example, that it could result from the trickle-down effects of competitiveness and profitability. Once again, however, nothing was laid down beyond this critical position. The alternative, which set the popular focus of development as the central criterion of action, might or might not be seen as socialism, according to how this was defined and to how one theorized the evolution of society. Such questions were precisely the ones left open for debate.

The meeting in Santiago also adopted a number of organizational proposals. One was that some of us should be given the task of starting up regional offices. I myself took charge of the African bureau, to be run from IDEP in Dakar where I was still director. Javier Alejo and Juan Somavía were given responsibility for the Latin American bureau, at ILET in Mexico City, and Godfrey Gunatileke for the Asian bureau, at the Marga Institute in Colombo. We were also asked to draw up a list of potential Forum members for each region, in line with the criteria defined above, to make proposals for Forum activities, and to explore ways in which they might be funded. I was further made responsible for coordination of the activities of the three bureaux, with the aim of holding a congress with at least enough members of the association to be representative. Some five hundred public figures were contacted and favourably considered, and it proved possible to invite more than a hundred of these to Karachi the following year.

In Santiago, only one exception was made to the rule that limited involvement in the Forum to third world nationals. The Swiss friend Marc Nerfin was consulted, first of all because he had shown by his actions that he was fully in solidarity with third world causes. (But fortunately he was by no means alone in this: competent activists dedicated to just causes in the third world may be counted by the thousand in Europe, North America and Japan.) The second reason, then, was that he made available a communications infrastructure that was extremely useful in getting the Forum off the ground. He was sensitive enough not to consider himself a Forum member, but simply to act as one of its friends and supporters in the countries of the North. He is a friend who has always been very dear to me; we all owe him a great deal.

Shortly after Santiago, the news reached us from Algiers that a group based at CREA intended to set up an 'Association of Third World

Economists'. Those of us who had some responsibility for the budding Forum were pleased to hear of this new initiative, which seemed likely to strengthen our common objective of encouraging critical debate on development. A first meeting took place in Algiers in 1979, at the invitation of CREA director Abdellatif Benachenhou. I took part in this interesting gathering, whose debates pointed in the same direction as those the Forum wished to develop, and the founding congress of the Association was held a little later in Havana. I personally regretted – and did not fail to say so to the people in charge – that the Association was giving too much weight to official government representatives; a Cuban minister was chosen as its chairperson, for example. The rush to attract sizeable funds (from the Algerian government, for example) also had considerable influence on the choice of people to fill positions. In my view – and history has sadly proved me right – these tendencies damaged the credibility of the Association more than they boosted it. The Association ceased to exist on the day when, for some reason, the Algerian government lost interest in it.

The Karachi congress in December 1974 marked the official birth of the Forum. As regards its essential role and functions, those in attendance adopted the principles worked out in Santiago – which was hardly surprising, given that its provisional membership had been selected on the basis of those principles. It was also natural enough, since if you want to do something you have a right to choose the means and strategy of achieving it. Those who disagree are perfectly free to do something else. Democracy means that everyone has a right to act in the same way.

The interesting thing about the Karachi congress was that it did not simply reaffirm the Santiago principles but began the work of putting them into practice. The quality of the participants made this possible, indeed necessary. The debates therefore mainly centred on the fundamental issues. What are the challenges facing the peoples of the third world? What is general and what is particular in these challenges? How are they defined by critical intellectuals from different regions, from different cultural and political backgrounds, and from different schools of thought? Which alternatives are being proposed, and what are the arguments for them? It was a very promising start for the Forum.

At the same time, of course, the congress adopted general statutes for the Forum. These called upon each of its regional bureaux to hold meetings at which the ways of pursuing the Forum's goals would be spelled out in greater detail. Thus, when I left IDEP – which had housed the Forum's African bureau between 1975 and 1980 – we lost no time in organizing an African assembly to adopt regional rules for the Forum, in conformity with the statutes of the organization. That was in Dakar in December 1980. Meanwhile the Karachi congress had ratified the creation of three regional bureaux and elected a chairman – Ismail Abdallah. It also confirmed my responsibility for coordination of the regional bureaux.

Each of the three bureaux developed in its own way. Javier Alejo and Juan Somavía, who were in charge of the Latin American bureau, perhaps did not see completely eye to eye with each other. Alejo was close to the Mexican regime and President Echeverría, whose third-worldist ambitions led him – after the end of his presidency – to help set up a well-endowed centre. Nevertheless, it was necessary to think again about the organization of the Latin American branch of the Forum, and it was Pablo González Casanova, based at UNAM university in Mexico City, who took responsibility for this. Pablo is not only a well-known intellectual producer but also a public figure respected throughout Latin America and beyond for his political integrity. As to the Caribbean area, my colleagues and friends Norman Girvan (Jamaica) and Gérard Pierre Charles (Haiti) helped to integrate it into the Forum in 1989. At first, the Colombo bureau was not very active and it was necessary to hand things over from the Marga Institute to Ponna Wignaraja, a talented Sri Lankan intellectual who, between 1980 and 1985, got a Forum network up and running for the whole of South Asia. But Asia was too huge and varied a continent for a single regional bureau to cover all the activities we wanted the Forum to sponsor there. A little later – I think it was in 1978 – I took the initiative of asking a small group of Southeast Asian intellectuals to establish a branch of the Forum in their region. George Aseniero, the brilliant and active Filipino

I had first met at a Goals, Processes and Indicators of Development programme run by Johan Galtung, agreed to coordinate this group, together with Suthy Prasartset, members of the Asian Regional Exchange for New Alternatives (ARENA) and of the East Asia/South Asia group based in Tokyo and Hong Kong and headed by our Japanese colleagues and friends Muto Ichiyo and Yoko Kitazawa. Later still, I brought into our networks a number of South Korean intellectuals working under the very difficult conditions of the dictatorship; they had invited me to Korea, I think in 1984. Already in 1980 the Chinese Academy of Social Sciences agreed to take part in the activities of the Forum, and its president, Pu Shan, along with a number of other Chinese intellectuals, did join our discussions on problems concerning changes in the international order, first in 1980 and then on two more occasions up to 1996. On the other hand, non-Arab Western Asia (Turkey, Iran, Afghanistan) and Central Asia (part of the USSR until 1991) remained outside the activities of the Forum. There were several reasons for this: the closed nature of the Soviet system, the war in Afghanistan, the pro-European stance of the Turkish intelligentsia, and the successive dictatorships in Iran. When I visited Iran in 1975, I tried to make some contacts who might fill this gap in the reach of the Forum, but the work of the Shah's terrible secret police, Savak, in stifling all critical intellectual activity, whether among the few elements of the Tudeh Party who were not in jail or among the new radical wing of the Islamist movement (the Fedayeen Khalq and the Mujahideen Khalq), did not make the task easy. After the victory of Khomeini, our friend Bani Sadr returned from his Parisian exile and even became president for a time, but he was unable to stem the autocratic drift of the Islamic Republic. Other Iranians who joined the Islamic movement – the Radzavi brothers, for example – were also soon forced to take the road of exile (the ambassador Radzavi was actually murdered abroad by Khomeini agents). Nevertheless, it may be that developments in the region will make it possible to create a regional bureau of the Forum in the near future. Our friend Fikret Baskaya has been running an Ankara-based Forum for Turkey and the Middle East, and some degree of tolerance might develop in Iran. We should also hope that one day the intellectuals of ex-Soviet Central Asia will break out of their isolation.

The president of the Third World Forum, Ismail Abdallah, himself has an office in Cairo, which serves as the base for activities in the Arab Middle East. Ibrahim Saadeddine shares with him responsibility for the work of the bureau.

The African bureau moved from IDEP to the CODESRIA building in June 1980, and it has had its own offices in Dakar since 1983. A number of colleagues from IDEP joined me there: Amoa (who retired a few years later), Lamine Gakou (who later returned to Bamako) and Bernard Founou. Bernard and I assumed joint and equal responsibility for the management direction of the bureau, while I continued to carry out the tasks of coordination among the different regions of the Forum.

The expansion of activities

In my opinion, the creation of the Third World Forum was a considerable success. The simple fact that it has survived – for more than twenty years at the time of writing – is testimony to this. For the cemetery holding institutions that were dead at birth, or that lived for only a couple of years, contains dozens if not hundreds of similar initiatives.

I have no hesitation in saying that the success was largely due to Olof Palme. In the early 1970s I got to know Rolf Gustavsson, then a consistent Maoist and a young researcher in social and economic history at Lund, who had invited me to Sweden to lecture at a number of universities. He had already translated into Swedish my *Accumulation on a World Scale*. He had also been to Dakar as a journalist, and boldly travelled to Guinea-Bissau to report on the liberation war. Our friendship has resisted the passage of time, although his subsequent political evolution – as director of Swedish television, then its correspondent in Brussels – has taken him in a highly moderate direction. In 1975, when the left wind was still blowing strong, Swedish academics had taken the initiative of creating a foundation to support independent critical research in the third world. The statutes of

SAREC, as the institution is called, had been drawn up in a typically Swedish spirit, with nothing quite like them anywhere else. Although publicly funded, SAREC was not in the business of carrying out government policy; it was a genuinely independent body. For the Swedish state, having chosen to support critical thinking in the third world, was courageous in drawing the consequences. Such cases are unfortunately all too rare.

Rolf introduced me to the top people at SAREC, and through them I had the opportunity to speak with Olof Palme in person about the Forum project (I think this was 1976). The idea convinced him on the spot. Palme was one of those politicians who knew how to listen, and who, having formed an opinion, really drew the practical consequences. He also had a broad vision of world affairs, strongly critical of actually existing capitalism and American–Atlanticist hegemonism. The positions that Sweden took in the Vietnam war were evidence of this, and the decision to support liberation struggles in the Portuguese colonies and South Africa sharply contrasted with the hypocrisy of all the other Western governments, which in reality preferred the Portuguese fascists and the apartheid oppressors. Sweden thereby gained a position on the global chessboard – alongside democratic and progressive forces – which was quite out of proportion to the small size of the country.

So, at the end of our discussion Palme asked me directly: 'How much do you need?' I explained that we did not want to succumb to the temptation to 'start off rich' – a temptation that is often fatal because of the easy opportunities it offers. I said that we would need something like $100,000 a year for a few years, after which we would have to prove the viability of the project and find more diverse sources of funding. Palme said: 'I'll double that and guarantee it for five or even ten years, if the voters stay with us that long.' And that is what happened: the Social Democrats continued to win the elections at regular three-yearly intervals, and SAREC did not waver in its mission until the end of the 1980s. The right, semi-neoliberal wind eventually prevailed, as the country drew closer to and eventually joined the European Union, and Stockholm's courageous decisions of the previous decades were watered down.

The fact remains that SAREC's generous support between 1978 and 1992 amounted to more than $2 million, mainly in allocations for the Forum's African programme, but also for the coordination activities for which I was responsible. This gave us enough time to look for other sources of support, chiefly from various institutions in Norway, Finland, the Netherlands, Canada and Italy, as well as the EU and the UN University.

The African bureau of the Third World Forum also associated some of its programmes with UN institutions such as the Institute for Training and Research (UNITAR), which managed the SAREC funds allocated to the Forum between 1978 and 1980. Philippe de Seynes was having an active retirement within UNITAR, whose director in those days was a gentleman from Sierra Leone by the name of Davidson Nichol. This arrangement, which enabled the UN to manage the Forum's budget, continued until 1987. Then Nichol's successor, Michel Doo Kingue, hastened to impose his bureaucratic views in line with his American bosses – something the Forum obviously could not accept. So, the arrangement was switched to the UN Research Institute for Social Development (UNRISD), whose successive directors were the Argentinean Enrique Oteíza and the Kenyan Dharam Ghai, both Forum members and valuable intellectuals of great intellectual and political integrity. Some of the Forum's African programmes were thus integrated into the UNITAR and UNRISD programmes, without the latter having to contribute any funding themselves; they simply managed some of the Forum's finances in keeping with the rules of the United Nations (for a fee of 14 per cent, under the famous category of 'overheads'). Of course, the whole budget – for which I remained responsible – was subject to an annual audit, in accordance with the general statutes and the rules of good management. The arrangement with UNRISD anyway came to an end when Bernard Founou and I reached retirement age and jointly decided to continue with our activities in the Forum.

In my capacity as IDEP director, I had participated each year in a meeting of directors of research and training institutes within the body of the United Nations. The agenda always included a point on the creation of a United Nations University, and opinions were always divided between those who wanted to incorporate their institute into the new UNU and those who wanted to leave out existing institutes and build something new from scratch. In the end, the formula used for the creation of the Tokyo-based UNU made it a kind of foundation to fund other people's programmes, rather than a real university in its own right. Neither its successive rectors nor its senate made much of an impression on me. And the institution was saved from mediocrity, for a while, only through the efforts of its Japanese vice-rector, Kinhide Mushakoji, an intelligent and extremely active man with an open and critical mind. He managed to implement 90 per cent of the UNU's actual programmes with 10 per cent of its budget. Mushakoji selected the Forum as a major partner in a programme of fundamental debates on the prospects for third world regions within the global system. Between 1980 and 1985 this programme was one of the Forum's principal axes of activity, and it was maintained in part until Mushakoji was forced out of the UNU in 1988: his efficient work was setting too bad an example! It goes without saying that Mushakoji became and has remained a dear personal friend.

Whereas the funding from Nordic countries was generally allocated to the Forum's programmes on sub-Saharan Africa, the contribution from Italy helped to expand its activities in the Arab world. In this respect, the most memorable event was the great European–Arab symposium at Naples in 1983, which brought together a hundred participants from countries in the southern Mediterranean. Giuseppe Santoro, then director-general of Italian overseas aid in Rome, worked together with me on the development of this programme. It was a bold and clear-sighted initiative, which unfortunately no other European politician whom one might have expected to take an interest in the views of critical Arab intellectuals thought it necessary to pursue – a failure especially remarkable in the cases of France and Spain.

Nevertheless, in the second half of the 1980s, the Forum reached what might be called its cruising speed. Its membership held steady at a figure around one thousand, a good half of whom were really very active in one programme or another. Over the past fifteen years the Forum has organized more than 150 working groups, gathered more than 2,500 written communications and published them under its own imprint and in numerous journals. The publication of work on Africa and the Middle East – in French, English and Arabic – has been running at the level of seven or eight books a year, and the eightieth title in the Forum's African collection (a book on South Africa) appeared in 1998. Given its volume of activity, the Forum's funding appears extraordinarily modest in comparison with that of institutions of similar scope. This modesty is actually quite intentional: the point is to prove that debates of great importance for the major issues of our time do not necessarily require the expenditure of large sums of money. The members of the Forum are high-quality intellectuals attracted by the debates themselves, not by any remuneration they may derive from them.

Dakar was certainly a happy choice for the Forum's headquarters. I suggested it to President Senghor a few months before I left IDEP. He encouraged me and promised the support of his government, and to its great credit it never ceased to show a real and sincere friendship towards us, without exerting the slightest pressure on the Forum. I do not know many other countries, in Africa or elsewhere in the third world, that have as much respect for intellectual freedom and take such pride in the importance of the debates that it makes possible.

The Forum often opened new directions in its work. For example, it departed from the costly and ineffectual formula of the conventional 'symposium', where 'papers' with varying status are presented, and gradually introduced the formula of smaller working groups, each with a coordinator (who spent 30 to 50 per cent of his annual work time on this activity) and four to six participants (who spent 10 to 20 per cent of their time on it). Over and above the personal views of its members, the 'dossier' drawn up by the group was supposed to take stock of the latest research on a particular topic. Most of the dossiers were substantial documents (200 pages or more) and were subjected to criticism by twenty to thirty people known for their competence in the area, their diversity of views and their eye for the practical consequences.

The Forum's programmes in the last fifteen years have mainly involved critical analysis of the ideas and practices associated with 'development', using a methodology that takes each region of the world as part of an integrated system. In other words, the principal unit of analysis is ultimately always the world system, rather than one of its geographical components. What this implies is not that the specificities of each society (country or region) at each point in its evolution should be ignored, but that these specificities acquire their full meaning only in relation to the world system. It is a compelling methodological choice in today's world, where rhetoric concerning 'the unavoidable constraints of the world market' dominates mainstream discourse. But fifteen years ago, when the Forum groups were starting their work, it was a pioneering approach that was poorly understood and often rejected.

This methodological choice meant analysing the evolution of each country within the broader category of the 'third world', itself a component of the world system; differentiation within the third world (the emergence of a 'fourth world', newly industrialized countries, regional North–South relations, etc.) was thus directly situated within the dynamic of the world system. This also meant giving special attention to the evolution of the world system itself, to the emergence of qualitatively new features and new forms of polarization (technological monopolies associated with the ongoing technological revolution, globalization of finance capital, intensive development of communications and the media, control of weapons of mass destruction, etc.), to the new kinds of 'social movement', and to the evolution of ideological debates (increased salience of cultural and religious dimensions, etc.). In other words, the idea was to study 'the world as seen from the South', rather than 'the South in the world'. Once again, the changes marking the end of the post-war era (1945–90) would validate the Forum's pioneering approach.

If the 1960s were marked by high hopes of an irreversible process of development throughout the third world, especially Africa, the present age is one of disillusionment. Development has ground to a halt, its theory in crisis and its ideology subject to doubt. The Forum starts from the fact that the options available within the limited macroeconomic schemas offer only trivial, predictable results, and that we need to raise the debate to a higher level by integrating all the economic, political, social and cultural dimensions of the problem, both in their local setting and as they interact globally. In doing this, the Forum has helped to challenge the North's monopoly on theoretical reflection concerning globalization and its uneven impact on its geographical components.

In its contribution to the debate on development in various parts of the third world and within the world system as a whole, the Forum seeks to go beyond the short-term preoccupations that are the main concern of the powers-that-be and to lay the stress on the medium to long term. The short-term 'structural adjustment policies' imposed by the institutions of the world system lead at best to a regressive equilibrium, and often aggravate the social problems of underdevelopment, since they channel long-term trends by whittling away the diversity of possible options.

To overcome the failure of development and the crisis of development theory, the Forum has been trying to encourage discussion of a polycentric world order not dominated by three or five 'great powers' and two military superpowers, so that Africa, Asia and Latin America are offered real prospects of development that take account of their existing economic inequality.

Over the past seventeen years, the Third World Forum has undergone continual expansion in spite of its modest resources. This achievement is all the more remarkable when we consider the well-known difficulties of the period. Many donors responded to the financial crisis by cutting sharply back on their contributions, and the first to go was usually anything that did not immediately lead to 'concrete action'. This unfortunate sense of priorities tended to reinforce the emphasis on temporary fashions and short-term viewpoints. Some quite simply gave up supporting any effort at critical thought. Yet this climate may now be passing, if only because the dominant policy recommendations have produced more chaos and regression than genuinely new departures. The need to reopen fundamental debates is already felt to be urgent, and the obsession with the 'immediately useful' (shared by many NGOs) is perhaps losing ground.

The activities of the Forum in Africa and the Middle East have passed through a series of phases, which can be followed in the fifteen issues of its *Bulletin* (later, *Information Letter*) published between 1983 and July 1998. The main programmes characterizing each of these phases were as follows: (1) regional perspectives (TWF/UNU) covering the whole of the third world (1981–85), geared to debate on the dialectic of national construction and transnationalization; (2) the Mediterranean project, funded by Italy, which analysed geostrategic and other aspects of relations between the Arab world and Western and Eastern Europe (1983–89); (3) the 'Third World and Global Development' project (TWF/UNU), developed on the basis of the regional perspectives, which focused on the critique of development paradigms (1989–92); (4) the three-year programme on 'Alternatives for sustainable, autonomous and democratic development in Africa and the Middle East' (1992–95); and (5) the three-year programme on the world system as seen from the South (1996–98).

A reading of what the Forum networks produced will show an early sharp critique of the theoretical conceptualization, strategic choices and institutional application of so-called development policies. It passed a severe verdict on the practices of the 'development decades', in both their 'socialist' and 'liberal' variants. The Forum's analyses reveal that their different ideological discourses masked their often shared weaknesses: a high degree of external financial dependence, agricultural failures, lack of an industrial revolution, undemocratic political regimes, a narrow vision of social 'modernization', and so on. The Forum's analyses therefore suggested an alternative to the dominant approach of short-term management, just as they proposed a holistic multidisciplinary method in contrast to the narrowness of the prevailing economism.

A large number of intellectuals became involved in the programmes. The diversity of analytic tools and theoretical–ideological attachments was a deliberately pursued end in itself. No attempt was made to ground different viewpoints on an exclusive 'theory', which would have been eclectic and unanimously rejected. It would have made no sense to 'integrate' the points of view of the strong personalities that the Forum brought together.

For the Forum is not a 'school': its purpose is to compel otherwise different thinkers to respond seriously to the arguments put to them, with the aim of enriching debate.

The Forum has always had a presence in the major international forums, as at the fiftieth anniversary of Bretton Woods (September 1994) and the opening of the discussion on global development, or at the social summit in Copenhagen (March 1995) that opened debate on the social dimensions of development, where the Forum was invited by the UN secretariat to present the main independent report on the issue.

On the occasion of the Cairo meeting in March 1997, a group of thirty leading figures from the five continents, North and South, took the initiative of creating a World Forum for Alternatives – of which the Third World Forum is proud to be an active part. The Forum shares the conviction that it is more necessary than ever to intensify global debate by linking up the different networks that are pursuing the same objective – the construction of a pluricentric and democratic world system.

TEN

Towards a Common Front of the World's Peoples?

All societies on earth, without exception, find themselves in an impasse where the only future ahead seems to be the destruction of human civilization. The reader of these memoirs will doubtless have come to the same conclusion – if, that is, he or she accepts the analyses I have offered of the third world, the former socialist countries and the 'first world'. It may seem pessimistic in the extreme, but that is not how I see it. The point, rather, is that the world capitalist system has reached the end of its historical trajectory and can no longer produce anything positive, if we assume that circumstances will allow it to survive at all. Human civilization is therefore at a dangerous crossroads: it can avoid destruction only by embarking on a new road, an 'alternative' as they say, which for me is synonymous with the long transition to world socialism. The neoliberal view of the world, though seemingly triumphant, is not viable. But the certainty of its collapse does not guarantee that what follows will automatically take the right path; the demise of liberal capitalism could produce only indescribable chaos, with consequences impossible to predict. This is not, however, the only exit from the impasse in which senescent capitalism imprisons humanity. More or less everywhere in the world, real forces exist which may initiate positive changes – forces visible today in the numerous struggles whose scale has already shaken neoliberal triumphalism.

Capitalism has built a world system and can really be overcome only at the level of the planet. Although national struggles have to be the starting point, without which no progress can be achieved at the level of the world, they are not sufficient because the scope for change that they can unleash is inevitably limited by the constraints of globalization. It is therefore absolutely necessary that these struggles should converge and open a way beyond the logic of capitalist accumulation, both in its national bases and at the regional and global levels.

The goal of the World Forum for Alternatives (WFA), founded in 1997, is precisely to assist this convergence of struggles. In this connection, the Third World Forum has a fairly dense network of committed intellectuals in each of the three continents (Asia, Africa and Latin America), which by no means belittles the importance of either networks, whether tricontinental (such as Via Campesina or the Third World Network), regional (e.g. CLACSO or the São Paulo Forum in Latin America, CODESRIA in Africa, ARENA and Focus on the Global South in Southeast Asia, or the Teaegu Forum in East and South Asia), or even national (a no less important level for large countries such as India or Brazil). The intellectuals involved in these networks have close, often organizational relations with many social movements, which in their respective countries sometimes have a support base running into the millions (the trade unions in Korea or South Africa, the Landless Workers Movement in Brazil, the neo-Zapatistas in Mexico, and so on). The same is true in many countries of the 'first world': for example, in France (CEDETIM[45] and the highly active alter-globalization movement ATTAC[46]), Switzerland (the 'Third World Centre', CETIM), Italy (Il Manifesto, Punto Rosso), Japan (Ampo), Canada (Alternatives) and elsewhere. Today's electronic means of communication have increased the scale and rapidity of the international exchange of views, especially between movements from different political-ideological traditions such as those of Europe (where political life is dominated by the major parties and trade unions) and the United States (where 'civil society' consists more of a plethora of small local associations, quite remote from the two almost identical establishment parties). This dense communication largely explains the success of the Seattle mobilization, which thwarted the plans for the WTO in January 2000. At the present moment, however, the WFA networks are still weakly implanted in the countries of the ex-Soviet world.

In the short space of a decade, these movements together have become a successful parallel force questioning the international organizations. I attribute particular importance to the organizations of the third world: among others, the Non-Aligned Movement (which I have suggested specifying as 'non-aligned over globalization'), the Organization of African Unity (whose current secretary-general, Salim Ahmed Salim, remains an anti-imperialist patriot), the Afro-Asian Peoples' Solidarity Organization (which, despite its initial difficulties, worked with the Third World Forum on the Cairo conference of April 1997 that gave rise to the WFA), the Asia-Pacific Peoples' Organization (which demonstrated its real strength at the various official meetings of APEC). Parts of the UN system are themselves sensitive to these trends: UNCTAD, for example, which was created by Raúl Prebisch and run by a number of directors known personally to me (Kenneth Dadzie, Gamani Corea, Rubens Ricupero); or the United Nations University, at the time when Kinhide Mushakoji was vice-rector; or UNESCO when Mahtar Mbow, well ahead of his time, was waging the struggle for a 'new international communications order'. The same was obviously not true of resolute opponents such as those G7 and US instruments, the World Bank, IMF and WTO, although even they are now forced to confuse matters with various verbal contortions. Nor is it true of the United Nations Organization itself, whose secretary-general, Kofi Annan, produced a 'Millennium Report' that seemed to come straight from the offices of the State Department. Other UN institutions – UNIDO, FAO or UNDP – have now been vassalized by Washington and its loyal allies in the triad, whereas the institutions of the EU, largely because of its elected parliament, are quite sensitive to these trends, even if the bureaucracy of the Brussels Commission remains subject to EU governments and has gone along with neoliberal globalization. The summits held under these conditions – like the one on poverty, in Copenhagen in 1995, where the

Third World Forum presented the only really independent report from Africa – have only a limited impact.

The last of the major UN conferences of this kind was held in Durban in August–September 2001. The importance of the event was due to the perspectives it opened up, for a wind of change was blowing there for the solidarity of Afro-Asian peoples. The building of such solidarity is indeed one of the main conditions, if not *the* main condition, for a world system more just than the one that the G7 and its North American boss wish to impose on the peoples of the world, through all means including the most violent.

The dominant establishment, consisting of the United States plus the World Bank (a kind of G7 propaganda ministry) and the UN bureaucracy, had previously controlled the expressions of 'civil society' that were invited to participate in these international conferences; it had managed to do this through its hold on the purse strings and its manipulation of NGOs sufficiently apolitical to sign up to the mainstream proposals, which in effect cancelled any impact of the protests and demands of the peoples in the countries where the NGOs originated.

The Durban conference had been planned along the same lines. The protest against 'racism and all other forms of discrimination' was to be an innocuous event at which all participants, both governments and NGOs, would be called upon to beat their breast over the 'vestiges' of discrimination afflicting 'indigenous peoples', 'non-Caucasian races' (to use the official US language), women and 'sexual minorities'. Some highly general recommendations were drawn up, in the spirit of North American legalism according to which an act of legislation is all that is required to solve a problem. The social and international inequalities generated by the logic of globalized capitalism, which are the essential causes of the main forms of discrimination, were left out of the original considerations.

This strategy of Washington and its allies was defeated by the massive participation of African and Asian organizations determined to pose the real questions. The issue of racism and discrimination, they argued, is not synonymous with the behaviour of people still suffering from 'outmoded' prejudices, who sadly are still present in large numbers in every society on earth. Contemporary racism and discrimination are produced and reproduced by the expansionist logic of actually existing capitalism, especially in its so-called liberal form. The forms of 'globalization' imposed by dominant capital and its political intermediaries (above all, the triad governments) can result in nothing other than 'global apartheid'.

Having sensed the danger at the meetings of the preparatory committee, the G7 governments decided to boycott the conference and to decree its 'failure' in advance. The Africans and Asians stood firm. In accordance with the strategy they had adopted, they ensured that there was discussion of the two issues that Western foreign ministries did not want to hear about.

The first concerned 'reparations' for the damage caused by the black slave trade. I have placed the word in inverted commas because of the attitude of American and European diplomats, who tried to undermine the whole discussion by condescending remarks about the 'amount' of reparations and the 'professional beggars' who were claiming them on behalf of formerly colonized peoples. Africans certainly did not see things in that way. For them the issue was not 'money' but a recognition that colonialism, imperialism and slavery were largely responsible for the 'underdevelopment' of the continent and the legacy of racism. It was these arguments which provoked the ire of the representatives of Western powers.

The second concerned the actions of the State of Israel. Here the Africans and Asians were clear and precise: the continuation of Israeli settlement in the occupied territories, the eviction of Palestinians in a process of veritable ethnic cleansing, the Bantustanization plan for Palestine directly inspired by the defunct apartheid regime in South Africa: these were but the latest chapter in its long history of evidently 'racist' imperialism. Characteristically, the Palestinian question unites people in Africa and Asia, whereas it divides them in other parts of the world.

The wind of Bandung is rising again. The original Bandung Conference in 1955, the founding moment of Afro-Asian solidarity and the Non-Aligned

Movement (which today is more and more 'non-aligned' behind liberal globalization and US hegemonism), ushered in a first cycle of national liberation. As always in history, there were limits to the systems that resulted from this period of popular emancipation from colonialism and the illusions bound up with it. But the exhaustion of those systems permitted a new offensive by capital in those parts of the world and the unfurling of a new imperialist globalization. The conditions for a second wave of liberation that will go further than before are maturing before our eyes. Durban was one proof of this.

It is because Durban was a victory for the peoples that the G7 tried to minimize its impact. Regrettably, most of the mainstream media simply reproduced what the United States and Israel wanted people to believe.

Durban, together with Seattle, Nice, Gothenburg, Genoa and Porto Alegre, was part of a chain of major positive events. It is time that all who condemn the strategy of global neoliberalism should understand that theirs is a single fight, that the struggle of the peoples of the South against imperialism and US hegemonism is no less important than that of victims of injustice in the developed capitalist countries. After the attack on the symbolic targets of the World Trade Center and the Pentagon, it is time to understand that there can be no united front against terrorism without a united front against social and international injustice.

The World Forum for Alternatives is located within this complex universe. It is therefore a forum in the true sense of the term – that is, a place of mutual encounter and debate, not an 'International' (Communist, Socialist, Christian Democrat, Islamic or Liberal). It brings together currents of thought and action which, though totally independent of one another (a good thing, in my opinion), share critical points of view about the application of liberal policies to such areas of social management as relations between the sexes, environmental issues, human rights or intercommunal problems. All these currents have a place in the WFA, whatever their ideological inspirations or practical choices. The WFA programme for debate on the objectives, instruments and achievements of social movements around the world – whether it is a question of regional balance sheets, the stimulation of alternatives to agribusiness, or systematic reflection on universal values concerning individual, social and collective rights – testifies to the openness which is a matter of principle for the Forum. The group of co-ordinators who appointed me chairman of the WFA did me a great honour, which is perhaps justified, if at all, by the fact that my activities over forty years familiarized me with a large number of organizations and leading personalities around the world. My colleagues in this group, including François Houtart, Pierre Beaudet, Giorgio Riolo and many others, lack neither exceptional qualities nor unlimited dedication.

The World Forum for Alternatives first appeared on the international stage when it organized the 'anti-Davos' in January 1999, on the occasion of the annual elite conference at Davos. We were, of course, denied access to the holy precinct itself, but we took up position fifty metres away, on the other side of the snow-covered street in this beautiful winter resort. Our small group included a number of committed intellectuals and figures from mass movements in the five continents, chosen for their high degree of representativeness: the farmers' organizations of Burkina Faso, Brazil and India; the labour unions of South Africa, Korea and Brazil; the neo-Zapatistas of Chiapas in Mexico; the activists of the World March of Women; the 'Sans' in France and the ATTAC group. Helped into Davos by *Le Monde Diplomatique*, we were there to say that it was we, not the club of billionaires, who represented the real world. The Davos organizers, like the narrow-minded Swiss authorities, were so furious that it was impossible to produce the surprise a second time round. Hence the idea of a World Social Forum, on a different scale, for which Porto Alegre seemed a natural choice because of the considerable resources that the Brazilian Workers Party could mobilize for it there.

The success of Porto Alegre I, in January 2001, did not feature on the front pages of the major Western newspapers. The enemy's chosen strategy was to boycott the whole initiative.

Nevertheless, the rich gentlemen at Davos grew a little worried and suggested opening a 'dialogue' with us. I was lucky enough to take part in the ten minutes of airtime set aside for it on the radio.

'*Monsieur*,' asked my Davos partner, 'how does it happen that an economist like yourself is not there with us in Davos?'

My answer was simple. 'There were three reasons. One: I don't have $20,000 to spend on entering paradise for three days. Two: I wasn't invited – which doesn't surprise me, as my opinions are well enough known. Three: if by some mistake I had been invited, I wouldn't have accepted, as I am not a billionaire and have no interest in joining the club of their servants.'

'But, *monsieur*,' he countered, 'I am not a billionaire.'

'I know, you are the public relations director of a company whose owners are billionaires.'

'What have you got against billionaires?'

'Simple arithmetic, *monsieur*. Their profits doubled in the 1990s, but the incomes of all the non-billionaires – and there are a lot of them – obviously did not increase in the same proportion. You want inequality, and I equality. So, we are enemies, and I don't see what we could have a dialogue about.'

Even so, Davos will not fail to 'make an effort' in the future, and from the wide spectrum of social organizations it will find some 'left-wing figures' to go consciously or unconsciously on a journey to the mountain of reconciliation.

The success of Porto Alegre had been prepared by the events in Seattle. And we know that 'anti-liberal-globalization' forces are today strong enough to express their anger at any occasion in the calendar of great international gatherings: European summits, G7 meetings, conferences of the IMF, World Bank and WTO, and so on.

All this is a clear indication that the climate is changing. The time when the peoples of the world were in disarray before the triumph of liberal discourse is now over, as that discourse has lost its credibility and been thrown on to the defensive. In this respect, the French movement of December 1995 may have marked a turning point. Isabelle, who took part in the great demonstration, has stuck up on the wall a photo of herself amid a crowd of railway workers.

Typically, in May 2001, the World Bank called off at the last minute its planned 'dialogue' in Barcelona with carefully selected NGOs, out of fear that some troublemakers might pose a few awkward questions. We therefore drew up a list of charges to replace that false debate between the World Bank and 'civil society'.

Our tasks and responsibilities have grown at a pace which I will not say is unexpected, but which certainly suggests that the future will not be as gloomy as it may have appeared a few years ago.

In January 2002, Porto Alegre II took a great step forward that was well expressed in the 'appeal' adopted at the final rally. The 'social movements' have been growing more political – in the good sense of the term. Beyond the organization of struggle against the disastrous social effects of neoliberalism, they are taking the measure of a system which already entails, and will increasingly entail, 'military' barbarism on the pretext of a 'war on terrorism'. It is true that the aftermath of 9/11 had amply demonstrated this. The Third World Forum and the World Forum for Alternatives were very active at Porto Alegre, leading five major seminars at which the whole criminal political logic of global neoliberalism was subjected to analyses and commentaries by hundreds of the most lucid intellectuals in the contemporary world.

This success has already begun to have an impact. Social democracy, itself complicit with neoliberalism and US hegemonism, is no longer in a position to boycott the World Social Forum, as we can see from the stream of French ministers, among others, who have put in an appearance. 'They want to buy us off' said a number of likeable young leftists. To which Gustave Massiah gave the right answer: 'Yes, they want to buy us off, precisely because we now count for something. We can't stop the enemy trying to buy us, but it's up to us to refuse to sell ourselves.'

The World Forum for Alternatives has a major intellectual responsibility. Our age has witnessed another *trahison des clercs*, in the sense that the overwhelming majority of academics and other 'experts' are no longer seeking an alternative to the present system. Not without a certain cynicism, they are closing their eyes to its destructive dimensions. Some do this in order to make a fortune, in the tradition of straightforward opportunism. Others draw the teeth of their own criticism by reducing it to the minimum compatible with the needs of the people in power. This betrayal does not surprise me. It is what happens at every end of an epoch, when the society in place is declining and the new society has not yet crystallized through qualitative breakthroughs.

Thus, the role of the World Forum for Alternatives is also to allow a centre of alternative thinking to take shape within it. The enemy knows the importance of this kind of systematic thought, since without it there can be no strategy for effective action. I have already had occasion to mention the Mont Pelerin Society (founded in 1947 by Friedrich Hayek and joined by such luminaries as Milton Friedman, Lionel Robbins, Ludwig von Mises and Karl Popper, the apostles of today's liberalism) and the Trilateral Commission (which features the names of David Rockefeller, Zbigniew Brzezinski, Cyrus Vance, Andrew Young and Paul Volcker, the architects of the strategy of the North American establishment). The enemy knows that the main problem it faces today is management of the unviable criminal system that it seeks to impose on the peoples of the world. The theme of 'governability', to use its own jargon, dominates the agenda of international institutions, and unfortunately many NGOs have taken it on board – whether out of sheer opportunism or because they lack the critical capacity to do otherwise. We are not fully aware of how the enemy's thinking is currently orchestrated, although Susan George – in her Lugano Report – has painted an impressively shrewd scenario.

The strongest argument for pessimism about the future is based on the lack of visible subjects capable of undertaking the necessary historical transformation and putting an end to the hugely destructive dimensions of senescent capitalism. To say that 'the workers' – or even wage and salary earners more generally – constitute such a subject is likely to cause smiles all round. But the optimist that I am will reply that active subjects appear only for relatively brief periods in history, when a favourable combination of circumstances allows the different logics of social existence (economic, political, geostrategic, etc.) to converge with one another. At such moments, in ways impossible to predict in advance, potential subjects may crystallize into decisive agents of change. Who could have foretold two thousand years ago that the great religions (Christianity, Islam, Buddhism) would become decisive subjects of history? Who predicted that the nascent bourgeoisie of the Italian and Dutch towns would become the decisive subject of modern history, a class for itself whose keen awareness of what it wanted and what it was capable of achieving has only occasionally been matched by its opponent – 'the proletariat' – at brief moments of struggle? And who predicted that certain 'peoples' in the periphery – the Chinese and Vietnamese peoples – would take over and become the most decisive subjects of transformation in the post-war world? This is not to say that present-day social movements will not occasionally constitute themselves into active subjects, whose precise shape is difficult to imagine. We need to give constant thought to the precise situations that might permit this, and to the strategies that would make it easier for their different elements to come together.

These questions can be answered only on the basis of accelerating trends at the national (or nation-state) level where the political and social choices are made. But, as I said before, the present degree of globalization requires that any major breakthroughs should spread at least regionally. Europe, China, India, Southeast Asia, the Arab world, Africa and Latin America are the most important regions in today's world for which a crystallization of alternatives seems a possibility.

As far as Europe is concerned, the question more than ever is what Europeans are able and willing to make of it. What they want at the present moment is not certain. It is less clear than one might think that they 'want' the Maastricht of Europe, the dilution of nations within that kind of Europe, which is itself doubly diluted by market globalization and support for the political and military hegemonism of the United States. Such a Europe would become a field for the anarchic intensification of local social conflicts, mafia-manipulated regionalist illusions (of the Basque or Corsican type), and reactionary populist nostalgia à la Haider, Le Pen or the Italian right-wing bloc. It would be ungovernable and powerless – which is what US strategy aims to achieve. If Washington has its way, Europe will look much more like what Hitler had in mind – one strong central nation, with a cluster of communities around it; the same analogy lies behind my use of the term 'Vichy' – or 'Quisling' – to describe the ideology of this variant. The 'Europeanness' invoked by the supporters of this project is not hugely different from that which rallied pro-German collaborators during the Second World War, except that the equivalent strong nation today is not geographically European but lies on the other side of the Atlantic, while Germany is reduced to the functions of a regional manager for the American global system. The other difference is that the *Führerprinzip* of open autocracy has been replaced with low-intensity democracy. But both projects share the need for a common enemy and a 'racist' logic to designate that enemy. It used to be (Soviet) communism and the Jew; now it is the non-European peoples, the 'third world'. A Europe integrated on this basis is part of a kind of global apartheid: the whites on one side (no longer French or German but simply 'white', except in the case of Americans who are able to be both American and white), 'the rest' on the other side. Of course, as in apartheid South Africa and any system based on the political use of racism, the classification has nothing to do with the (dubious) reality of 'races' or 'peoples'. Israelis, though Jewish, are now white, whereas the equally semitic Arabs are not. Indians, though speaking an Indo-European language (supposedly superior because of the Eurocentric myth of Greek ancestry), are 'coloured'. Japanese are 'honorary whites', Latin Americans 'degenerated whites' (because of real or imaginary cross-breeding with native Americans). In this perspective, the European project becomes the European constituent of the American project.

It is clear to me that the alternative is a Europe which is non-imperialist in its relations with the rest of the world, and which therefore defines itself outside the 'triad'. Its construction would require genuinely democratic federal institutions, not the reactionary technocratic illusions of the European Commission and the European Central Bank. I think that such a Europe is possible. The generous third-worldism that inspired young Europeans in the 1960s, now replaced by a European identity ranging from vapidity to racist arrogance, is evidence that a sense of universality could one day be reborn on the continent.

China is the second pole whose various possibilities are fraught with significance for the future of the world system. China's advantage is not only its huge size but also the fact that it is the only third world country (together with Korea) to have made advances in the construction of an auto-centred economy, which give it a considerable degree of autonomy and bargaining power. Although success is not guaranteed in advance, China could eventually become inserted into the perspective of the long transition to socialism, which would require the blossoming of popular democracy. That is not impossible, even if it is not the option of the autocratic nationalist regime or of the new 'pro-Western' comprador bourgeoisie.

For all regions of the capitalist third world, the construction of an auto-centred economy is the unavoidable precondition for any further progress. This requires that external relations are subordinated to the priorities of internal development, not that the internal economy is 'adjusted' to the external constraints (as mainstream economic discourse repeats ad nauseam). I have not changed my views about 'delinking': the last half-century of world history has strengthened me in this fundamental conviction. Yet it is an obvious fact that the specific forms of delinking are not laid down once and for all. The construction of an auto-centred economy – which remains indispensable at national level – would encounter serious obstacles if it was not reinforced by forms of regional integration capable of enhancing its positive effects. I am speaking here not of regionalization as it appears in mainstream economics – common markets, and so on – which is unable to contemplate anything other than the logic of capitalist accumulation; but rather of regionalization where the political dimensions are decisive and can challenge the scientific, financial and military monopolies through which the first world imposes its project of world capitalist expansion. Regions such as the Arab world, Latin America, Africa and Southeast Asia, or vast countries such as India or Brazil, can capitalize on certain advantages that history has bequeathed to them (a common language or culture, for example), but also, and above all, on the fact that they have a common enemy. Here again the choices of the ruling powers do not go in the direction I have suggested. The fact that scarcely any of the regimes in question has any real legitimacy is already proof that an alternative is possible. But it will become more than a possibility only when the culturalist illusions fuelling many protest movements are dissipated – for such illusions are perfectly manipulated by those who run the capitalist order. It will certainly be easier to overcome them in some countries than in others (in the Islamic world, for example), and in some social milieux than in others.

Widespread demands for democracy and for the running of society in the interests of the popular classes would create the most favourable conditions for a way out of the present impasse. The geometry of these two dimensions varies from one time and place to another. But the art of politics, in the noble sense of the term, is not simply to adjust to them passively or actively – in the manner of power-hungry politicians – but to act in such a way as to transform them. As always, the future remains uncertain: it is not programmed in advance in accordance with some linear determinism, such as the rationality of the market; both the worst and the best outcome are possible. There will probably be some breakthroughs in the right direction, although it is impossible to predict where with more than a middling degree of probability. If these breakthroughs occur in a sufficient number of places and a concentrated period of time, they may snowball and radically transform the world situation. That is what we have to work towards.

After 9/11

The 11th of September 2001 did not change the course of history. It is only one event leading to the more violent assertion of options that the entire US establishment, Republican and Democrat, has been pursuing since 1990. Washington always thought that the USA would dominate the planet, and even that God had entrusted it with that mission. After 1945 it resolutely applied itself to the task, by deploying the bases and creating the network of alliances for the United States to control the global system militarily. The communist devil (the 'evil empire') was merely the pretext for this project. Of course, this had nothing to do with defending or spreading democracy, as the cynicism of the US foreign policy establishment clearly demonstrated. 'Liberal' doctrine was invoked only when it served the interests of dominant sections of capital, the only interests that have the right to a say in this monstrous society.

The disappearance of the Soviet Union convinced the US establishment that the time had come to complete the work it had begun in 1945 (in using the atom bomb, let us recall). Far from opening a new 'era of peace', the unification of the planet within a capitalist framework led to an increase in US military expenditure, underlining once again the dominant role that such spending plays in this model of capital accumulation.

Systematic exploitation of 'terrorism' to justify barbaric aggression against the peoples of the South: that is all the United States has to offer humanity. This needs to be known.

In this criminal enterprise, Washington has one absolutely unconditional ally at its disposal: Israel. The two countries have the same founding ideology (genocidal colonization), the same vision of the world (mercantile and contemptuous of peoples' rights) and the same enemy (all the peoples of the South). Those peoples understand very well what the 'Palestine question' is about; it is, I repeat, a unifying issue in Asia and Africa. Unfortunately the same is not true in Europe or even Latin America (with its largely 'European' culture): there Palestine is a divisive issue, because it is the object of a dreadful amalgam with 'the Jewish question'. This is an exclusively European matter, in the sense that both anti-Semitism and the criminal behaviour it sometimes inspires are the work of Europeans, and in no case of the poor Palestinian people. Yet Europeans – and their American offspring – have eased their guilty conscience at the expense of the Palestinian people, while making Israel the spearhead of their permanent aggression against the peoples of the Arab world and, more generally, the Afro-Asian South. As always in history, these sometimes respond in an intelligent and effective manner (as in China or Vietnam, for example), but sometimes by opposing a derivative barbarism of their own to the main barbarism of the capitalist triad. This is what Gilbert Achcar has called the 'clash of barbarisms', not the 'clash of civilizations'.

Washington's other allies – the Europeans – are potentially capable of ceasing to follow the North American sheriffs. It is up to us to convince them that the humanist ideals at the root of modern civilization are a dead letter in today's obsolescent capitalism.

Notes

1. An aniseed-based alcoholic drink, similar to the Greek ouzo.
2. A variant of backgammon popular in France.
3. A type of preserved feta cheese.
4. A strong-smelling salted fish.
5. Shredded filo dough used as the basis for various Middle Eastern pastries.
6. Seasoned minced meat, baked in the oven.
7. A green, unripened wheat popular in the Middle East.
8. Lamb broth with bread, often cooked during Ramadan.
9. Lucien Bodard, *The French Consul*, trans. B. Bray, W.H. Allen, London, 1977.
10. Many years later Saad Zahrane, a former leader of the Egyptian Communist Party, made to me the apposite remark: British money during the war brought the *gonella*; Saudi money today is bringing the *hijab*.
11. A pewterware serving tray.
12. Samir Amin, *Re-reading the Postwar Period: An Intellectual Itinerary*, Monthly Review Press, New York, 1994.
13. The Egyptian name for buffaloes.
14. The Mussolini-like character in Chaplin's *The Great Dictator*.
15. PCF: Parti Communiste Français; SFIO: Section Française de l'Internationale Ouvrière (France's original Socialist party); MRP: the Christian democrat Mouvement Républicain Populaire.
16. The Tudeh (People's) Party of Iran was founded in 1941 as a successor to the banned Communist Party.
17. Colonel Marcel Bigeard: a prominent French military figure during the wars in Vietnam (most notably at Dien Bien Phu) and Algeria. See his *Ma guerre d'Indochine*, Hachette, Paris, 1994.
18. Published as Samir Amin, *Accumulation on a World Scale*, Monthly Review Press, New York, 1974.
19. The term *gospodin*, used before the revolution as the equivalent of 'mister', is today again used in Russia in place of *tovarishch* ('comrade').
20. Ismail Abdallah: a fellow editor of the *Moyen Orient* journal and future leader of the Egyptian Communist Party.
21. Yves Bénot, born Édouard Helman (1920–2005): journalist and historian who special-

ized in the experiences of liberation and independence in the African continent. Among his most noted works is *Indépendances africaines. Idéologies et réalités*, 2 vols, Maspero, Paris, 1975.
22. Maxime Rodinson (1915–2004): Marxist historian and sociologist, specialist in Islam and the politics of the Middle East.
23. Charles Diané, ed., *Les Grandes heures de la FEANF*, Chaka, Dakar, 1990.
24. Yves Bénot, *Les députés africains au Palais-Bourbon de 1914 à 1958*, Chaka, Dakar, 1989.
25. My own later view of these clashes is briefly presented in *Re-reading the Postwar Period*.
26. *Shilal* ('clan'), a term familiar to anyone who knows the age-old habits of management in Egypt.
27. SEEF: Service des Études Économiques et Financières, whose functions were later taken over by the INSEE.
28. Richly spiced slices of dried beef.
29. Boubou: a large gown with long sleeves or a shirt that slips over the head.
30. Beast of Gévaudan: a wild animal that terrorized a region in the southern Auvergne in 1764, causing many deaths among humans and animals. The attacks ceased after a huge wolf, and another large she-wolf, were killed, but doubts continued about the precise identity of the creature, and some even speculated that it had been a man dressed to look like a wolf.
31. A large-scale irrigation scheme initiated in the colonial period, in 1932.
32. Leader of the Mouvement Populaire Sénégalais, the Senegalese section of the African Democratic Rally.
33. That is, Europeans.
34. ADEMA: Alliance for Democracy in Mali, then an opposition movement, since 2001 the government party in Mali.
35. CNID: National Congress for Democratic Initiative.
36. Mamadou El Béchir Gologo, *Le Rescapé de l'Ethylos*, Présence Africaine, Paris, 1963. Gologo, a noted drinker, was Malian information minister between 1962 and 1968.
37. Mário Pinto de Andrade (1928–1990): Angolan poet and politician, founder-member of the Angolan Communist Party and later active in the liberation movement.
38. The novel by Monique Wittig, first published to great acclaim in 1964 and translated into English as *The Opoponax*, trans H. Weaver, Simon & Schuster, New York, 1966.
39. Naturally, it is not possible to go here into the question of whether the devaluation was justified or not.
40. Benny Lévy died in 2003, after these lines were written.
41. *L'Homme et la Société*: international sociological journal, first published in 1966.
42. *Les Lettres françaises*, left-wing literary weekly published between 1942 and 1972, in its latter years as a supplement to the Communist *L'Humanité*.
43. André Gauron: economist; author of an important history of the 1970s, *Années de rêves, années de crises, 1970–1981*, La Découverte, Paris, 1988; and adviser to the Socialist government of Pierre Mauroy (1981–83).
44. Alioune Diop: well-known Senegalese editor and cultural theorist, founder of the journal *Présence Africaine*.
45. CEDETIM: a movement (or cluster of movements) of international solidarity, whose origins go back to the 1960s (Centre socialiste d'études du tiers monde). See the article by Bernard Dreano at www.reseau-ipam.org/article.php3?id_article=930.
46. ATTAC: Association pour la Taxation des Transactions pour l'Aide aux Citoyens.

These memoirs were largely written during the 1990s. I did not consider it useful to update the book to take into account later events. The reader may find such considerations in my recent writings, a bibliography of which is available on http://thirdworldforum.net.

Index

Abbé Pierre, 66
Abdallah, Ismail, 63–4, 67, 83–5, 87, 90, 93, 225, 231
Abdallah, Bouli, 63–4, 67, 79, 90
Abdel Sayed, Mikhail, 2
Abidjan, 12
Abu Chakra, Sana, 191
Academey of Sciences, USSR, 63
Accumulation on a World Scale, 231
Achcar, Gilbert, 254
Addis Ababa, 151; ECA headquarters, 200
Adedeji, Adebayo, 156, 201, 209–10
ADEMA, Mali, 122
Afana, Osende, 68–9
Afghanistan, Daud regime, 175
Africa: development disillusionment, 236; Lebanese immigrants, 123–4
African Democratic Alliance, 124
African Democratic Rally (ADR), 68–9, 108, 120; PDG section, 132
African Institute for Economic Planning and Development, UN (IDEP), 151–3, 155–6, 159, 169, 198, 199–205, 208–13, 215, 220–21, 224–5, 229, 231, 235; administrative expenditure, 206; Dakar, 227; pan-African seminars, 202
African Democratic Alliance, 124
Afro-Asian Peoples' Solidarity Organization, 242
Aghion, Raymond, 63, 93, 106, 141
agronomists, 119
Ahidjo, Ahmadou, 69
Ake, Claude, 225
Alavi, Hamza, 184

Alejo, Javier, 229
Algeria: FLN, 50–51; French FLN support networks, 120; independence, 140, liberation war, 60, 72, 147, 170; 1958 crisis, 33; Sétif massacre, 32
Allende, Salvador, 176, 208, 225
Alsace, 4, 6
Amin, Isabelle, 18, 37–8, 43, 46, 55–8, 64–8, 75, 80–82, 90–92, 100, 107, 109–11, 120, 122, 125–9, 137–8, 140–41, 150, 181, 191, 199, 210, 218–19
Amoa, Kwame, 200, 203, 209–10, 231
Ancelot, Augustine, 121
Ancelot, Jacqueline, 121
Andakkah, Ismail, 201
Anders, General, 18
Annan, Kofi, 242
Anta Diop, Cheikh, 68
Anthropos, publishing house, 189, 203
anti-authoritarian theories, 195
anti-semitism, 254
Anticolonialist Students Liason Committee, France, 61
Apithy, Sourou-Migan, 69
Applied Economics Research Centre, Algiers (CREA), 225–8
Arab communism, 102
Arab League, 87–8
Arab unity, issue of, 94–5
Arusha Charter, 172
Asian Peoples' Solidarity Organization (AAPSO), 221, 242
Asian Regional Exchange for New Alternatives (ARENA), 230, 241

Asniero, George, 225, 229
assimilation, 72
Aswan, 7; High Dam project, 84–5
Athens, 76
Atlantic pact 1949, 32
ATTAC organization, France, 241, 246
Attali, Jacques, 183
Auschwitz, concentration camp, 45
Averof, warship mutiny, 20
Aw, Mamadou, 141

Ba, Ousmane, 121, 146
Baathism, 75, 102, 171; party foundation, 51
Babu, Abdulrahman Mohamed, 74, 184
Baby, Jean, 54, 185
Bagchi, Amiya, 225
Bagdash, Khaled, personality cult, 102
Baghdad pact, 50
Bamako, Mali, 59, 82, 107, 109; cinemas, 126; daily life, 125; Niger river, 110
Bandung: Conference 1955, 47, 60, 169, 244; period/project, 50, 52–3, 64, 97, 102, 168, 174–5, 180, 218
Bangladesh, 179
Bani Sadr, Abolhassan, 230
Bao Dai, 74
Barre Raymond, 160
Barre, Syad, 172
Baskaya, Fikret, 230
Bastouly, Nadra, 80–82, 90
Bastouly, Reda, 80–82, 90
Batsa, Kofi, 134, 137
Bayoumy, Lily, 124–5
Béard, Guy, 38, 40
Béart, Robert, 122
Bénard, Jean, 105, 107, 113, 118, 140, 143, 146, 159, 161–3
Bénard, Sylvie, 140
Bénot, Yves, 63, 70, 134, 137, 141
Beaud, Michel, 166
Beaudet, Pierre, 246
Ben Bella, Ahmed, 60
Ben Salahist organization, Tunisia, 74
Ben Youssefist prganization, Tunisia, 74
Benachenhou, Abdellatif, 228
Benin (Dahomey), 153, 172
Bereci, André, 92
Besse, Annie, 62
Bettelheim, Charles, 107, 125
Bigeard, R., 60
Bir Hakeim, battle of, 18
Bitat, Rabah, 184
Blessed Revolution, Egypt, 78
Böhm-Bawerk, Eugen von, 65
Bodard, Lucien, 16
Boeringer, Albert, 4
Bogomolov, Oleg, 63

Borna, Bertin, 205
Boserup, Ester, 154
Boserup, Mogens, 154
Bouhired, Djemila, 140
Boumédienne, Henri, 170
Bourdon, Renée, 185
Bourguiba, Habib, 60
Brandt, Willy, 188
Braun, Oscar, 202
Brazil, 178, 252; farmer organizations, 246; Landless Workers Movement (MST), 241
Brezhnev, Leonid, 97, 188
Britain, 50
Brzezinski, Zbigniew, 249
Budapest, 1949 youth festival, 46
Bugincourt, Jacques, 154, 202, 207
Bujra, Abdalla, 203, 207
Burkina Faso, 172; farmer organizations, 246
Bush, George H., 52
Byé, Maurice, 65

Cairo: Al-Azhar University, 88, 100; Dokki district, 3; geography, 89; 1952 fire, 50, 60; Rod Al-Farag, 27; Shepherd's hotel, 7; University, 21
Cambodia, 74; war on, 170
Camélinat, Zélie, 4
Camelots de Roy, 20
Cameroon, 68, 72; People's Union, 69–70
Camp David Accords 1977, 171
capitalist crisis, 1980s' world, 139
Cardoso, Fernando Henrique, 199, 204, 224
Carioca, Tahia, 18
Carney, David, 154–6
Casablanca African nations group, 131; 1952 riots, 60
Casanova, Pablo González, 204, 225, 229
caste, prejudices, 146
Castellina, Luciana, 187, 189, 191
Castro, Fidel, 175
Cavtat, Yugoslavia, annual symposium, 191–2
Césaire, Aimé, 75
CEDETIM group, France, 241
Centre d'Études et de Programmation Économique, 158
Centre National des Indépendants, 33
CGT, French trade union federation, 120, 194
Charaffedine, Fahima, 191
Charles, Gérard Pierre, 204, 229
Chatelet, François 167
Chattopadhay, Presh, 225
Chile: Allende government, 225; Pinochet dictatorship, 176
China, 48, 51–3, 93, 102, 169, 177–8, 180, 216, 223; Academy of Sciences, 230; Cultural Revolution, 94, 164, 182; evolution, 99, 169; Sino-Soviet dispute, 107

Chou Enlai, 78
Christie, Agatha, 7, 27
Churchill, Winston, 20
Cissokho, Bernard, 122
CNID, Mali, 122
Cold War, 33, 35, 62
Colin, Geneviève, 206
Cominform, 44–5, 55, 61
Communist parties: anticolonial, 48; Arab, 75; Chinese, 94, 170; Egypt, 78–9, 93, 96, 98; India, 224; Latin American, 223; Soviet Union, see CPSU
computers, 65, 117
Conference of African Planners, 209
Congo, 68, 86, 108, 172; Lumumbaism, 171
Conkary, 131, 134, 136
Conseil de l'Union Française, 69
Coopération, 203
Copenhagen social summit 1995, 239, 242
Coptic aristocracy, 1
Coquery-Vidrovitch, Catherine, 203
Corcondilas, Adrien, 22
Corea, Gamani, 225, 242
Corenthin, Henri, 121
Cormon, Jacques, 38, 40
Coulibaly, Daniel Ouezzin, 69
Council for the Development of Social Science Research in Africa (CODESIRA), 207–9, 221, 224, 231, 241
CPSU (Communist Party of the Soviet Union), 94, 96; 'non-capitalist path' theory, 102; ideological censorship, 63; ideology, 118; Twentieth Congress, 35, 43, 47
Cuba, 172, 175, 178, 221, 228; 'Tricontinental', 222
Curiel, Henri, 24
Czechoslovakia, 42, 44, 56

D'Arboussier, Gabriel, 69, 72
Debeauvais, Michel, 54
D'Estaing, Giscard, 192
da Cruz, Viriato, 184
da Nobrega, Nicole, 120, 124
da Nobrega, Ruy, 120, 124
Dachau, concentration camp, 40
Dadzie, Kenneth, 242
Dahomey, see Benin
Dakar, 123, 163; TWF HQ, 235; University, 161, 164, 166, 199
Damas, Léon-Gontran, 75
Damascus, 1945 bombing of, 32
Davos: annual gatherings, 223; anti-conference 1999, 246
de Andrade, Elisa, 141
de Andrade, Mário, 141
De Brunhoff, Suzanne, 160
de Gaulle, Charles, 33–4, 182, 188, 220

de Seynes, Philippe, 151, 156, 198–9, 205, 218, 233
Démoulin, Zélie, 3
Démocratique Nouvelle, 107
Dène, Oumar, 121
Debeauvais Institute of Political Science, France, 54
Debray, Régis, 161
Deif, Nazih, 85–6
Deleuze, Gilles, 167
'delinking', 252
Delta Mort, Niger river, 119
Dembélé, Kari, 122
dependency theory/school, 204, 223–4
Depestre, René, 75
Derrida, Jacques, 167
Destour Party, Tunisia, 74
development theory, crisis of, 237
Dia, Mamadou, 68
Diallo, Demba, 121
Diallo, Ogo Kane, 68
Diallo, Samba, 121
Diallo, Sayfoullaye, 133
Diané, Charles, 68
Diarra, Idrissa, 111, 113, 121
Dien Bien Phu, 60
Dieng, Amady, 68
Diop, Alioune, 212
Diori, Hamani, 69
Diouf, Abdou, 208
Diplôme d'Études Supérieures, 163, 164
'diploma rent', 143
Diuzet, Alice, 20
Diuzet, Yvonne, 20
Djibou, Bakari, 69
Do Dai Phuoc, 56
dollar US, gold convertibility break, 188
dos Santos, Theotónio, 204
Dreyfus Affair, 183
Drouet, Jean-Baptiste, 3
Dubkova, Stania, 44–5
Duclos, Jacques, 35
Dumont, Bernard, 127
Dumont Reneé 119
Durban UN Conference 2001, 243–5

École Nationale d'Administration (ENA), 54
East Asia: capitalist development, 170: financial 'crisis' US use of, 177
East Berlin, 56; workers' revolt 1953, 35
Ebeid, Makam, 13
Efflatoun, Hamdy, 79
Efflatoun, Inji, 79, 90–91
Egypt, 179; British army, 2; communist movement, 63, 95, 96; English schools, 25; European capital, 83; French culture, 25; Industrial Bank, 87; military defeat 1967,

168; Nasser period, *see* Nasser(ism); National Bank, 86; planning failures, 158; progressive Jews of, 94; Upper, 6, 37
Egypt–Syria unity vision, 87
El Alamein, battle, 18
El Atrebi, Sobhi, 84
El Imam, Mohamed Mahmoud, 153
El Said, Rifaat, 93
Eleish, Gamal, 154
Elejo, Javier, 227
elitism, 54
Environment for Development in Africa (ENDA), 207, 209, 221
Ethiopia, Italian invasion, 11, liberation army, 28
Étudiants anticolonialistes, 57
eurocentrism, pluralist critique, 224
Europe: alternative future, 251; European Central Bank, 251; European Defence Community project of, 32; Economic Community (EEC), 149; Parliament, 222; European Union, 188
Ewing, Arthur, 151
external debt, 117
Ezzet, Mohamedrachid, Amina, 90
Ezzet, Zeinab, 90, 92

Fahmy, Mansour, 45
Farhi, André, 203
fascism, 11
Faure, Marcel, 18
Faure, Maurice, 113, 120, 125, 127
Faure, Solange, 120
Fédération des étudiants d'Afrique noire en France, 68
feminism, 196
Fifth Republic, France, 33
Florenzo, Monique, 160
Focus on the Global South, 241
Force Ouvrière, 34
Forum for Turkey and the Middle East, 230
Foucault, Michel, 167
Founou, Bernard, 202, 231, 233
Fourah Bay College, Sierra Leone, 154
'fourth world', 179–80
France, 50; Communist Party, *see* French Communist Party; December 1995 movement, 247; foreign policy, 217; Fourth Republic, 31, 33; Free France movement/army, 18, 43, 120, 154; imperialist chauvinism, 62; Libre, 5; Socialist Party, 192; universities, 54, 161–2
Franco, Marco, 203
Frank, André Gunder, 6, 204
Frankfurt School, 195
Franqui, Carlos, 184
Free officers, Egypt 1952, 18, 50, 78–9, 83, 97

French Centre for the Study of Economic Prgrammes, 201
French Communist Party (PCF), 31, 34, 37, 44, 51, 55, 59, 61–2, 66, 71–2, 74, 93, 106–7, 111, 135, 185, 192, 194
French Sudan, 116
French Union, African idea of, 72
French West Africa, 115
French West Indies, 71
Friedlander, Paul (Saul), 38
Friedman, Milton, 249
Frisch, Ragnar, 104
Furtado, Celso, 199, 201, 224

Gabillard, J., 161–2, 181
Gabra, Samiz, 13
Gakou, Lamine, 122, 203, 231
Galtung, Johan, 230
Gambas, Pierre, 122
game theory, 184
Garaudy, Roger, 186
Gardiner, Robert, 151, 154, 156, 200–201, 205, 209
Gariballah, Hamid, 203
Gauche Prolétarienne, 185–66
Gauron, André, 189
Gawlik, Akwilina, 45
Geismar, Alain, 185
Genoa, demonstrations, 245
George, Susan, 249
Germany, 1948 tripartite agreement, 32; unified, 189
Ghaffour, Abdel, 6, 28
Ghai, Dharam, 233
Ghali, André, 90, 107
Ghana (ex-Gold Coast), 73, 86, 128, 131, 135; Accra, 134; Accra 'market women', 137; independence, 171; national plan, 136
Ghandar, Leila, 26
Ghattas, Wadie, 23
Girvan, Norman, 202, 229
globalization, neoliberal, 215
Godard, Jean-Luc, 182
Goethe Institute, 90
Gologo, Mamadou, 121, 124, 144, 184
Gonzague, Louis de, 109
Gorbachev, Mikhail, 184, 188–90
Gothenburg, demonstrations, 245
Gréco, Juliette, 40
Great Leap Forward, China, 43
Greece, civil war, 76; EAM movement, 20
Group of 77, 203, 218
Gruson, Claude, 86, 92, 104, 107
Guèye, Doudou, 69, 121
Guèye, Marie Louise, 121
Guinea, 73, 130–33
Guinea-Bissau, 231

Gulf War 1991, 190
Gustavsson, Rolf, 231–2
Guyot, Raymond, 62

Hadeto communist party, Egypt, 63–4, 79, 92–3, 96–8
Hadj, Messali, 74
Haïdra, Mahamane, 129
Haile Selassie, overthrow of, 172
Haiti, 75
Hamza, Awatef, 22
Hamza, Malika, 22
hashish, 27; trafficking, 16
Hayek, Friedrich von, 249
Hazan, Mimi, 92
Hazan, Youssef, 92
Hedayat, Naguib, 154, 202
Hedayet, Wahiba, 154
Hettata, Sherif, 93
'hippy' ideology, 182
Ho Chi Minh, 70; Association, 56
Houphouët-Boigny, Félix, 69, 72
Houtart, François, 246
Huchard, Marcelle, 205–6
Hughes, Jean, 154
Hungary, 1956 uprising, 35, 47
Hussein, Ahmad, 3, 77–9

Ibrahim, Hassan, 83
Ichiyo, Muto, 230
Idriss, Youssef, 13
Iglesias, Enrique, 225
ILET, Mexico, 227
IMF (International Monetary Fund), 148–9, 155, 177, 242
import-substitution industries (ISIs), 135
India, 169, 174, 178–9, 223, 252; Communist parties, 224; Congress Rule, 52; farmer organizations, 246
Indochina, war, 32
Indonesia, 221
Institute of Social History, Amsterdam, 93
Iran, 175, 178, 230; Islamic Revolution 1978–9, 174
Iraq: Communist Party, 102; monarchy overthrow, 95
Islam: Islamization, 113; political, 17, 88, 99, 151, 175, 230; traditionalist, 100, 170, 180
Ismail, Khedive, 2–3, 79
Israel, 245, 251; creation of, 50; global role of, 254; state actions, 244
Istiqal party, Moroccan, 74
Italy: Communist Party (PCI), 45, 93 187; IRI, 83; 1968 movement, 186; overseas aid, 234
Ivory Coast, 13, 68, 70, 73, 117, 121, 128–9, 135–6, 143, 179; 'miracle', 181

Jagan, Cheddi, 184
Japan, 216
Joliot-Curie, Frédéric, 38, 45

Kabe, Francine, 203
Kadri, Naguib, 131, 212
Kalsoum, Oum, 27
Kane, Abdouslam, 203
Kaya, Paul, 205
Kérékou, Mathieu, 172
Keita, Fodeba, 133
Keita, Founeké, 122
Keita, Madeira, 108, 111, 113, 127, 133, 146
Keito, Modibo, 108, 128, 130, 133, 142, 146, 148; murder of, 144
Kenya, 179; Mau Mau revolt, 72–3
Keynes, J.M., 65
Khalil, Hassan, 202–3
Khieu Samphan, 75
Khrushchev, Nikita, 35, 175, 184, 188
Kien, N., 184
Kingue, Doo, 205, 233
Kitazawa, Yoko, 230
Kodsy, Constantin, 38
Komo, 112–13, 122
Konate, Mamadou, 69, 108
Koné, Jean Marie, 147
Korean War, 35, 49, 170
Kouyaté, Seydou Badian, 145–6, 203
Kune, Chane, 66

Labica, Georges, 167
Lacarrè, Andrée
La Fontaine, fables, 10
Langevin, Paul, 38
Latin America, 175; Council for the Social Sciences (CLASCO), 207, 223–4, 241
Le Marc, Viviane, 56
Le Pen, Jean-Marie, 59, 250
Lévy, Benny, 185–6
Lebanon, 76–7; emigrants, 123–4
Lefebvre, Henri, 167, 189, 191
Legassik, Martin, 184
Lesseps, Ferdinand de, 15
'Letter in Twenty-Five Points', Chinese Communist Party, 94
Lin, Paul, 225
Lindon, Jerôme, 195
Lobel, Élie, 106, 113, 120, 125, 154, 156, 160
Lopez, Henri, 68
Los Angeles University, 203
Louis XVI, arrest of, 4
Ly, Baidi, 68

Maastricht Treaty 1992, 189
Macalou, Oumar, 121, 150
Madagascar, 60, 72, 86, 172; 1947 insurrection,

32; political trials, 70
Magdoff, Harry, 191
Magri, Lucio, 187
malaria, 6
Malek, Anouar Abdel, 191
Mali, 46, 76, 86, 106, 118, 131, 133, 135, 143, 145–6, 150–51, 158; African Democratic Rally, 18; archives, 116; banking system, 121; education system, 149; Federal Republic of, 108–9; –France dispute, 147; Manantali dam project, 141; national currency creation, 148; planning department, 210; planning difficulties, 142; state, 115; Timbuktu, 129
Mallebay Vacquer, Raymonde, 121
management, 85; Keynesian public finance, 104
Manifesto Group, Italy, 187, 189
Mansour, Fawzy, 79, 91, 202
Mao Zedong, 43, 48; Maoism, 62, 93, 107, 180, 185; *New Democracy*, 49, 74, 96, 98
Maqar, Jacqueline, 90
Marcuse, Herbert, 195
Marga Institute, Colombo, 227, 229
Marini, Ruy Mário, 204
Mars, John, 153–4
Marshall Plan, 32, 47
Martin, Victor, 23
Marx, Karl, 24, 65; historical materialism, 194; Marxism, 43, 99, 130, 183
Marxism–Leninism, 42, 52, 151
Massaga, Tchaptchet, 68–9
Massaga, Woungly, 68
Massiah, Gustave, 206, 248
Maublanc, René, 38
Mauritius, 71
Mauthausen, concentration camp, 21
May 1968, events of, 181, 193, 195
M'Bow, Mahtar, 68, 242
McCarthyism, 52
Meadi, Franco-Egyptian lycée, 90
Meillassoux, Claude, 123, 154, 156
Meir, Golda, 218
Mensah, J.H., 134
Menzaleh Lake, Egypt, 28, 37
Meppiel, Jacqueline, 66
Messageries Maritimes, 15
Messouaq, Hadi, 74
Mexico, 178; neo-Zapatistas, 241, 246
Michelena, Héctor Silva, 202
Mills, Cadmn Atta, 203
Mises, Ludwig von, 249
Misr al-Fatta, 3
Mitterrand, François, 188, 192–3
Mkandawire, Thandika, 203, 207
MNA, Algerian party, 74
Mohammed Ali, 3
Mohi el Dine, Khaled, 93

Molle, Blanche, 120
Molle, Jean, 113, 115, 120, 125
Mollet, Guy, 34, 60
Monrovia Group, African nations, 131
Mont Pelerin Society, 249
Montasser, Essam, 210
Morocco, 32; monarchy, 51
Moscow: Patrice Lumumba University, 122; 1930s show trials, 42
Mossadegh, Muhammad, 51; CIA coup against, 60, 174; coup against, 174
Mossé, Éliane, 56, 160
Mottin, Melle, 207
Moumie, Félix, 69
Moumouni, Abdou, 56, 59, 68, 73, 133, 181
Moursi, Fouad, 64, 93
Moussa, Farag, 55–9, 67
Moustapha, Yousry Ali, 84
Moyen Orient, 63–4, 93
MRP, French resistance party, 31
Mukerjee, Ramkrishna, 225
Mushakoji, Kinhide, 234, 242
Muslim Brotherhood, 28, 77–9
Mwasasa Iqtisadia (economic institution, Egypt), 83–6, 106, 210

Naguib, Muhammad, 77
Nanterre University, Paris X, 167
Nasser, Gamal Abdel, regime 3, 20, 77–8, 80, 85, 87, 94, 96–7, 130, 153; Al Azhar policy, 100; democratic deficit, 99; *coup d'état*, 60; Nasserism, 48, 50, 98, 169–70, 181; nostalgia for, 103; religious courts, 101; USSR attitude, 107
national accounting, 156; categories, 116; systems difference, 157
National Bank of Pakistan, 208, 225
national bourgeois project(s), 102, 176–7, 196
'national bourgeois stage', 98–9
nationalist parties, anti-colonialist, 48;
'national question', the, 71
NATO (North Atlantic Treaty Organisation), 33, 188; formation, 47
Ndiaye, Samba, 184
Nègre, Louis, 150
négritude, 73
Nehru, Jawaharlal, 52, 78, 169, 174
neoliberalism, 55, 105, 117, 193; fundamentalist, 223
Nerfin, Marc, 227
Netherlands, the, 104; Navigation Company, 15
'New International Economic Order', 176
New Zealand, 216, 219
Niamey, solar energy laboratory, 59
Niang, Babacar, 68
Nice demonstrations, 245

Nichol, Davidson, 233
Niger, 68, 133
Nikolic, Milos, 191
Nkrumah, Kwame, 73, 128, 131, 133, 136
Noël, Yvon, 24
Noema, Adib, 191
Noirot, Paul, 107
Non-Aligned Movement, 221, 223, 242, 245
'non-capitalist path', theories of, 190
North Korea, 169, 178
Norway, 104
Nyerere, Julius, 139, 172
Nyobé, Ruben Um, 69

OAS (Organisation Armée Secrète), 107
Obeng, Anthony, 203
OECD (Organization for Economic Cooperation and Development), 119
Ogaden conflict 1978, 172
Oinay, Antoine, 33
Omaboe, E.M., 134
Organization of African Unity (OAS), 242
Oteíza, Enrique, 207, 224, 233
Ovanissian, Vazguen, 38

P&O Company, 15
Pakistan, 179
Palestine: ethnic cleansing, 244; first War 1948, 50; global issue, 94, 254; intifada, 17; partition, 95; radicalism, 171
Palme, Olof, 208, 231–2
Papendreou, George, 76
Paris: Lycée Henri IV, 26, 36–9; Père Lachaise cemetery, 30; Quatorze Juillet, 58; restaurants, 41
Parlato, Valentino, 187
Parti Africain d l'Indépendance, 72
Perroux, François, 65
Picasso, Pablo, 45
planning, 115, 117–18; concept of, 87–8; Ghana, 136; macroeconomic coherence need, 158; Mali difficulties, 141–7; models, 86; social dimension, 116; techniques, 156
Poitiers University, 161–3
Poland, 45
Politi, Melle, 90, 107
Popper, Karl, 249
Port Said, 5–6, 8–10, 13–17, 21, 23, 75–7, 79, 82, 91–2; beaches, 11; cemetery, 30; Christian Brothers school, 24; cinemas, 27; Coptic church, 29; Manakh district, 15; 1956 violence against, 15, 22, 80; wartime, 18–19
Porto Alegre, Brazil, 245–6, 248
Portugal, colonialism collapse, 170
postmodernism, 195
Poznan, workers' revolt 1956, 35

Prasartset, Suthy, 225, 230
Prebisch, Raúl, 199, 223, 225, 242
Prenant, Marcel, 38
prestige projects, 142
Pronteau, Jean, 189, 192
Pronteau, Jonas, 189
Prou, Anne Françoise, 140
Prou, Charles, 86, 88, 92, 105, 118, 140, 201
Prou, Suzanne, 140
Pu Shan, 230
public sector accounts, 150

Qassim, Abdel Karim, 96
Qift, Upper Egypt, 6–7
Quijano, Aníba, 204
'quotation method', 96

Rabesahala, Gisèle, 69
Rabie, Taha, 92
racism, 244, 251
Radwan, Fathi, 78
Radzavi brothers, 230
Raseta, Joseph, 70
Ratsiraka, Didier, 86, 172
Ravoahangy, Joseph, 70
Rawlings, Jerry, 86
Rayan, 'Islamic' finance company, Egypt, 157
Razek, Hassan Abdel, 87
Réunion, 56–7, 66, 71
Révolution, 184
Reagan, Ronald, 52, 193
regionalization, 252
Reich, Wilhelm, 196
revolutions, 36
Rey, Pierre Philippe, 203
Reysen, Joseph van den, 68
Riad, Hassan (Samir Amin), 87, 184
Ricardo, David, 65
Ricupero, Rubens, 242
Ridgeway, Matthew, 35
Rifaat, Adel, 185
Riolo, Giorgio, 246
Rivet, Paul, 20
Robbins, Lionel, 249
Rockefeller, David, 249
Rodinson, Maxime, 63–4, 213
Rolin, Jean, 185
Rolin, Olivier, 185
Rommel, Erwin, 3, 17
Rosensztroch, Lazare, 38, 42, 44, 66
Rossanda, Rossana, 187, 189
Russian Revolution, 183
Rweyemamu, Justinian, 225

São Paulo Forum, 241
Saadeddine, Ibrahim, 231

Sadat, Anwar, 15, 84, 97, 170, 210; *infitah* policy, 99, 101, 171, 181
Safouan, Moustapha, 90, 93, 130
Said, Edward, 25
Saigal, Jagdish, 203
Saigon, American defeat, 60
Sakho, Momar, 121
Salim, Salim Ahmed, 242
Sall, Alioune, 203
Saloth Sar (Pol Pot), 75
Samir, Leila, 26
Samuelson, Paul, 165
San Fransisco, 1951 Treaty of, 47
Sandinista movement, Nicaragua, 176
Sangaré, Malik, 56, 68
Sankara, Thomas, 172
'Sans' group, France, 246
Santporo, Giuseppe, 234
SAREC, Sweden, 232–3
Sartre, Jean-Paul, 34, 186
Schumann Plan, European Coal and Steel Community, 33
Seattle mobilization, anti-WTO, 242, 245
Seck, Assane, 68
Sedki, Atef, 84
Seers, Dudley, 201
Senegal, 13, 68, 108, 133, 135, 199; planning ministry, 154
Senghor, Léopold, 69, 72–3, 199, 208, 211–12, 235
September 11th attacks, 253
Service des Études Économiques et Financières (SEEF), 92, 104, 106–7, 115, 117, 120, 158, 162, 203, 210
SFIO, French resistance party, 31, 72
Shanghai, 16
Sharwaby, Mohamed, 90
shiga, disease, 82
shura, 112
Sid Ahmed, Mohamed, 21, 99
Sino-Soviet split, 61
'small is beautiful', discourse, 135
Smith, Adam, 65
social democracy, 248
Socialist Union of Popular Forces, Morocco, 74
Soliman, Sedki, 83–4
Somalia, 179
Somavía, Juan, 225, 227, 229
Somoza, Anastasio, overthrow, 176
South Africa, 17, 173–4, 179, 251; apartheid, 244; post-apartheid, 181; trade unions, 241, 246
South Korea, 119, 178; economic success, 177; intellectuals, 230; state industrial intervention, 136; trade unions, 241, 246
South Yemen, 171
Sow, Samba, 202

Stalin, Josef, 24, 52; death of, 47; Stalinism, 35, 43
Stiglitz, Joseph, 155
Stockholm, 1972 environment conference, 207
Strasbourg, 6; University, 28
Stuckey, Barbara, 203
Students' and Workers Committees, Egypt, 21
Sudan, 78, 171; independence, 73; Republic of, 107; Unionists, 95
Sudanese Republic, 109
Sudanese Union, 111, 121, 124, 146–7; class composition, 112–13; Congress of, 108; programme, 114–15
Suez Canal: Company, 14, 20, 37; nationalization, 3, 23, 50, 60, 78, 80; 1956 military adventure, 32, 34, 65
Suez Crisis, Franco–British–Israeli aggression, 32, 34, 65, 80
Sukarno, 78, 169
Sultan Ben Youssef, deposition of, 60
Sussex University, Institutue of Development Studies, 201
Sweden: foreign policy, 232; International Cooperation Development Agency, 205, 208; UN supporter, 217
Sweezy, Paul, 191
Sylla, Djim, 111, 113, 121, 125
Sylla, Oumou, 121
Syria, 95; Communist Party, 102; –Egypt union failure, 170

Tagamu (Party of the Egyptian Left), 93, 102
Taiwan, economic success, 177
Tall, Mountaga, 122
Tawfik, Abu, 3
Tchaptchet, J-M., 69
Tchicaya, Félix, 69
Teaegu Forum, Asia, 241
Telli, Diallo, 133
Tenants Federation, France, 38, 55, 66
Thalieux, Melle, 25–6
Thatcher, Margaret, 193
Theeravit, Kien, 225
Third International, 94, 178, 194
third world: diplomacy, 219; auto-centred economies, 252; Western Third Worldism, 196
Third World Forum, 125, 169, 191, 209–10, 221, 224, 231, 237, 241, 248; achievments, 234–5; beginnings, 227; founding conference Karachi, 208, 228–9; methodology, 236; programmes, 238
Third World Network, 241
Thorez, Maurice, 62
Tinbergen, Jan, 104
Tito, Josip Broz, 41, 55, 128, 138; Titoism, 42, 44, 139

Togo-Dahomey, 68, 108
Touraine, Alain, 167
Touré, Bakary, 121
Touré, Mamadou, 155
Touré, Sékou, 69, 72, 131–2, 134, 136
Touré, Thérèse, 121
Traoré, Denis, 122
Traoré, Lamine, 121, 142
Traoré, Moussa, 150, dictatorship of, 122
Treaty of Rome 1957, 33
Trilateral Commission, 223, 249
Trotskyism, 42; Trotskyists, 185
Tsiranana, Philibert, 172
Tudeh Party, Iran, 38, 51, 75, 230
Tunisia, 32, 66; bourgeoisie, 51
Turkey, 51; intellectuals, 230, 238

U Thant, 155
Ul-Haq, Mabbub, 225
UN (United Nations), 95, 118, 153, 214, 219; apparatus, 213, 217–18; CIA infiltration, 215; Commission on Trade and Development (UNCTAD), 218, 225, 242; Development Programme (UNDP), 155–6, 205; Economic Commission for Africa (ECA), 148, 151, 156, 199–200, 209; Economic Commission for Latin America (ECLA), 119, 198, 201, 223; Education, Social and Cultural Organisation (UNESCO), 68, 242; IDEP, *see* African Institute for Economic Planning and Development; Institute for Training and Research (UNITAR), 233; Research Institute for Social Development, 233; University, 233–4, 242; US instumentalisation, 216; US policy, 210
UNAM University, Mexico, 229
'underdetermination', 194
United Arab Republic, 95
University of Dar es Salaam, 203
Upper Volta, 68
USA (United States of America), 176, 188–9, 243, 245; 'civil society', 241; CIA, 208; foreign policy establishment, 253–4; hegemonism, 34, 47–8, 215–16, 232, 248, 250
USSR (Union of Soviet Socialist Republics), 6, 17, 22, 51–3, 93, 169; as model, 43; collapse, 102, 188, 254; Communist Party, *see* CPSU; foreign policy, 190; Mali financial support, 149; Maoist critique, 194; multinational, 71; Palestine policy, 95; top-down nature, 97

Vance, Cyrus, 249
Van den Reysen, Joseph, 203

Vanoli, André, 56
'variable prices model', 106, 117
Vergès, Jacques, 43–6, 56–7, 107, 140, 184
Vergès, Paul, 43
Vergès, Raymond, 44
Vergopoulos, Kostas, 166
Verne, Jules, 37
Via Campesina, 241
Vietnam, 51, 169; liberation model, 70
Vietnam, War on, 32, 60, 170; American opposition to, 182; first, 49; mobilization against, 34
Vieyra, Chistian, 153–4
Vincennes University, Paris VIII, 161, 166–7
Vitrolles, France, 23
Vo The Quang, 56
Voivodic, Ljubomir, 22
Volcker, Paul, 249
Vu Van Thai, 155

Wade, Abdoulaye, 165
Wafdism/political party, 3, 6, 13, 17–18, 77–8, 95; electoral victory, 50
wakfs (religious trusts), wealth of, 87
Walras, Leon, 65
welfare state model, 187
West African Students Union, 73
West Indies, 56, 75; British, 71
Wieworka, Annette, 161
Wignaraja, Ponna, 225, 229
Workers Party (PT), Brazil, 246
World Bank, 85, 88, 106, 114, 117–18, 135, 139, 155, 158, 181, 225, 242–3, 247–8; Berg Report, 136; 'Society for International Development', 222
World Federation of Democratic Youth (WFDY), 41
World Forum for Alternatives (WFA), 241–2, 245–9; Cairo beginning, 239
World March of Women, 246
World Social Forum: Porto Alegre I, 246; Porto Alegre II, 248

Yeltsin, Boris, 97
Young, Andrew, 249
Yugoslavia, 46, 138, 189; break-up, 140; self-management, 139; Zagreb–Belgrade highway, 41

Zambia, Kaunda regime, 172
Zanzibar, revolution, 74, 172
Zarb, Mizou, 26
Zhadanov, Andrei, doctrine, 61–4
Zimbabwe, Lancaster House Agreement, 173, 181
Zionism, 94–5, 120

www.ingramcontent.com/pod-product-compliance
Lightning Source LLC
Chambersburg PA
CBHW030533230426
43665CB00010B/873